MIND SCIENCE
of the
PSALMS

Discovering the Power of Your Thoughts

Interpretation & Analysis

Volume 1: Books 1-50

By
David E. Smith Jr.

Aspoonful Publishing

NORTH CAROLINA

Copyright © 2019 by **David E. Smith Jr.**

All rights reserved. No part of this publication may be reproduced, distributed or transmitted in any form or by any means, without prior written permission.

Aspoonful Publishing
PO Box 1168
Davidson, NC 28036
www.aspoonful.com

Book Layout © 2019

Mind Science of the Psalms/ David E. Smith Jr.. -- 1st ed.
ISBN 978-1-891641-02-2

Dedicated to all seekers of truth.

For in the volume of the book of the gospel, the book of the Law, it is written of you and your ways. It is for you to delight in the will of God. Yes, it is the Law of the Creator that should occupy your mind.

"And saying the time is fulfilled, and the kingdom of God is at hand: repent ye and believe the gospel."

Mark 1:15

Meaning:

"The time is now at hand. The wonderful human Imagination is the Kingdom of God; where he resides. Radically change your mind and believe in the laws of scripture; for scriptures are the words of the Absolute".

David E. Smith Jr.

Page Intentionally Left Blank

CONTENTS

INTRODUCTION 9
PART ONE 12
VOLUME 1 12
PSALM 1 16
PSALM 2 21
PSALM 3 27
PSALM 4 31
PSALM 5 36
PSALM 6 42
PSALM 7 46
PSALM 8 53
PSALM 9 57
PSALM 10 65
PSALM 11 74
PSALM 12 78
PSALM 13 82
PSALM 14 86
PSALM 15 90
PSALM 16 94
PSALM 17 99
PSALM 18 106
PSALM 19 122
PSALM 20 128
PSALM 21 132
PSALM 22 138

PSALM 23	149
PSALM 24	158
PSALM 25	163
PSALM 26	171
PSALM 27	176
PSALM 28	184
PSALM 29	188
PSALM 30	192
PSALM 31	197
PSALM 32	206
PSALM 33	211
PSALM 34	219
PSALM 35	227
PSALM 36	238
PSALM 37	243
PSALM 38	256
PSALM 39	263
PSALM 40	269
PSALM 41	277
PSALM 42	283
PSALM 43	289
PSALM 44	292
PSALM 45	301
PSALM 46	308
PSALM 47	313
PSALM 48	317
PSALM 49	322
PSALM 50	330

UNDERSTANDING THIS BOOK

Here are preliminary aspects to consider when reading this book.

Recognition of the Names for God:

You can use any of these names below throughout the text of the Psalms interchangeably in the place of "Lord" or "God".

God; Jesus Christ; Allah; Brahma; Jehovah; Krishna; Christos; Lord; Imagination; Law; Universal Law; Universal Mind; Mind; Creator; Infinite Intelligence; Higher Mind; Divine; Divine Mind; the Force; Absolute; Spirit; among many other names.

In this book, you will see that all names apply, and that such names can be used interchangeably. You will see that God has no specific name. A "Holy" name is only used in the world for man to associate with.

Psalms truly reflects the laws of thought, interpreted correctly. Read them for yourself including the Commentary and Analysis, and I trust you will find the many gems that pertain to you; gems that will enhance your life.

In this book, the King James Version has been used and kept in the original format despite the difference in modern English as well as grammar and spelling. Thus, the Original Text has been unedited, and the interpretation remains as close as possible to the format of the original biblical text.

The breakdown of this work is as follows:

- **Psalm Number**
- **Original Text** – Here, the King James Version was used for this text.
- **The Theme** - Concept
- **Power of the Psalm** – Use the Psalm when experiencing the attributes mentioned, or what you consider similar attributes
- **Thought for the Psalm** – Giving you a thought about the Psalm before reading the Interpretation

- **Interpretation of the Psalm** – Gives you a verse by verse interpretation as to what the Psalm is trying to demonstrate regarding your thoughts. The text has been kept intact as close as possible, including the punctuation.
- **Analysis of the Scripture** – A break-down of the verse by verse interpretation and how it may apply to you. As you will see, I have chosen to use pronouns that reflect you personally using "I," or left the pronoun as "me" depending on what pronoun would give greater impact in the Analysis.

In this first volume of the one hundred and fifty books, there is much leeway for you to personalize the Psalms and meditate on them for even greater understanding.

INTRODUCTION

Why should you consider the Psalms as your own personal improvement program? The books of the Psalms clearly demonstrate that, no matter what your circumstance, situation, color, religion, disability, age or culture, you possess the same power the God power, within you. You are an individual that is more powerful than you've been taught. You are more powerful than you know; more than you ever imagined you could be; and Psalms proves this. Whether you associate yourself with Buddha, Krishna, Yahweh, Christ, Allah, Brahma, or even if you are an atheist, you will find this material useful. You are the power spoken of in many scriptures of the world; including the books of the Psalms.

The Psalms are an autobiography of you, not about something separate and outside of you. Thus, from you, all scriptures of the world flow forth. It is you that come from Consciousness, meaning God. Not a separation of Consciousness, but a part of the whole of Consciousness. The Universal Mind (God), has declared that he is absolute and indivisible. Thus, Psalms demonstrates that the only way you can be separate from God, is if your Conscious Mind, a part of the Universal Mind, convinces you that you are separate from it, and not worthy of the blessings of the One called God.

As for all the things that happen in your lifetime, or what can be called your existence, you are the source for who, what, where, when and why you are. In your lifetime in this dimension, you are the continuation and the end. For it is the God in you, that that came as you that sends all manifestations forth from your own imagination; the temple of God's abode. You are entitled to all that you desire, and to be told anything else would be mocking God. In scripture, he distinctly tells man:

"As a man thinketh in his heart, so is he."
Proverbs 23:7

Thus, Psalms clearly shows the reader that God is "Thought." God said there is nothing that is impossible unto you. Thus, if your circumstances demonstrate to you a lack of money, a faulty relationship, or unemployment, for example, you are the operant power through your thought to correct it.

In reading the Psalms, it is my hope that you discover that the books are not about literal history of characters that walked the Earth, but that they are books, like many other scriptures, about Divine history. You are the Divine. The Psalms demonstrate that there is no religion, there is only you; for you are God as it says in the 82nd Psalm. The Psalms create the blueprint for using the science of thought, or in other words, the science of mind. The book of Psalms is all about thought, and what you think, you will manifest; that is the power of God.

"I and my Father are one."

John 10:30

As many books of classical literature demonstrate in their allegories or parables, it is for you to discover that you are existing in a dream of separation. You are to discover from the Psalms, that it is your thinking that makes you believe in the perception of separation from the One Mind, the Universal Mind, God, Spirit, or whatever name you may choose to identify.

When this illusion of separation ends, the same conceived separation that is veiled or clouded by your physical organ senses and outer ego, you will return unto yourself, the One Mind or what may be termed your Father.

Into thine hand I commit my spirit: thou hast redeemed me, O LORD God of truth.

Psalm 31:5

God has come as man, only for man to become as God. The veil of darkness makes it hard to see, but in reading the Psalms, hopefully you will see how your thoughts are explained throughout the classical hymns.

For scripture tells us:

1 *In the beginning was the Word, and the Word was with God, and the Word was God.*

² The same was in the beginning with God.

³ All things were made by him; and without him was not any thing made that was made.

⁴ In him was life; and the life was the light of men.

⁵ And the light shineth in darkness; and the darkness comprehended it not.

John 1:1-5

If we take the first verse:

1 *In the beginning was the Word, and the Word was with God, and the Word was God.*

This verse tells us that, in the beginning was the Thought, and the Thought was with God, and the Thought was God. Thus, before you can have Word or Speech, you must have Thought. Before you can have Thought, you must have Mind. The Universal Mind (God), creates Thought through man's imagination and manifests the Word (Speech or Expression).

Thus, in your imagination where Thought takes place, is God: God in action. The books of the Psalms are all about your thoughts; for your thoughts are God; he in you, and you in him. Thus, you are not divisible; for without thought, you cannot be.

Thus, you are not separate from God the Father, and he is not a deity outside of yourself, which many religious orders teach you. To worship a deity outside of yourself is to give away your power to something other than yourself. That is what is meant by sin in each and every holy scripture. To "sin" only means to "miss the mark."

PART ONE

VOLUME 1

"He who tills his land shall have plenty of bread."

Proverbs 12:11

This is one true secret power in using Psalms. Understand this, and you will harness many powers contained within the book of the Psalms. If you choose not to prepare your mind, then you may understand the Proverb in scripture that says:

"The lazy man will not plow because of winter; He will beg during harvest and have nothing."

Proverbs 20:4

The book of the Psalms are for those who are not lazy, but are ready to learn a science, a science of mind that contains within it a treasure that is priceless. That treasure is the treasure of Mind; particularly, your Mind. The Mind of God.

Master Engineers of Thought

Psalms teaches us that we are all Master Engineers of "Thought." Thus, when reading the Psalms, think of your mind as a fertile field on a farm. In order to prepare for a harvest, the Master Engineer (the farmer) must till, cultivate and condition the land for the harvest. The same goes for your mind. You must till the land within your mind, cultivate your mind, and condition it for prosperity and success. As a farmer plants the seeds of corn in the appropriate season, he will witness an identical harvest; a crop of corn that, in turn, can repeat the cycle, season after season. Plant the seeds of success and prosperity in your mind as the Psalms do, and you will reap an identical harvest of success and prosperity in your outer world. This is an unwavering principle. If you want to fail, all you must do is nothing; as we found in the words of the *lazy* man in the Proverbs scripture.

Understand that everyone is the Master Engineer of their own mind. Salvation is in the realm of the mind; salvation is in cultivating the powers which God has put within your mind. If you don't use the powers given to you by God, then you are destined for failure. The books of the Psalms set out instructions, axioms, foundational truths and positive reinforcement to aid you in being who you desire you want to be and to have what it is that you desire.

> *"And all things, whatsoever ye shall ask in prayer, believing, ye shall receive.."*

Matthew 21:22

**(Note: Not some things, no exceptions, not maybe; but all things whatsoever are to be yours if you desire them to be yours.)

Conditions the Mind for Success

The Psalms not only disciplines your mind, but cultivates it, creates a pattern within it, and conditions it for the success you desire to have. Allowing the Psalms to do these things, you shall have plenty of bread. Not maybe, not perhaps, not probably; but with certainty you will have food, or money or whatever you consider your bread to be.

Reading the Psalms provides you with the axioms that tell you that the world has plenty of whatever you condition your mind for. It is a fact that your mind cannot escape conditioning. Whether it be from people of so-called authority, clergy, media or whatever organization of influence you surround yourself with, your mind is susceptible to conditioning; positive or negative.

If you do not condition your mind positively for wealth, love, health, success and prosperity, then the world will condition it negatively for you. This will be done at no expense to you. In other words, it won't cost you a dime, for others are glad to condition you negatively for free.

In this world, the world of governments, taxes, crime, corruption, diseases and all the horrors of the world you've been exposed to, Caesar's World, you may come to the conclusion that such a world offers you nothing to enhance yourself. For nothing you've invested, gives you nothing in return. *There is no such thing as free.* In fact, people never look to charge you for telling you that you can't do something you desire to do. They can tell you the negative all day, and they can do it with a smile.

However, if you desire to request the positive conditioning from the world, the answers to many of the questions that you may have, the world will not provide you that free of charge. Understanding the mind science of the Psalms, you will have discovered the secret to your own prosperity. The cost to you is only the time and effort you spend with reading and practicing. There is no blood, sweat and tears. No sophisticated or theological education. There is only your willingness and intent to be who you truly desire to be using your own wonderful human imagination. Psalms uses several universal principles to communicate the laws of God, thus I believe it to be wise to begin your journey with understanding the power of your thought as detailed in the text of

Psalms. The books of Psalms, interpreted correctly, will help you with thought, creation and manifestation for all your desires.

CHAPTER ONE

PSALM 1

ORIGINAL TEXT

1 Blessed is the man that walketh not in the counsel of the ungodly, nor standeth in the way of sinners, nor sitteth in the seat of the scornful.

2 But his delight is in the law of the Lord; and in his law doth he meditate day and night.

3 And he shall be like a tree planted by the rivers of water, that bringeth forth his fruit in his season; his leaf also shall not wither; and whatsoever he doeth shall prosper.

4 The ungodly are not so: but are like the chaff which the wind driveth away.

5 Therefore the ungodly shall not stand in the judgment, nor sinners in the congregation of the righteous.

6 For the Lord knoweth the way of the righteous: but the way of the ungodly shall perish.

THEME

ALIGNMENT OF MIND (SELF) WITH THE LAW OF GOD

POWER OF PSALM

Confidence, Seeking Independence, Alignment of Mind, Meditation, Faith

THOUGHT FOR THE PSALM

In aligning oneself, it begins with the attitude of mind. A person must be consciously selective in what they think; for the secret of all power, all experiences, possessions and achievements depend on how one thinks. Their thinking must be righteous.

INTERPRETATION OF EACH VERSE

1 Blessed is the man that walketh not in the counsel of the ungodly, nor standeth in the way of sinners, nor sitteth in the seat of the scornful.

1. Rewarded is the man that doesn't travel accompanied by negative and unloving thoughts, nor stands in the way of thoughts that miss the mark, nor hold a place for the contemptuous.

² But his delight is in the law of the Lord; and in his law doth he meditate day and night.

2. The joy of man is in the law governed by the use of his Imagination, Infinite Intelligence. And in the law, be silent with self, throughout the good times and the darkest of periods you encounter.

³ And he shall be like a tree planted by the rivers of water, that bringeth forth his fruit in his season; his leaf also shall not wither; and whatsoever he doeth shall prosper.

3. And man must be like a root (silent, strong, ready to receive) that stands by truth (water), only to await the harvest of fruits of his own wonderful human Imagination; in its appointed time. Man's thought must not consist of doubt. In turn, whatsoever he does must prosper.

⁴ The ungodly are not so: but are like the chaff which the wind driveth away.

4. The unloving, negative thoughts are not to be entertained, for they are not what they appear to be: for they are like the seed coverings and other debris that are distant from the love of God, which the Spirit of you and within you are to drive away or banish.

⁵ Therefore the ungodly shall not stand in the judgment, nor sinners in the congregation of the righteous.

5. Therefore, neither negative thinking nor unloving thoughts must stand in comparison of the conscious mind, nor those who miss the mark in the thoughts of the God-like.

⁶ For the LORD knoweth the way of the righteous: but the way of the ungodly shall perish.

6. For the Lord, your own wonderful human Imagination, Infinite Intelligence, knows the way of God: but the way of the unloving thoughts will cease to exist.

ANALYSIS OF THE SCRIPTURE

In order to be rewarded by the blessings of God, you must align yourself with the Law of God. You must align the way you think about yourself and others. Change your thoughts, and you will change your mind. Thus, scripture tells us:

Rewarded is the man of God, meaning you, that is aware of the company of negative, doubtful, deceitful, fearful and unloving thoughts you are to refuse to keep with you.

The conscious or aware man, who knows he is a Spirit indivisible of God, neither chooses to stand in the company of such negative thoughts, nor the thoughts of others who miss the mark in their negative thoughtful desires. Rewarded is the man that chooses not to maintain a place in their mind filled with hate; but have forgiveness of self and others.

Your loving thought manifestation will find joy in the laws of Mind, which is God, (Infinite Intelligence, Universal Mind, The Absolute) or whatever name you desire to give - in action. To understand the laws of mind, be silent with self through meditation, all day and all night. Be silent in meditation, throughout the great times as well as the bad. Meditation is the key to understanding.

You must stand firm in your faith as a root does in the ground; silent in its undertaking, strong and always seeking truth (water). In the appropriate time, the fruits of your harvest shall manifest. All this is done by using your own wonderful human Imagination. There must be no doubt in your desires. In imagining, whatever you desire will come to pass. This is the Law.

You should never entertain any unloving, doubtful or negative thoughts. They do not reflect your true self; and are nothing more than an illusion of what you might think of them as good. Ungodly thoughts, thoughts not of God or Goodness, are to be cast away from your mind.

> *"And if it seem evil unto you to serve the LORD, choose you this day whom ye will serve; whether the gods which your fathers served that were on the other side of the flood, or the gods of the Amorites, in whose land ye dwell: but as for me and my house, we will serve the LORD".*
>
> *Joshua 24:15*

Unloving thoughts should never be kept alive in your mind. For only love is to exist in your heart; meaning your mind. Thoughts that miss the mark of your desires are not to be kept, for you are to imagine only the thoughts that reflect the love of God.

It is your own wonderful human Imagination that is God; God in action. Mind, Universal Mind, always knows the way, but you must be conscious not to keep the way of unloving or negative thoughts. For Mind will return whatever it is you think about.

CHAPTER TWO

PSALM 2

2 Why do the heathen rage, and the people imagine a vain thing?

² The kings of the earth set themselves, and the rulers take counsel together, against the LORD, and against his anointed, saying,

³ Let us break their bands asunder, and cast away their cords from us.
⁴ He that sitteth in the heavens shall laugh: the LORD shall have them in derision.

⁵ Then shall he speak unto them in his wrath, and vex them in his sore displeasure.

⁶ Yet have I set my king upon my holy hill of Zion.

⁷ I will declare the decree: the LORD hath said unto me, Thou art my Son; this day have I begotten thee.

⁸ Ask of me, and I shall give thee the heathen for thine inheritance, and the uttermost parts of the earth for thy possession.

⁹ Thou shalt break them with a rod of iron; thou shalt dash them in pieces like a potter's vessel.

¹⁰ Be wise now therefore, O ye kings: be instructed, ye judges of the earth.

¹¹ Serve the LORD with fear, and rejoice with trembling.
¹² Kiss the Son, lest he be angry, and ye perish from the way, when his wrath is kindled but a little. Blessed are all they that put their trust in him.

THEME

ILLUSORY THINKING

POWER OF PSALM

Denial, Bondage; Breaking Bad Thoughts; Assertiveness, Declaration of Oneness with God; Inheritance; Focus; Concentration; Seeking Wisdom

THOUGHT FOR THE PSALM

False thinking leads to false powers of thought. False thinking reflects false ideas about oneself. Placing your thoughts into things other than your own self is false thinking. The only way to secure the possession of power within oneself, is to become aware, or conscious of the power that one has. Illusory thinking continues in man, until he learns that all the power he possesses, comes from within himself.

INTERPRETATION OF EACH VERSE

2 Why do the heathen rage, and the people imagine a vain thing?

1. Why do the many thoughts of man possess such anger and violence, and people continue to imagine undue or excessive pride in what they see before them?

² The kings of the earth set themselves, and the rulers take counsel together, against the LORD, and against his anointed, saying,

2. The rulers, and their many negative manifestations set themselves upon the earth, take advice in congregation of such thoughts, all against the Imagination of Good, and denies his oily substance, a substance that God creates for manifestation.

³ Let us break their bands asunder, and cast away their cords from us.

3. Let us break such binds of negative, doubtful, conceited thoughts on good manifestations into pieces, and throw away their twisted strands that bind us.

⁴ He that sitteth in the heavens shall laugh: the LORD shall have them in derision.

4. Man, that places his attention within his own mind shall entertain the Good: whereby the Imagination will have negative thoughts ridiculed.

⁵ Then shall he speak unto them in his wrath, and vex them in his sore displeasure.

5. Man must speak, within his own mind, to negative thoughts within him. He is to express his anger of them, as well as his disapproval of their existence.

⁶Yet have I set my king upon my holy hill of Zion.

6. Yet, I have placed my rulership in the holy temple of the Mind of man, where Imagination takes place.

⁷ I will declare the decree: the LORD hath said unto me, Thou art my Son; this day have I begotten thee.

7. I will declare the rule of law: The Universal Mind tells me, that the conscious mind, man, is born of the Universal Mind, and brought into being by the Mind; here and now.

⁸ Ask of me, and I shall give thee the heathen for thine inheritance, and the uttermost parts of the earth for thy possession.

8. Ask God, Infinite Intelligence, Brahma, Allah, and he must give you the nature of your thoughts for your own self, and the ultimate of things of the earth. Your manifested thoughts will become yours for inheritance.

⁹ Thou shalt break them with a rod of iron; thou shalt dash them in pieces like a potter's vessel.

9. You must break through the negative and doubtful thoughts with extreme focus and concentration upon them; you must

scatter them to pieces like that of a potter of clay at his wheel who chooses not to enjoy his latest creation.

¹⁰ Be wise now therefore, O ye kings: be instructed, ye judges of the earth.

10. Use your wisdom here and now, for you are a ruler of mind. Thus, be instructed by your thoughts. You are judges of the earth; the place where from your thoughts, manifestation occurs.

¹¹ Serve the LORD with fear, and rejoice with trembling.

11. Follow the Law with an emotion of awareness, using your Imagination, and rejoice in your thoughts with a vibration of proof.

¹² Kiss the Son, lest he be angry, and ye perish from the way, when his wrath is kindled but a little. Blessed are all they that put their trust in him.

12. Show love to the Conscious Mind, despite his displeasure with you, along with its negative thoughts; for those thoughts will wither from the chosen path within the conscious mind: for his anger with you will wither also. Rewarded, are all men who put their trust in their own Imagination, the temple of God.

ANALYSIS OF THE SCRIPTURE

False thinking leads to illusory thinking. Believe in yourself and love yourself, for God is in you and you are in God. Thus, scripture says:

You are asked, why do the thoughts of men reflect such anger and violence at any time? Why do people imagine negative or attach negative things to the "I AM"? Scripture continues to ask, why does man go on to imagine thoughts that are unnecessary and pride themselves in such works they see before them; more so than that of God?

Every man is a ruler of his own thoughts. Many men consciously or unconsciously have so many negative and misguided manifestations already on earth before them. As for you personally, you place too many negative thoughts before you.

Unnecessarily, you allow the conscious mind to interact with all those negative thoughts, which devour all the good thoughts Imagination has to offer. You should not allow that to happen. For man continues to deny the oily substance that every man has within them for creation. Negative thoughts in congregation will certainly overcome good thoughts, unless you are conscious of them, and choose to change your way of thinking.

Break such binds of negative, doubtful, conceited thoughts of manifestation into pieces, and throw away their twisted strands that bind you.

Man, that places his attention within his own mind, shall entertain the Good. The Imagination, God, will have negative thoughts ridiculed. For you must speak, within your own mind, to negative thoughts within. You are to express your anger of them, as well as your disapproval of their existence.

Yet, in you, already exists your place of rulership; the kingdom of heaven. In the holy temple of the Mind of man, is where Imagination takes place. You are to declare the rule of law. You are to understand that the Universal Mind brings forth to you, knowledge that the conscious mind of man cannot conceive or comprehend. Man is born of the Universal Mind, and brought into being by the Mind, here and now. Trust in the Universal Mind and ask the God within you, to rid your mind of such negative thinking.

Ask God, Infinite Intelligence, Brahma, Allah, or whatever name you give the Absolute, and he must give you the nature of your thoughts for your own self. Imagine what it is you desire. He will provide you with the ultimate of things of the earth. Your manifested thoughts will become your inheritance. Proper thinking is to take place in your kingdom; in your mind. In scripture we find:

> *"an inheritance that is incorruptible, and undefiled, and that fadeth not away, reserved in heaven for you."*

Peter 1:4

You must break through the negative and doubtful thoughts with extreme focus and concentration upon them. You must scatter them to pieces, like that of a potter of clay at his wheel who chooses not to enjoy his latest creation. For you are the potter, and in your Imagination is the clay in which you shape your thoughts.

> *"So I went down to the potter's house, and I saw him working at the wheel. But the pot he was shaping from the clay was marred in his hands; so the potter formed it into another pot, shaping it as seemed best to him".*

Jeremiah 18:3-4

Use your wisdom here and now, for you are a ruler of mind. Be instructed by your thoughts. You are judge of the earth; the place from where your thoughts, manifestations occur. Follow the Law, the Law of God with strong emotion. Use your Imagination and rejoice in your thoughts with a vibration of proof of goodness.

Show love to the Conscious Mind, despite its thoughts of displeasure within you. In time, your negative thoughts will wither from their chosen path, and their anger will wither also. Rewarded, are all men who put their trust in their own Imagination, the temple of God. Their Imagination is their salvation.

CHAPTER THREE

PSALM 3

ORIGINAL TEXT

3 Lord, how are they increased that trouble me! many are they that rise up against me.

2 Many there be which say of my soul, There is no help for him in God. Selah.

3 But thou, O Lord, art a shield for me; my glory, and the lifter up of mine head.

4 I cried unto the Lord with my voice, and he heard me out of his holy hill. Selah.

5 I laid me down and slept; I awaked; for the Lord sustained me.

6 I will not be afraid of ten thousands of people, that have set themselves against me round about.

7 Arise, O Lord; save me, O my God: for thou hast smitten all mine enemies upon the cheek bone; thou hast broken the teeth of the ungodly.

8 Salvation belongeth unto the Lord: thy blessing is upon thy people. Selah.

THEME

DEALING WITH TIMES OF DESPAIR

POWER OF PSALM

Overwhelmed, Challenge of Faith, Guiding Light, Salvation

THOUGHT FOR THE PSALM

Create harmony and peace in your way of thinking. Creating harmony and peace within, can be accomplished by controlling your thoughts, and determining for yourself how any experience affects you. Peace and harmony within yourself will reflect the identical harvest outside of yourself; which includes your environment, circumstances, situations, conditions and experiences. It is the foundation that determines abundance or despair.

INTERPRETATION OF EACH VERSE

3 Lord, how are they increased that trouble me! many are they that rise up against me.

1. Infinite Intelligence, there are growing negative thoughts that aggravate me! There are so many of them that are rising up against me.

² Many there be which say of my soul, there is no help for him in God. Selah.

2. Many of those thoughts are describing or depicting who I am and tell me, God will not help me. Selah

³ But thou, O LORD, art a shield for me; my glory, and the lifter up of mine head.

3. But me, in my own wonderful human Imagination, God is a shield for me; my glory, and one that lifts my head upward.

⁴ **I cried unto the LORD with my voice, and he heard me out of his holy hill. Selah.**

    4. I, with feeling, call unto my own Imagination with my thought, and I know he answers me out of my Imagination. Selah.

⁵ **I laid me down and slept; I awaked; for the LORD sustained me.**

    5. I laid me down, became still and slept; I became conscious; for Infinite Intelligence holds me up without fail.

⁶ **I will not be afraid of ten thousands of people, that have set themselves against me round about.**

    6. I will not be afraid of the thousands of negative thoughts created by myself or what appears to be thoughts of others; thoughts that have set themselves against me directly or indirectly.

7. Arise, O LORD; save me, O my God: for thou hast smitten all mine enemies upon the cheek bone; thou hast broken the teeth of the ungodly.

    7. Come forth Infinite Intelligence, save me, for you are my God within me. For you can deeply affect my enemies that affect me, and even in your word; you will have broken the glee of the ungodly.

⁸ **Salvation belongeth unto the LORD: thy blessing is upon thy people. Selah.**

    8. Salvation belongs to my Imagination: my blessing is upon my thoughts. And those that are saved, knowing the oneness of God, are the people that are rewarded.

ANALYSIS OF THE SCRIPTURE

Acknowledge to Infinite Intelligence within you, that there are growing negative and doubtful thoughts that aggravate you. Acknowledge that are so many of them revolting against you. It is from your thoughts in which good and evil thoughts arise.

> *"I have set before thee this day life and good, and death and evil."*
>
> *Deuteronomy 30:15*

Many of those thoughts will describe or depict who you are and tell you, God will not help you. Selah (**Selah – this is foundational truth, the axiom, wherein this true statement is self-evident.**)

For you, in your own wonderful human Imagination, God is a shield for you. God is your glory, and the One that lifts your head upward.

You with feeling, must call unto your own Imagination with your good thoughts. You are to know that he answers you; for he acts through your Imagination. (Selah)

You are to lay down, become still, meditate and sleep. You are certain to become conscious; for Infinite Intelligence holds you up without fail.

> *"Ye shall know the truth, and the truth shall set you free."*
> *John 8:32*

You are to declare that you will not be afraid of the thousands of negative and doubtful thoughts created by your own self, or what appears to be thoughts of others. For those thoughts are the same ones that have set themselves against you directly or indirectly.

Call upon and ask Infinite Intelligence to come forth and save you. Declare that he is the God, the Jesus Christ, Jehovah within you. For God can deeply affect your enemies that affect you, and through the Word of God, he will break the glee of the ungodly.

Salvation belongs to your Imagination, and not something or someone outside of yourself. To believe in anything outside of yourself is a lie. Your blessing is upon your thoughts. And those that are saved, knowing the oneness of God, are the people that are rewarded. (Selah)

CHAPTER FOUR

PSALM 4

ORIGINAL TEXT

4 Hear me when I call, O God of my righteousness: thou hast enlarged me when I was in distress; have mercy upon me and hear my prayer.

2 O ye sons of men, how long will ye turn my glory into shame? how long will ye love vanity, and seek after leasing? Selah.

3 But know that the Lord hath set apart him that is godly for himself: The Lord will hear when I call unto him.

4 Stand in awe, and sin not: commune with your own heart upon your bed and be still. Selah.

5 Offer the sacrifices of righteousness and put your trust in the Lord.

6 There be many that say, Who will shew us any good? Lord, lift thou up the light of thy countenance upon us.

7 Thou hast put gladness in my heart, more than in the time that their corn and their wine increased.

8 I will both lay me down in peace, and sleep: for thou, Lord, only makest me dwell in safety.

THEME

Receiving Counsel

POWER OF PSALM

Wealth; Health; Joy; Distress; Guidance; Lies; Seeking Truth; In Need of Advice; Abundance

THOUGHT FOR THE PSALM

In receiving counsel from God, go into the heaven of your mind, the Kingdom of God, when you desire something. Know that it is your secret closet, and when you shut the door of that closet, desire or pray to your Father which only you and God the Father know about. Your Father, God, will see in secret, and reward you openly. For the world of all your desires will be given unto you.

> *"But thou, when thou prayest, enter into thy closet, and when thou hast shut thy door, pray to thy Father which is in secret; and thy Father which seeth in secret shall reward thee openly."*

Matthew 6:6

INTERPRETATION OF EACH VERSE

4 Hear me when I call, O God of my righteousness: thou hast enlarged me when I was in distress; have mercy upon me, and hear my prayer.

1. Hear me mind upon my thought, in my Imagination, Infinite Intelligence which is all right: you have appreciated me when my mind was possessed with turmoil or troubled thoughts. Have compassion for me and hear my desire.

² O ye sons of men, how long will ye turn my glory into shame? how long will ye love vanity, and seek after leasing? Selah.

2. All sons of manifestations, all men of the Most High, how long will you turn the glory of the God within you into shame? How long will you see yourself in reflection to only love your own vanity, and resort to lies of your own thoughts? Selah.

³ But know that the LORD hath set apart him that is godly for himself: the LORD will hear when I call unto him.

3. Know that God, Infinite Intelligence, your own wonderful human Imagination has set apart the man that is acting in godlike for himself: The Divine, Universal Mind will hear when man calls upon himself (the Infinite Intelligence, Higher Mind) within self.

⁴ Stand in awe, and sin not: commune with your own heart upon your bed, and be still. Selah.

4. Stand in wonder of the sacred truth, and don't miss the mark: commune with your own heart (desires) upon your bed and be silent. Selah.

⁵ Offer the sacrifices of righteousness, and put your trust in the LORD.

5. Surrender yourself to the Good, to God, and put your trust in the Imagination.

⁶ There be many that say, Who will shew us any good? LORD, lift thou up the light of thy countenance upon us.

6. There will be many negative thoughts that will say unto you, who will show us any good or prosperity? Divine Mind lift me up and shine your truth upon me.

⁷ Thou hast put gladness in my heart, more than in the time that their corn and their wine increased.

7. You have placed joy within my mind, many more times than food and drink has been abundant.

⁸ I will both lay me down in peace, and sleep: for thou, LORD, only makest me dwell in safety.

8. I will lay myself down in peace, and sleep: for I, Lord, am the one that dwells in the safety of my own being.

ANALYSIS OF THE SCRIPTURE

All our answers are just a visualization away. Be still and ask for the answer you desire.

Ask the Mind to hear your thoughts, in your Imagination, which is all right. Praise the Lord, the Law, in acknowledgement that you are appreciative of the fact that he was there for you in times of turmoil and troubled thoughts. Ask to have compassion, and that he hears your desires.

All sons of manifestations, all men of the Most High, including you, are asked the specific question as to how long will you turn the glory of the God within you into shame? The question is then followed up with the second question: How long will you see yourself in the reflection of a mirror to only love your own vanity, and resort to lies about yourself? Is what you see in the mirror truly who you are, or are you more or less than what you think? Selah. Is that question not true of yourself when you look in mirror?

Know that God, Infinite Intelligence, your own wonderful human Imagination has set apart the man that is acting in godlike, in goodness for himself. The Divine, Universal Mind will hear when you call upon yourself; the Infinite Intelligence, the Christ, the Krishna, the Mohammad, within yourself.

Stand in wonder of the sacred truth, and don't miss the mark. Commune with your own heart (desires) upon your bed at night and be silent. Silence is your meditation. Selah.

> *"Then he openeth the ears of men, and sealeth their instruction."*

Job 33:15-16

Surrender yourself to the Good, to the Law, and put your trust in the Imagination; for your Imagination is the Supreme. There will be many negative and doubtful thoughts that will say unto you: Who will show us any good or prosperity? Divine Mind will, and the Divine Mind will lift you up and shine truth upon you.

God has placed joy within your mind, many more times than food and drink has been abundant. Lay yourself down in peace, and sleep: for you are to know that the Lord dwells in the safety of your own being.

CHAPTER FIVE

PSALM 5

ORIGINAL TEXT

5 Give ear to my words, O LORD, consider my meditation.

² Hearken unto the voice of my cry, my King, and my God: for unto thee will I pray.

³ My voice shalt thou hear in the morning, O LORD; in the morning will I direct my prayer unto thee, and will look up.

⁴ For thou art not a God that hath pleasure in wickedness: neither shall evil dwell with thee.

⁵ The foolish shall not stand in thy sight: thou hatest all workers of iniquity.

⁶ Thou shalt destroy them that speak leasing: the LORD will abhor the bloody and deceitful man.

⁷ But as for me, I will come into thy house in the multitude of thy mercy: and in thy fear will I worship toward thy holy temple.

⁸ Lead me, O LORD, in thy righteousness because of mine enemies; make thy way straight before my face.

⁹ For there is no faithfulness in their mouth; their inward part is very wickedness; their throat is an open sepulchre; they flatter with their tongue.

¹⁰ Destroy thou them, O God; let them fall by their own counsels; cast them out in the multitude of their transgressions; for they have rebelled against thee.

¹¹ But let all those that put their trust in thee rejoice: let them ever shout for joy, because thou defendest them: let them also that love thy name be joyful in thee.

¹² For thou, LORD, wilt bless the righteous; with favour wilt thou compass him as with a shield.

THEME

Considering Imagination

POWER OF PSALM

Meditation; Desires; Prayer; Grace; Purity; Mistakes; Direction of Thought; Unwise Decisions; Trusting Self; Inner Mind Conversations

THOUGHT FOR THE PSALM

Practice using the Imagination all day, every day. In good times and bad times, you must practice. For all desires are expressed through the Imagination. The Imagination is God in Action.

INTERPRETATION OF EACH VERSE

5 Give ear to my words, O LORD, consider my meditation.

1. Listen to my words, consider the Imagination the meditation of God.

² Hearken unto the voice of my cry, my King, and my God: for unto thee will I pray.

2. Give attention unto the sound of your call with feeling, the One, Imagination in action, for unto the Imagination you will place your desires.

³ My voice shalt thou hear in the morning, O LORD; in the morning will I direct my prayer unto thee, and will look up.

3. You must hear my voice in the Imagination where it all begins. You will direct your desires unto it, and will look up (to the eye of Imagination/in the Kingdom of Heaven)

⁴ For thou art not a God that hath pleasure in wickedness: neither shall evil dwell with thee.

4. For you are not a God that takes pleasure in evil doing, or wickedness; and such thoughts must not dwell within your being.

⁵ The foolish shall not stand in thy sight: thou hatest all workers of iniquity.

5. The foolish or unwise must not stand in your vision; no love is to be given to any thoughts of wickedness.

⁶ Thou shalt destroy them that speak leasing: the LORD will abhor the bloody and deceitful man.

6. God will destroy thoughts that speak falsehood or lies. The wonderful human Imagination, God in Action, will detest the non-spiritual and deceitful manifestations that come to mind.

⁷ But as for me, I will come into thy house in the multitude of thy mercy: and in thy fear will I worship toward thy holy temple.

7. But as for me, I will come unto myself, in the great numbers of thoughts of compassion. And in myself, feeling with emotion will I worship my holy temple; my own wonderful human Imagination.

⁸ Lead me, O LORD, in thy righteousness because of mine enemies; make thy way straight before my face.

8. Lead me, Lord, in Imagination, in my Goodness. Because of my negative thoughts; make my path true before me.

⁹ For there is no faithfulness in their mouth; their inward part is very wickedness; their throat is an open sepulchre; they flatter with their tongue.

> 9. For there is no substance of things hoped for, but their evidence is only in what is seen from where negative thoughts speak. The conscious mind's inner conversation with you is very evil; for the conscious mind's passageway is an open grave or burial place for you. Negative thoughts flatter with their voice as they converse in your head.

¹⁰ Destroy thou them, O God; let them fall by their own counsels; cast them out in the multitude of their transgressions; for they have rebelled against thee.

> 10. Destroy those negative thoughts Lord. He is to hear truth with your Imagination. Let the negative thoughts fall by their own advice. Throw them out in the multitude of their violation of laws; for they have rebelled against God, meaning you.

¹¹ But let all those that put their trust in thee rejoice: let them ever shout for joy, because thou defendest them: let them also that love thy name be joyful in thee.

> 11. But let all those that put their trust in God, your own wonderful human Imagination, rejoice. Let your positive and loving thoughts shout for joy, because you are to protect those thoughts. Let them also that love the name of God, be joyful in Him.

¹² For thou, LORD, wilt bless the righteous; with favour wilt thou compass him as with a shield.

> 12. For your Imagination, God in Action, will reward righteousness, and positive thoughts; with friendly regard, guiding you as leading the way as your protector.

ANALYSIS OF THE SCRIPTURE

Test the Law of God yourself by imagining that which you desire; with earnest feeling and without doubt. See the desire already fulfilled in your mind's eye and hold to the faith night and day.

Listen to the words of God, and consider the Imagination, the meditation of God. Give attention unto the sound of his words with feeling. He is the One, Imagination in action, for unto the Imagination you are to place all your desires.

You must hear his voice in the Imagination, where it all begins. You will direct your desires unto it and will look up (to the eye of Imagination in the Kingdom of Heaven; the Kingdom of your own mind).

For you are not a God that takes pleasure in evil doing or wickedness. Such thoughts must not dwell within your being. For the foolish or unwise must not stand in your vision. No love is to be given to any thoughts of wickedness.

You must destroy all thoughts that speak falsehood or lies of you. The wonderful human Imagination, God in Action, will detest the non-spiritual and deceitful manifestations that come to mind.

But as for you, you will come unto yourself, in the great numbers of thoughts of compassion. And in yourself, feeling with emotion, will you worship your holy temple; your own wonderful human Imagination.

Ask the Lord, to lead you, in your own Imagination, in your Goodness. Because of your negative thoughts; ask the Lord to make your path true before you. Create your personal conversation with God. Make God personal to you.

For there is no substance of things hoped for, but their evidence is only in what is seen from where negative thoughts speak. The conscious mind's inner conversation with you is very evil; for the conscious mind's passageway is an open grave or burial place for you if you are not an aware man. Negative thoughts flatter with their voice as they converse in your head.

"Now faith is the substance of things hoped for, the evidence of things not seen."

Hebrews 11:1

Destroy your negative thoughts. Hear truth with your Imagination. Let the negative thoughts fall by their own advice. Throw them out in into the pasture for their multitude of violation of laws; for they have rebelled against God; meaning you.

But let all those that put their trust in God, your own wonderful human Imagination, rejoice. Let your positive and loving thoughts shout for joy, because you are to protect those thoughts. Let them also that love the name of God, be joyful in Him.

For your Imagination, God in Action, will reward righteousness, positive thoughts; with friendly regard, guiding you as he leads you to protection.

CHAPTER SIX

PSALM 6

ORIGINAL TEXT

6 O Lord, rebuke me not in thine anger, neither chasten me in thy hot displeasure.

2 Have mercy upon me, O Lord; for I am weak: O Lord, heal me; for my bones are vexed.

3 My soul is also sore vexed: but thou, O Lord, how long?

4 Return, O Lord, deliver my soul: oh save me for thy mercies' sake.

5 For in death there is no remembrance of thee: in the grave who shall give thee thanks?

6 I am weary with my groaning; all the night make I my bed to swim; I water my couch with my tears.

7 Mine eye is consumed because of grief; it waxeth old because of all mine enemies.

8 Depart from me, all ye workers of iniquity; for the Lord hath heard the voice of my weeping.

9 The Lord hath heard my supplication; the Lord will receive my prayer.

10 Let all mine enemies be ashamed and sore vexed: let them return and be ashamed suddenly.

THEME

Healing

POWER OF PSALM

Self-Conviction, Health, Illusory Thought, Finding Your Way, Clouded Vision, Sudden Change

THOUGHT FOR THE PSALM

The Lord, your Imagination, heals all thoughts; all situations in all circumstances.

INTERPRETATION OF EACH VERSE

6 O LORD, rebuke me not in thine anger, neither chasten me in thy hot displeasure.

1. Infinite Intelligence, don't let me disapprove of myself in anger, nor let me suffer in displeasure.

² Have mercy upon me, O LORD; for I am weak: O LORD, heal me; for my bones are vexed.

2. Have compassion for me, Infinite Intelligence; for I do not stand affirmed. Infinite Intelligence, heal me; for my body is sick.

³ My soul is also sore vexed: but thou, O LORD, how long?

3. My inner being is also in distress: but I, Infinite Intelligence, how much longer must I endure this?

⁴ Return, O LORD, deliver my soul: oh save me for thy mercies' sake.

4. Imagination, return unto me. Divine Mind, bring forth my desires not of old. Have mercy upon me.

⁵ **For in death there is no remembrance of thee: in the grave who shall give thee thanks?**

5. In death, I cannot remember who I am: in the grave who must I give thanks to?

⁶ **I am weary with my groaning; all the night make I my bed to swim; I water my couch with my tears.**

6. I groan with exhaustion; though throughout the darkness I create a lasting feeling; I lay down in the comfort of truth along with my own being.

⁷ **Mine eye is consumed because of grief; it waxeth old because of all mine enemies.**

7. My vision is clouded because of my grief; the cloud increases due to the long standing of all my negative thoughts.

⁸ **Depart from me, all ye workers of iniquity; for the LORD hath heard the voice of my weeping.**

8. Leave me, all you thoughts of evil; for the Divine Intelligence, Creator, God, has recognized the expression of my feeling.

⁹ **The LORD hath heard my supplication; the LORD will receive my prayer.**

9. My Imagination has heard my humble call; the Imagination will receive my desire.

¹⁰ **Let all mine enemies be ashamed and sore vexed: let them return and be ashamed suddenly.**

10. Let all my negative thoughts be ashamed and be sorely irritated: let them return and be ashamed of the abruptness of the manifestation to come.

ANALYSIS OF THE SCRIPTURE

Healing comes from within. Right thinking and faith will bring about the healing of both mind and body. Have Infinite Intelligence guide you, so you don't disapprove of yourself in anger, nor let you suffer in displeasure. Have Infinite Intelligence respond to you with compassion, as your actions of faith in yourself has not been strong. Ask for Infinite Intelligence to heal you as you recognize that your body is not aligned with the Universal Mind.

Your inner being may be in distress, but you may want to ask Infinite Intelligence, how much longer must you endure this? Though things come to harvest in the appropriate time, and the time is not for you to know, you may still request of Infinite Intelligence to come forth and reward you with the Lord's grace. You are to request from your inner being, to see the good within you.

Upon the death of your negative thoughts, you may not remember what led you to think that way. However, give praise to God even though the circumstances you are currently in are dire.

"And He was casting out a demon, and it was mute; when the demon had gone out, the mute man spoke; and the crowds were amazed."
Luke 11:14

Cast away all your thoughts of evil; for the Divine Intelligence, Creator, God, has recognized the expression of your feeling. Your Imagination has heard your humble call. The Imagination will receive your desire. Let all your negative thoughts be ashamed and be sorely irritated. Let the ungodly thoughts return and be ashamed of the abruptness of the good manifestation to come. Let the good thoughts speak.

"You may groan with exhaustion; though throughout the darkness you've created a lasting feeling; a feeling that will have you lay down in the comfort of truth along with your own being. Your vision is clouded because of your grief; the cloud increases due to the long standing of all your negative thoughts."
Deuteronomy 30:19-20

CHAPTER SEVEN

PSALM 7

ORIGINAL TEXT

7 O Lord my God, in thee do I put my trust: save me from all them that persecute me, and deliver me:

2 Lest he tear my soul like a lion, rending it in pieces, while there is none to deliver.

3 O Lord my God, If I have done this; if there be iniquity in my hands;

4 If I have rewarded evil unto him that was at peace with me; (yea, I have delivered him that without cause is mine enemy:)

5 Let the enemy persecute my soul, and take it; yea, let him tread down my life upon the earth, and lay mine honour in the dust. Selah.

6 Arise, O Lord, in thine anger, lift up thyself because of the rage of mine enemies: and awake for me to the judgment that thou hast commanded.

7 So shall the congregation of the people compass thee about: for their sakes therefore return thou on high.

8 The Lord shall judge the people: judge me, O Lord, according to my righteousness, and according to mine integrity that is in me.

9 Oh let the wickedness of the wicked come to an end; but establish the just: for the righteous God trieth the hearts and reins.

10 My defence is of God, which saveth the upright in heart.

11 God judgeth the righteous, and God is angry with the wicked every day.

12 If he turn not, he will whet his sword; he hath bent his bow, and made it ready.

13 He hath also prepared for him the instruments of death; he ordaineth his arrows against the persecutors.

14 Behold, he travaileth with iniquity, and hath conceived mischief, and brought forth falsehood.

15 He made a pit, and digged it, and is fallen into the ditch which he made.

16 His mischief shall return upon his own head, and his violent dealing shall come down upon his own pate.

17 I will praise the Lord according to his righteousness: and will sing praise to the name of the Lord most high.

THEME

HAVING TRUST IN SALVATION

POWER OF PSALM

Trust, Lost Hope, Creation of Evil, Declaring, Judgment, Protection, Forgetfulness,

THOUGHT FOR THE PSALM

Place your trust in the Imagination, and regardless of what you see in front of you, on your screen of space, is not to deter your thought of your desires already fulfilled. Hold to your thoughts, for your perseverance is your salvation.

INTERPRETATION OF EACH VERSE

7 O Lord my God, in thee do I put my trust: save me from all them that persecute me, and deliver me:

1. Infinite Intelligence, my God, in you do I place my trust: help me from all the negative thoughts that persecute me, and set me free:

² Lest he tear my soul like a lion, rending it in pieces, while there is none to deliver.

2. For such thoughts will tear my being apart like a lion, shredding it into pieces, then there will be nothing left of me to set free.

³ O LORD my God, If I have done this; if there be iniquity in my hands;

3. Divine Mind, if I have created this; if there is guilt in my hands;

⁴ If I have rewarded evil unto him that was at peace with me; (yea, I have delivered him that without cause is mine enemy)

4. If I have granted evil unto my thoughts that were at peace with me; (yes, I have set free that which without cause is my own enemy)

⁵ Let the enemy persecute my soul, and take it; yea, let him tread down my life upon the earth, and lay mine honour in the dust. Selah.

5. Let the negative thought afflict my soul, and take it; yes, let him walk down my path of life upon the earth, and lay my honor in the dust. Selah. (Selah – this is foundational truth, the axiom, wherein this true statement is self-evident.)

⁶ Arise, O LORD, in thine anger, lift up thyself because of the rage of mine enemies: and awake for me to the judgment that thou hast commanded.

6. Awaken, Christ Jesus, in the anger of negative thoughts, lift me up due to the rage of my negative thoughts: and awake for me to judge them as you have commanded me to do so.

⁷ So shall the congregation of the people compass thee about: for their sakes therefore return thou on high.

7. So must the congregation of negative thoughts direct me about: for their cause will alas come before me while I command from the most high.

⁸The LORD shall judge the people: judge me, O LORD, according to my righteousness, and according to mine integrity that is in me.

8. My Imagination must judge the thoughts: the thoughts that judge me, my Imagination, according to my Good, God, and according to my honor that is in me.

⁹ Oh let the wickedness of the wicked come to an end; but establish the just: for the righteous God trieth the hearts and reins.

9. Let the corrupt of the wicked thoughts come to an end; create justice: for the Good God tests the hearts and feelings.

¹⁰My defence is of God, which saveth the upright in heart.

10. My armor is God, which embraces the one with a just heart.

¹¹ God judgeth the righteous, and God is angry with the wicked every day.

11. God judges the good within man, and God is angry with the daily negative thoughts.

¹² If he turn not, he will whet his sword; he hath bent his bow, and made it ready.

12. If man stands his ground, he will sharpen his mind; prepare his weapon and make it ready for action.

¹³ He hath also prepared for him the instruments of death; he ordaineth his arrows against the persecutors.

13. God has prepared the tools of death; and man establishes order (in his mind) with arrows against the negative thoughts.

¹⁴ Behold, he travaileth with iniquity, and hath conceived mischief, and brought forth falsehood.

14. Observe, he that walks with evil, and has conceived a source of harm, and brought forth untruth.

¹⁵ He made a pit, and digged it, and is fallen into the ditch which he made.

15. God made a hole, carved it out, and (the thoughts of evil) is fallen into the ditch which he made.

¹⁶ His mischief shall return upon his own head, and his violent dealing shall come down upon his own pate.

16. His source of harm must return upon his own head (thinking), and his violent actions must come down upon his own head.

¹⁷ I will praise the LORD according to his righteousness: and will sing praise to the name of the LORD most high.

17. I will praise God within me according to his good: and will sing praise to the name of God within me, most high.

ANALYSIS OF THE SCRIPTURE

Declare Infinite Intelligence, God, in you do you place your trust. Declare delivery of all negative thoughts that persecute you and set you free. For such thoughts will tear your being apart like a lion, shredding it into pieces. For you believe that if that happens, there will be nothing left of you to set free.

Declare to Divine Mind, that if you have created all that persecutes you, that is, if this is true; then evil comes from your hands. If you have granted evil unto your thoughts that were at peace with you; (yes, you have set free that which without cause is your own enemy)

"If the world hates you, keep in mind that it hated me first."

John 15:18

Let the negative thought afflict your feelings and consume them. Yes, let him walk down your path of life upon the earth, and lay your honor in the dust. Selah. **(Selah – this is foundational truth, the axiom, wherein this true statement is self-evident.)**

Then, awaken, Christ Jesus within you, in the anger of negative thoughts. Ask Christ Jesus, Universal Mind to lift you up due to the rage of your negative thoughts. Awaken Christ Jesus for you to judge them as he has commanded you to do so.

So must the congregation of negative thoughts direct you about. For their cause will soon enough come before you while you command from above; your Imagination. Your Imagination must judge the thoughts: the thoughts that judge you. Judgment by your Imagination, is judgment according to your Good, God, and according to your honor that is in you.

Let the corrupt of the wicked thoughts come to an end. Create justice for the Good. God tests the hearts and feelings of men. Your armor is God, which embraces the one with a just heart. God judges the good within man, and God is angry with the daily negative thoughts.

If man stands his ground, he will sharpen his mind. He will have prepared his weapon and make it ready for action. God has prepared the tools of death; and man establishes order (in his mind) with arrows against the negative thoughts.

Observe, the man that walks with evil, and has conceived a source of harm. Look at the man that has brought forth untruth. God made a hole, carved it out, and (the thoughts of evil) fall into the ditch which he has made.

His source of harm must return upon his own head (thinking), and his violent actions must come down upon his own head. In other words, man's harm comes from his own thinking, and his violent actions manifest themselves on earth. Therefore, you are to praise God within you according to his good: and shall sing praise to the name of God within you, the Most High.

"Let them alone; they are blind guides of the blind And if a blind man guides a blind man, both will fall into a pit."

Matthew 15:14

CHAPTER EIGHT

PSALM 8

ORIGINAL TEXT

8 O Lord, our Lord, how excellent is thy name in all the earth! who hast set thy glory above the heavens.

2 Out of the mouth of babes and sucklings hast thou ordained strength because of thine enemies, that thou mightest still the enemy and the avenger.

3 When I consider thy heavens, the work of thy fingers, the moon and the stars, which thou hast ordained;

4 What is man, that thou art mindful of him? and the son of man, that thou visitest him?

5 For thou hast made him a little lower than the angels, and hast crowned him with glory and honour.

6 Thou madest him to have dominion over the works of thy hands; thou hast put all things under his feet:

7 All sheep and oxen, yea, and the beasts of the field;

8 The fowl of the air, and the fish of the sea, and whatsoever passeth through the paths of the seas.

9 O Lord our Lord, how excellent is thy name in all the earth!

THEME

REJOICE

POWER OF PSALM

Imaginative Power; Strength Against Negative Thoughts; Forgetfulness; Thinking; Conscious Thought; Mind Power; Domination Over All Thoughts

THOUGHT FOR THE PSALM

The use of the Imagination is where the Lord delights. Rejoice in the Imagination and you rejoice in the Lord.

INTERPRETATION OF EACH VERSE

[8]O LORD, our Lord, how excellent is thy name in all the earth! who hast set thy glory above the heavens.

1. Divine Intelligence, our Infinite Intelligence, how perfect is your name in all the earth! who has placed his glory into the infinite.

[2] Out of the mouth of babes and sucklings hast thou ordained strength because of thine enemies, that thou mightest still the enemy and the avenger.

2. Out of the mouth of the children and newborn has man been given ministerial authority with strength over those negative thoughts, to silence and stop those thoughts that seek to avenge the silenced.

[3] When I consider thy heavens, the work of thy fingers, the moon and the stars, which thou hast ordained;

3. When I consider my own heaven, my Imagination, the work of my own hands, the hidden and the illumined, God has provided me authority over;

⁴What is man, that thou art mindful of him? and the son of man, that thou visitest him?

4. What is man that is not mindful of the God within his own being? and the Conscious Mind that partakes the action within him?

⁵For thou hast made him a little lower than the angels, and hast crowned him with glory and honour.

5. For God has made the Conscious Mind a little less in stature, and has given its power, glory and honor for use.

⁶Thou madest him to have dominion over the works of thy hands; thou hast put all things under his feet:

6. The Conscious Mind has been given power to have say over the works of my own hands; giving claim to all that is before me.

⁷All sheep and oxen, yea, and the beasts of the field;

7. All created thoughts and the ones that have been just initiated breath, yes, and the matured thoughts in your environment;

⁸The fowl of the air, and the fish of the sea, and whatsoever passeth through the paths of the seas.

8. The thoughts that take flight, and those that lurk, and whatever may come your way.

⁹O LORD our Lord, how excellent is thy name in all the earth!

9. Imagination, our Imagination, how perfect God is in all that manifests!

ANALYSIS OF THE SCRIPTURE

For Divine Intelligence, our Infinite Intelligence, knows how perfect His name is in all the earth! It is He within you that has placed his glory into the infinite. Out of the mouth of the children and newborn (thoughts that have been created and newly created thoughts) has man been given ministerial authority with strength over those negative thoughts. This strength allows man to silence and stop those thoughts that seek to avenge the silenced (the good thoughts that desire to fully manifest).

When you consider your own heaven, your Imagination, the work of your own hands, the hidden and the illumined, God has provided you authority over all thoughts. What is man that is not mindful of the God within his own being or the Conscious Mind that partakes the action within him?

For God has made the Conscious Mind a little less in stature for man to live by alone, and has given its power, glory, and honor for a specific purpose. The Conscious Mind has been given power to have say over the works of your own hands; giving claim to all that is before you (part of the illusion that escapes your knowing that you and the Absolute are one).

> *"And God raised the Lord and will also raise us up by his power."*
> 1 Corinthians 6:14

All created thoughts and the ones that have been just initiated breath, seek maturity on your screen of space; in your immediate environment. The thoughts that take flight, and those that lurk, and whatever may come your way are to be addressed by you. For Imagination, our Imagination, how perfect God is in all that manifests!

CHAPTER NINE

PSALM 9

ORIGINAL TEXT

9 I will praise thee, O LORD, with my whole heart; I will shew forth all thy marvellous works.

² I will be glad and rejoice in thee: I will sing praise to thy name, O thou most High.

³ When mine enemies are turned back, they shall fall and perish at thy presence.

⁴ For thou hast maintained my right and my cause; thou satest in the throne judging right.

⁵ Thou hast rebuked the heathen, thou hast destroyed the wicked, thou hast put out their name for ever and ever.

⁶ O thou enemy, destructions are come to a perpetual end: and thou hast destroyed cities; their memorial is perished with them.

⁷ But the LORD shall endure for ever: he hath prepared his throne for judgment.

⁸ And he shall judge the world in righteousness, he shall minister judgment to the people in uprightness.

⁹ The LORD also will be a refuge for the oppressed, a refuge in times of trouble.

¹⁰ And they that know thy name will put their trust in thee: for thou, LORD, hast not forsaken them that seek thee.

¹¹ Sing praises to the LORD, which dwelleth in Zion: declare among the people his doings.

¹² When he maketh inquisition for blood, he remembereth them: he forgetteth not the cry of the humble.

¹³ Have mercy upon me, O LORD; consider my trouble which I suffer of them that hate me, thou that liftest me up from the gates of death:

¹⁴ That I may shew forth all thy praise in the gates of the daughter of Zion: I will rejoice in thy salvation.

¹⁵ The heathen are sunk down in the pit that they made: in the net which they hid is their own foot taken.

¹⁶ The LORD is known by the judgment which he executeth: the wicked is snared in the work of his own hands. Higgaion. Selah.

¹⁷ The wicked shall be turned into hell, and all the nations that forget God.

¹⁸ For the needy shall not always be forgotten: the expectation of the poor shall not perish for ever.

¹⁹ Arise, O LORD; let not man prevail: let the heathen be judged in thy sight.

²⁰ Put them in fear, O LORD: that the nations may know themselves to be but men. Selah.

THEME

Miracles

POWER OF PSALM

Miracles; Praise; Troubled Mind; Doubt; Concern; Destroy Enemy Thought; Remembrance

INTERPRETATION OF EACH VERSE

9 I will praise thee, O LORD, with my whole heart; I will shew forth all thy marvellous works.

1. I will honor God, through my Imagination with my entire heart; In using my Imagination, I will manifest marvelous works.

² I will be glad and rejoice in thee: I will sing praise to thy name, O thou most High.

2. I will be glad to rejoice in my Imagination: I will express praise to the name of God, Infinite Intelligence, Creator, the Most High.

³ When mine enemies are turned back, they shall fall and perish at thy presence.

3. When my negative thoughts are turned away, they will fall and die in their presence before me.

⁴ For thou hast maintained my right and my cause; thou satest in the throne judging right.

4. For God has maintained my truth of me and my actions; sitting enthroned in the temple, Imagination, the righteousness of God prevails.

⁵ Thou hast rebuked the heathen, thou hast destroyed the wicked, thou hast put out their name for ever and ever.

5. You have condemned the unrighteous thoughts; you have destroyed such evil thoughts; you have cast the ungodly created thought manifestations forever.

⁶ O thou enemy, destructions are come to a perpetual end: and thou hast destroyed cities; their memorial is perished with them.

6. Listen, your negative thoughts, your enemy, face destruction and will face an ongoing end: and you will have destroyed their congregations; and your memory of them will die along with them.

⁷ But the LORD shall endure for ever: he hath prepared his throne for judgment.

7. The Imagination will endure forever: for he has prepared his throne, your Imagination, the place of all judgment.

⁸ And he shall judge the world in righteousness, he shall minister judgment to the people in uprightness.

8. And, he must judge the world in the view of goodness, and he will delegate his word to the thoughts of the Imagination in Goodness.

⁹ The LORD also will be a refuge for the oppressed, a refuge in times of trouble.

9. Infinite Intelligence, Imagination, is a haven for those that suffer, for it is their haven too in times of trouble.

¹⁰ And they that know thy name will put their trust in thee: for thou, LORD, hast not forsaken them that seek thee.

10. Those that know the name of God, Allah, Buddha, Confucius, Yahweh, Brahma, the name you have chosen to associate with, will put their trust in that name, their Imagination within self: for your Imagination will not let you down for all that seek its use.

¹¹ Sing praises to the LORD, which dwelleth in Zion: declare among the people his doings.

11. Express praises to God, Infinite Intelligence, which dwells in your own Imagination: declare among your thoughts the things that are capable of God in Action using your Imagination.

[12] When he maketh inquisition for blood, he remembereth them: he forgetteth not the cry of the humble.

12. When one makes an inquiry of a spiritual principle, he will remember what he needs to know: he will not forget the humble feeling.

[13] Have mercy upon me, O LORD; consider my trouble which I suffer of them that hate me, thou that liftest me up from the gates of death:

13. Have compassion upon me, hear me Imagination, Father; consider my troubled mind, thoughts which I suffer from that display displeasure with me, Father, lift me up from the gates of sure destruction.

[14] That I may shew forth all thy praise in the gates of the daughter of Zion: I will rejoice in thy salvation.

14. I desire to show my praise in the gates of subconscious mind, the receiver of the Holy Temple: and I will express happiness in your salvation of me.

[15] The heathen are sunk down in the pit that they made: in the net which they hid is their own foot taken.

15. The ungodly thoughts are ensnared in a pit that they created for themselves: in the web in which they once traveled.

[16] The LORD is known by the judgment which he executeth: the wicked is snared in the work of his own hands. Higgaion. Selah.

16. The Imagination is known by the thoughts one creates: for evil thoughts are ensnared in the work of the creator of such thoughts. Meditate. (Selah – this is foundational truth, the axiom, wherein this true statement is self-evident.)

¹⁷ **The wicked shall be turned into hell, and all the nations that forget God.**

> 17. The wicked thoughts will be subjected to suffering, and all the thoughts that forget God.

¹⁸ **For the needy shall not always be forgotten: the expectation of the poor shall not perish for ever.**

> 18. For the those in need of the truth, will not be forgotten: those faithful, that lack wisdom, will never die.

¹⁹ **Arise, O LORD; let not man prevail: let the heathen be judged in thy sight.**

> 19. Awaken, hear me Imagination, no manifestation prevails, for those that are ungodly judge their world by sight, and let them do so.

²⁰ **Put them in fear, O LORD: that the nations may know themselves to be but men. Selah.**

> 20. Place them in fear by wisdom and hear me Father: the many thoughts I have, may know themselves, that they are only manifestations. Selah. (Selah – this is foundational truth, the axiom, wherein this true statement is self-evident.)

ANALYSIS OF THE SCRIPTURE

You are to honor God, through your Imagination, with your entire heart. In using your Imagination, you will manifest marvelous works; meaning miracles. You are to be glad to rejoice in your Imagination. You are to express praise to the name of God, Infinite Intelligence, Creator, the Most High.

When your negative thoughts are turned away, they will fall and die in their presence before you. For God has maintained your truth of you and your actions. God sits enthroned in your temple, Imagination, where the righteousness of God prevails.

> *"Neither shall they say, Lo here! or, lo there! for, behold, the kingdom of God is within you."*

Luke 17:21

Acknowledge that he has condemned the unrighteous thoughts within you. Know that God is the one within you, that has destroyed such evil thoughts you manifested in the past. Know that he is the one that has cast the ungodly thought manifestations you have created, forever.

Listen and know that your negative thoughts, your enemy, face destruction and face an ongoing end. You will in time, have destroyed their congregations. Your memory of them will also die along with them.

The Imagination will endure forever, for he has prepared his throne within you. Your Imagination, the place of all judgment is where he resides. He shall judge the world in the view of goodness. He will delegate his word to the thoughts of the Imagination in goodness.

Infinite Intelligence, Imagination, is a haven for those that suffer; for it is their haven too in times of trouble. Those that know the name of God, Allah, Buddha, Confucius, Yahweh, Brahma, the name you have chosen to associate with, will put their trust in that name. It is for men to trust their Imagination within self. Your Imagination will not let you down, for all that seek its use.

> *"But seek ye first the kingdom of God, and his righteousness; and all these things shall be added unto you."*

Matthew 6:33

Express praises to God, Infinite Intelligence, which dwells in your own Imagination. Declare among your thoughts, that all things are capable by you, the God in Action, using your Imagination.

When one makes an inquiry of a spiritual principle, he will remember what he needs to know, and he will not forget the humble feeling. Asking God is visualizing. Thus, in your vision, ask for him to have compassion for you. Ask, hear me Imagination, Father: consider my troubled mind, the wicked thoughts which I suffer from that display their displeasure with me. Father lift me up from the gates of sure destruction.

Express your desire to show your praise in the gates of the subconscious mind, the receiver of the Holy Temple. Declare that you will express happiness in your salvation. Understand that the ungodly thoughts that you have created, are ensnared in a pit that they created for themselves: in the web in which they once traveled.

The Imagination is known by the thoughts one creates: for evil thoughts are ensnared in the work of the creator of such thoughts. Meditate. (Selah – this is foundational truth, the axiom, wherein this true statement is self-evident.)

The wicked thoughts must be subjected to suffering, including all the thoughts that forget God. For those in need of the truth, shall not be forgotten. Those that are faithful, and even lack wisdom, will never die.

> *"But turning around and seeing His disciples, He rebuked Peter and said, "Get behind Me, Satan; for you are not setting your mind on God's interests, but man's."*

Mark 8:33

Awaken, and declare that the Imagination hear you. Manifestation will not prevail for those that are ungodly and judge their world by sight. If they do, let them do so. Place your negative thoughts in fear of wisdom and ask your Father to hear your call. The many negative thoughts you have, are to know themselves, that they are only manifestations. Selah.

CHAPTER TEN

PSALM 10

ORIGINAL TEXT

10 Why standest thou afar off, O LORD? why hidest thou thyself in times of trouble?

² The wicked in his pride doth persecute the poor: let them be taken in the devices that they have imagined.

³ For the wicked boasteth of his heart's desire, and blesseth the covetous, whom the LORD abhorreth.

⁴ The wicked, through the pride of his countenance, will not seek after God: God is not in all his thoughts.

⁵ His ways are always grievous; thy judgments are far above out of his sight: as for all his enemies, he puffeth at them.

⁶ He hath said in his heart, I shall not be moved: for I shall never be in adversity.

⁷ His mouth is full of cursing and deceit and fraud: under his tongue is mischief and vanity.

⁸ He sitteth in the lurking places of the villages: in the secret places doth he murder the innocent: his eyes are privily set against the poor.

⁹ He lieth in wait secretly as a lion in his den: he lieth in wait to catch the poor: he doth catch the poor, when he draweth him into his net.

¹⁰ He croucheth, and humbleth himself, that the poor may fall by his strong ones.

¹¹ He hath said in his heart, God hath forgotten: he hideth his face; he will never see it.

¹² Arise, O LORD; O God, lift up thine hand: forget not the humble.

¹³ Wherefore doth the wicked contemn God? he hath said in his heart, Thou wilt not require it.

¹⁴ Thou hast seen it; for thou beholdest mischief and spite, to requite it with thy hand: the poor committeth himself unto thee; thou art the helper of the fatherless.

¹⁵ Break thou the arm of the wicked and the evil man: seek out his wickedness till thou find none.

¹⁶ The LORD is King for ever and ever: the heathen are perished out of his land.

¹⁷ LORD, thou hast heard the desire of the humble: thou wilt prepare their heart, thou wilt cause thine ear to hear:

¹⁸ To judge the fatherless and the oppressed, that the man of the earth may no more oppress.

THEME

TROUBLED MIND

POWER OF PSALM

Troubled Mind; Doubt; Economy of Thought

THOUGHT FOR THE PSALM

The only thoughts that one should keep, are loving and positive thoughts. For the Lord delights in righteous thinking to ease a troubled mind. He sets arrows upon those thoughts that are sinful.

INTERPRETATION OF EACH VERSE

10 Why standest thou afar off, O LORD? why hidest thyself in times of trouble?

1. Why be distant when it comes to hearing the Lord, to knowing the power of your Imagination? Why do you hide from the Imagination, God in Action when there are troubled times?

² The wicked in his pride doth persecute the poor: let them be taken in the devices that they have imagined.

2. Evil thoughts, wicked heart, prides itself on persecuting those that are without what it is they desire: allow those that think such thoughts be taken by their own instruments of destruction, for that is what they imagined in.

³ For the wicked boasteth of his heart's desire, and blesseth the covetous, whom the LORD abhorreth.

3. For those thoughts that are evil in their ways, meaning wicked thoughts, may brag about their doing until their heart's desire, and reward themselves with something they believe in and

others don't. The Lord, God the Father does not tolerate such actions.

⁴ The wicked, through the pride of his countenance, will not seek after God: God is not in all his thoughts.

4. The evil, through the pride of his own expression, will not seek after God: God is not what he thinks about; righteous is not what he thinks about.

⁵ His ways are always grievous; thy judgments are far above out of his sight: as for all his enemies, he puffeth at them.

5. His ways are always referring to suffering; his judgments are even out of reach of what he can see: as for all his thoughts, he tries to maintain them.

⁶ He hath said in his heart, I shall not be moved: for I shall never be in adversity.

6. He has said within his own heart, with his evil ways, he will not be moved from such thoughts: for he must never be against himself.

⁷ His mouth is full of cursing and deceit and fraud: under his tongue is mischief and vanity.

7. His mouth is full of hateful words and lies, and even fraud: his tongue speaks of evil doings and is concerned with the appearance of things.

⁸ He sitteth in the lurking places of the villages: in the secret places doth he murder the innocent: his eyes are privily set against the poor.

8. He resides in darkness of his many evil thoughts: in hidden places he exposes himself to commit murder of his good and loving thoughts; his eyes are set only to recognize the lack and suffering that his thoughts have created for himself or others.

⁹ **He lieth in wait secretly as a lion in his den: he lieth in wait to catch the poor: he doth catch the poor, when he draweth him into his net.**

9. The wicked secretly lieth in wait within the darkness of the Imagination, as a lion does in his den: looking to catch those that are weak or lack: and by his will of his dark thoughts, he draws them into his trap, and consumes them.

¹⁰ **He croucheth, and humbleth himself, that the poor may fall by his strong ones.**

10. The wicked, hunkers down and contains his self-assertiveness, expecting that those thoughts of himself or others that lack faith in their actions, will be overcome by his own dominating evil thoughts.

¹¹ **He hath said in his heart, God hath forgotten: he hideth his face; he will never see it.**

11. Convinced and declares in his own mind, God doesn't recognize him: and that God hides his face of truth; never to be seen.

¹² **Arise, O LORD; O God, lift up thine hand: forget not the humble.**

12. However, awaken and hear the Lord, your Imagination, for he lifts the hand of truth: doing so in a humble fashion.

¹³ **Wherefore doth the wicked contemn God? he hath said in his heart, Thou wilt not require it.**

13. Where is the place that disrespect is shown of God? One knows, in his Imagination, but the wicked will not require the use of Imagination.

¹⁴ **Thou hast seen it; for thou beholdest mischief and spite, to requite it with thy hand: the poor committeth himself unto thee; thou art the helper of the fatherless.**

14. You have seen it, now witness the wrong- doing and ill will of a wicked thought, claim by his own ability and commitment to

repay the poor through his own means. For he is the one that claims he is the helper of the lost thoughts or people.

¹⁵ Break thou the arm of the wicked and the evil man: seek out his wickedness till thou find none.

15. Do not conform to the strength of evil, who claim to do righteous for the poor. For those thoughts that lack faith, identify with all wicked thoughts until there are none left to find.

¹⁶ The LORD is King for ever and ever: the heathen are perished out of his land.

16. Infinite Intelligence, Universal Mind, Imagination is the Ruler forever more; the ungodly thoughts are banished from the mind.

¹⁷ LORD, thou hast heard the desire of the humble: thou wilt prepare their heart, thou wilt cause thine ear to hear:

17. Infinite Intelligence, you have heard the prayer of the humble: you will prepare their heart to hear good news, the good news of Spirit, the good news of God.

¹⁸ To judge the fatherless and the oppressed, that the man of the earth may no more oppress.

18. No longer should there be need to judge unattended thoughts or thoughts of oppression, for change of thought will wipe away all oppression.

ANALYSIS OF THE SCRIPTURE

Why be distant when it comes to hearing the Lord, to knowing the power of your Imagination? Why do you hide from the Imagination, God in Action when there are troubled times? Evil thoughts, wicked hearts, pride themselves on persecuting those that are without what it is they desire. Allow those that think such thoughts be taken by their own instruments of destruction, for that is what they imagined.

> *"Can a man hide himself in hiding places So I do not see him?" declares the LORD "Do I not fill the heavens and the earth?" declares the LORD.*
>
> *Jeremiah 23:24*

For those that are evil in their ways, having wicked thoughts, may brag about their conduct until their heart's desire. They reward themselves in things they believe in, that others don't have. Other than goodness, the Lord, God the Father does not tolerate such actions.

The evil thought, through the pride of his own expression, will not seek after God. God is not what he thinks about. Righteousness is not what he thinks about. His ways are always referring to suffering; his judgments are even out of reach of what he can see: as for all his troubling, negative thoughts, he tries to maintain them.

He has said within his own heart, within his own mind with his evil ways, he will not be moved from by obstacles: for such a person must never be against himself. His mouth is full of hateful words and lies, and even fraud. His tongue speaks of evil doings and is concerned with the appearance of things.

He resides in darkness of his many evil thoughts: in hidden places he exposes himself to commit murder of his good and loving thoughts. His eyes are set only to recognize the lack and suffering that his thoughts have created for himself or others.

The wicked secretly lieth in wait within the darkness of their Imagination, as a lion does in his den, looking to catch those that are weak or lack. And by his will of his dark thoughts, he draws them into his trap, and consumes them.

> *"Now when he had gone, a lion met him on the way and killed him, and his body was thrown on the road, with the donkey standing beside it; the lion also was standing beside the body. And behold, men passed by and saw the body thrown on the road, and the lion standing beside the body; so they came and told it in the city where the old prophet lived. Now when the prophet who brought him back from the way heard it, he said, "It is the man of God, who disobeyed the command of the LORD; therefore the LORD has given him to the lion, which has torn him and killed him, according to the word of the LORD which He spoke to him." Then he spoke to his sons, saying, "Saddle the donkey for me." And they saddled it. He went and found his body thrown on the road with the donkey and the lion standing beside the body; the lion had not eaten the body nor torn the donkey."*
>
> **1 Kings 13:24-28**

The wicked, hunkers down and contains his self-assertiveness, expecting that those thoughts of himself or others that lack faith in their actions, will be overcome by his own dominating evil thoughts.

Convinced and declaring in his own heart, God doesn't recognize him: thus, a man of wicked thoughts hides his face of truth so God will never see it. However, awaken and hear the Lord, your Imagination, and use your ability to Imagine with humbleness.

Where is the place that disrespect is shown of God? One knows, in his Imagination, but the wicked will not require the use of Imagination. You have seen it, now witness the wrong- doing and ill will of a wicked thought, claim by his own ability and commitment to repay the poor through his own means. For he is the one that claims he is the helper of the lost thoughts or people.

Do not conform to the strength of evil, who claim to do righteous for the poor. For those thoughts that lack faith, identify with all wicked thoughts until there are none left to find.

Infinite Intelligence, Universal Mind, Imagination is Ruler forever more. With the help of Infinite Intelligence, the ungodly thoughts are banished from the mind.

Know that Infinite Intelligence, has heard the prayer of the humble. You are to prepare your heart to hear good news, the good news of Spirit, and the good news of God. No longer should there be need to judge unattended thoughts or thoughts of oppression; for change of thought will wipe away all oppression.

CHAPTER ELEVEN

PSALM 11

ORIGINAL TEXT

11 In the Lord put I my trust: how say ye to my soul, Flee as a bird to your mountain?

² For, lo, the wicked bend their bow, they make ready their arrow upon the string, that they may privily shoot at the upright in heart.

³ If the foundations be destroyed, what can the righteous do?

⁴ The Lord is in his holy temple, the Lord's throne is in heaven: his eyes behold, his eyelids try, the children of men.

⁵ The Lord trieth the righteous: but the wicked and him that loveth violence his soul hateth.

⁶ Upon the wicked he shall rain snares, fire and brimstone, and an horrible tempest: this shall be the portion of their cup.

⁷ For the righteous Lord loveth righteousness; his countenance doth behold the upright.

THEME

TRUST

POWER OF PSALM

When in Doubt; Need of Confidence; Feeling of Betrayal; Emotional Strength

THOUGHT FOR THE PSALM

If you trust in God, the God within you and not something separate and apart from you, your life will change forever.

When Moses conversed with God in the Christian scripture of the Book of Exodus 3:13-14, Moses asked the question: "Indeed, when I come to the children of Israel and say to them, 'The God of your fathers has sent me to you,' and they say to me, 'What is His name?' what shall I say to them?" And God replied unto Moses: "I AM WHO I AM." And He said, "Thus you shall say to the children of Israel, 'I AM has sent me to you.'" You are to trust the "I AM".

The "I AM" is you and the God within you.

INTERPRETATION OF EACH VERSE

1 1 In the LORD put I my trust: how say ye to my soul, Flee as a bird to your mountain?

    1. In my Imagination I place my trust: this is what you tell your soul, your being. Run from your own obstacles?

² For, lo, the wicked bend their bow, they make ready their arrow upon the string, that they may privily shoot at the upright in heart.

    2. Understand, the wicked or evil thoughts try your patience, and they set ready to sting you like an arrow, knowing that they will hit you right where it hurts most.

³ **If the foundations be destroyed, what can the righteous do?**

    3. If you let them hit their mark and destroy the base of what is to be built by you, how much can God help you?

⁴ **The Lord is in his holy temple, the Lord's throne is in heaven: his eyes behold, his eyelids try, the children of men.**

    4. The Imagination is the holy temple of God, for it is the throne of heaven in every man: for Infinite Intelligence, God, sees and has man bear witness of what is possible, for in the sight of God, you will find all thoughts as manifestation.

⁵ **The Lord trieth the righteous: but the wicked and him that loveth violence his soul hateth.**

    5. The Imagination, Lord Jesus, Mohammad, Krishna, test those that seek the Good: but the evil thoughts and the man that loves such thoughts of violence hates his own mind, and his mind does not actually seek the Good.

⁶ **Upon the wicked he shall rain snares, fire and brimstone, and an horrible tempest: this shall be the portion of their cup.**

    6. Upon the evil thoughts, man must create his own traps, his own pain and suffering, and face horrible storms of his creation; this must be the cup they drink from.

⁷ **For the righteous Lord loveth righteousness; his countenance doth behold the upright.**

    7. For those that seek God, loving good; his expression is to be one that seeks to witness the truth.

ANALYSIS OF THE SCRIPTURE

In your Imagination is where you are to place your trust: this is what you tell your soul, your mind. Run from your own obstacles? Understand, the wicked or evil thoughts try your patience, and they set ready to sting you like an arrow, knowing that they will hit you right where it hurts most.

If you let them hit their mark and destroy the base of what is to be built by you, how much can God help you? The Imagination is the holy temple of God, for it is the throne of heaven in every man. Infinite Intelligence, God, sees and has man bear witness of what is possible. In the sight of God, you will find that all thoughts can manifest.

The Imagination, Lord Jesus, Mohammad, Krishna, test those that seek the Good. But the evil thoughts and the man that loves such thoughts of violence hates his own mind. Such a man that thinks ill thoughts is a person where his mind does not actually seek Goodness.

Upon the creation of evil thoughts, man will encounter his own traps, his own pain and suffering, and face horrible storms of his own creation; this must be the cup they drink from. For those that seek God, loving good; their expression is to be one that seeks to witness the truth.

> *"Have I not commanded you? Be strong and courageous. Do not be afraid; do not be discouraged, for the LORD your God will be with you wherever you go."*
>
> *Joshua 1:9*

CHAPTER TWELVE

PSALM 12

ORIGINAL TEXT

12 Help, Lord; for the godly man ceaseth; for the faithful fail from among the children of men.

² They speak vanity every one with his neighbour: with flattering lips and with a double heart do they speak.

³ The Lord shall cut off all flattering lips, and the tongue that speaketh proud things:

⁴ Who have said, With our tongue will we prevail; our lips are our own: who is lord over us?

⁵ For the oppression of the poor, for the sighing of the needy, now will I arise, saith the Lord; I will set him in safety from him that puffeth at him.

⁶ The words of the Lord are pure words: as silver tried in a furnace of earth, purified seven times.

⁷ Thou shalt keep them, O Lord, thou shalt preserve them from this generation for ever.

⁸ The wicked walk on every side, when the vilest men are exalted.

THEME:

Congregation of the Wicked Speaking to You

POWER OF PSALM:

Wicked Lip Service; Inner Conversation of the Wicked;

THOUGHT FOR THE PSALM

When the congregation of wicked thoughts continually speak to you, causing trouble in your mind, send them to the Lord.

INTERPRETATION OF EACH VERSE

12 Help, LORD; for the godly man ceaseth; for the faithful fail from among the children of men.

1. Universal Mind, I ask for help, for my good manifestations, my good creations have stopped; for the faithful thoughts I once had, have succumb to doubt and mistrust; leading me to unwanted results.

² They speak vanity every one with his neighbour: with flattering lips and with a double heart do they speak.

2. They are now judged by their appearance, their actual manifestation and one negative thought tends to share with another; and from my mouth, I may believe I speak the word of good, when actually I'm not.

³ The LORD shall cut off all flattering lips, and the tongue that speaketh proud things:

3. It is the Imagination that shall cut off the words of the false prophet, and have man speak of things he can once again be proud of:

⁴ Who have said, With our tongue will we prevail; our lips are our own: who is lord over us?

4. Who has told you that from your tongue, your good thoughts will prevail; for the words come from your thoughts, and your thoughts alone, thus the question becomes who is lord over those thoughts?

⁵ For the oppression of the poor, for the sighing of the needy, now will I arise, saith the LORD; I will set him in safety from him that puffeth at him.

5. As for the cruelty of the thoughts that lack faith, take a deep breath as to imagine what you need, and maintain what faith you have, and your Imagination will awaken; for God will take such thoughts of man and lead him to safety from those that seek to lead him astray.

⁶ The words of the LORD are pure words: as silver tried in a furnace of earth, purified seven times.

6. The words of the Christ are pure words: awareness brought forth despite suffering manifestations, too, will be rewarded by divine spirit.

⁷ Thou shalt keep them, O LORD, thou shalt preserve them from this generation for ever.

7. Keep your thoughts, hear Imagination, you must keep such thoughts from that evil generation forever.

⁸The wicked walk on every side, when the vilest men are exalted.

8. Evil thoughts are all around, but even the most morally despicable man too can be exalted.

ANALYSIS OF THE SCRIPTURE

From Universal Mind, you are to ask for help. Your good manifestations, your good creations have stopped manifesting your inner desires. For the faithful thoughts you once had, have succumb to doubt and mistrust, leading you to unwanted results. It is because of your prior negative manifestations that your good thoughts have been stifled.

Negative manifestations, thoughts, judge you by sight and by your appearance. All the negative, doubtful and deceitful thoughts tend to share with one another; and from your mouth, you may believe you speak the word of good, when you are not. You must be conscious of your thoughts.

> *"But they became disobedient and rebelled against You, And cast Your law behind their backs And killed Your prophets who had admonished them So that they might return to You, And they committed great blasphemies."*
>
> *Nehemiah 9:26*

It is the Imagination that shall cut off the words of the false prophet, and have man speak of things he can once again be proud of. You are to know, in order to answer the question: who has told you that from your tongue, your good thoughts will prevail? From the words you speak, come from your thoughts; and your thoughts alone. Thus, the question becomes, who is lord over those thoughts?

As for the cruelty of the thoughts that lack faith, take a deep breath and imagine what you desire. Maintain what faith you have, and your Imagination will awaken; for God will take such thoughts of man and lead him to safety from those that seek to lead you astray. The words of the Christ are pure words. Awareness is brought forth despite suffering manifestations; and they too, will be rewarded by Divine Spirit.

Keep your good thoughts. Hear your Imagination. You must keep such thoughts from an evil generation or congregation forever. Evil thoughts are all around you, but even the most morally despicable man too can be exalted.

CHAPTER THIRTEEN

PSALM 13

ORIGINAL TEXT

13 How long wilt thou forget me, O LORD? for ever? how long wilt thou hide thy face from me?

² How long shall I take counsel in my soul, having sorrow in my heart daily? how long shall mine enemy be exalted over me?

³ Consider and hear me, O LORD my God: lighten mine eyes, lest I sleep the sleep of death;

⁴ Lest mine enemy say, I have prevailed against him; and those that trouble me rejoice when I am moved.

⁵ But I have trusted in thy mercy; my heart shall rejoice in thy salvation.

⁶ I will sing unto the LORD, because he hath dealt bountifully with me.

THEME

Change in Favor of the Lord

POWER OF PSALM

Change. Change in circumstances or situations. Desire a change within yourself or someone else.

THOUGHT FOR THE PSALM

When confused about your existence, needing to know what to do in a circumstance or situation, seek salvation in the Lord God.

INTERPRETATION OF EACH VERSE

13 **How long wilt thou forget me, O LORD? for ever? how long wilt thou hide thy face from me?**

1. Hear me Infinite Intelligence. How long will you forget me? Will this continue forever? How long will you hide your truth from me?

² How long shall I take counsel in my soul, having sorrow in my heart daily? how long shall mine enemy be exalted over me?

2. How long must I seek advice of my own inner being, as I suffer in my heart daily for lack of your knowing? How long shall the conscious or reasoning mind that is against me, be given power over me?

³ Consider and hear me, O LORD my God: lighten mine eyes, lest I sleep the sleep of death;

3. Account for and hear me, Infinite Intelligence, your Imagination, your God: expose my eyes so I no longer experience the darkness of the sleep of death;

⁴ Lest mine enemy say, I have prevailed against him; and those that trouble me rejoice when I am moved.

4. Let your enemy, your negative thoughts tell you that I, your Imagination, God, has prevailed; and those thoughts that once troubled you, will be no longer, for you will be happy when I am moved to answer your prayers.

⁵ But I have trusted in thy mercy; my heart shall rejoice in thy salvation.

5. Trusting in mercy, your heart will rejoice in your salvation.

⁶ I will sing unto the LORD, because he hath dealt bountifully with me.

6. Praise be unto the Lord, the God in me, because God has provided abundantly for me.

ANALYSIS OF THE SCRIPTURE

The question is, how long will you forget me? This question was being directed to the use of your own Imagination. You are asking this question of yourself.

The judgment you have created upon yourself of being forgotten, begs you to recognize what are you asking of yourself: will this continue forever? Seeking truth, you also ask, how long will God hide his truth from you? The truth is that you have failed to use your own Imagination to fulfill your desire to stop all the negative thoughts that besiege you.

> *However, at that time, when you did not know God, you were slaves to those which by nature are no gods. But now that you have come to know God, or rather to be known by God, how is it that you turn back again to the weak and worthless elemental things, to which you desire to be enslaved all over again?*
>
> *Galatians 4:8-9*

As time passes, your questions will continue. The questions such as, how long must you seek advice of your own inner being, as you suffer in your mind daily for lack of your knowing? How long shall the conscious or reasoning thoughts in your mind that are against you, be given power over you?

In asking these questions, it is up to you to lift your head up and receive counsel from Higher Intelligence. Ask Higher Intelligence to account for and hear your call. Ask Infinite Intelligence, your Imagination, God, to expose your eyes. You should no longer look to experience the darkness of the sleep of death.

Let your enemy, your negative thoughts tell you that your Imagination, God, has prevailed over such them. And those thoughts that once troubled you, will no longer do so; for you will be happy when you are moved with answered prayers.

Trusting in the mercy of God, your heart will rejoice in your salvation. Praise be unto the Lord, the God in you, because God has provided abundantly for you.

CHAPTER FOURTEEN

PSALM 14

ORIGINAL TEXT

14 The fool hath said in his heart, There is no God. They are corrupt, they have done abominable works, there is none that doeth good.

² The LORD looked down from heaven upon the children of men, to see if there were any that did understand, and seek God.

³ They are all gone aside, they are all together become filthy: there is none that doeth good, no, not one.

⁴ Have all the workers of iniquity no knowledge? who eat up my people as they eat bread, and call not upon the LORD.

⁵ There were they in great fear: for God is in the generation of the righteous.

⁶ Ye have shamed the counsel of the poor, because the LORD is his refuge.

⁷ Oh that the salvation of Israel were come out of Zion! when the LORD bringeth back the captivity of his people, Jacob shall rejoice, and Israel shall be glad.

THEME

LACKING FAITH IN THE GOD THAT YOU ARE AND THE GOD WITHIN YOU

POWER IN PSALM

Build faith in God; Doubting; Seeking God; Self Confidence

THOUGHT FOR THE PSALM

Faith is required in all things. When one has faith, they are to understand that the world was created by the word of God. Thus, things that are seen on your screen of space, are made out of that which does not appear before you.

"Now Faith is the assurance of things hoped for, the evidence of things not seen."

Hebrews 11:1

INTERPRETATION OF EACH VERSE

14 The fool hath said in his heart, There is no God. They are corrupt, they have done abominable works, there is none that doeth good.

1. The one that lacks righteous judgment says in his mind, that there is no God. They are bad character in thought, for they are responsible for hatred or unpleasant works, and none of the bad thoughts can do good.

² The LORD looked down from heaven upon the children of men, to see if there were any that did understand, and seek God.

2. God, residing within your own Imagination, the Universal Mind, sees all the thoughts of many manifestations (men), to see

if any good thoughts exist, understanding and seek God in the midst of all the thoughts created by man (manifestation).

³ They are all gone aside, they are all together become filthy: there is none that doeth good, no, not one.

3. When it comes to negative thoughts, they have all gone astray, and are considered not worthy, but vile: and none of the negative thoughts can be identified to the good of God.

⁴ Have all the workers of iniquity no knowledge? who eat up my people as they eat bread, and call not upon the LORD.

4. The question is, do wicked thoughts have any wisdom? Such thoughts are responsible for consuming the thoughts of manifestations (men), who take from the substance of source from which all thoughts, good, bad or indifferent come from; but never call upon the Lord, the Imagination for righteousness.

⁵ There were they in great fear: for God is in the generation of the righteous.

5. Fearing (negative thoughts) of being overcome where they eat their bread: for God, is responsible for creating for thoughts that do good.

⁶ Ye have shamed the counsel of the poor, because the LORD is his refuge.

6. You have placed guilt among the thoughts you have that are lacking, because the Imagination is your haven of all thoughts.

⁷ Oh that the salvation of Israel were come out of Zion! when the LORD bringeth back the captivity of his people, Jacob shall rejoice, and Israel shall be glad.

7. See enlightened thoughts, thoughts that have manifested from Imagination! When man, God, creates order among his thoughts, the higher consciousness (Jacob) will rejoice, and all enlightened thoughts of God will rejoice.

ANALYSIS OF THE SCRIPTURE

The one that lacks righteous judgment says in his mind that there is no God. They are bad character in thought, for they are responsible for hatred or unpleasant works, and none of their bad thoughts can do good.

God, residing within your own Imagination, the Universal Mind, sees all the thoughts of many manifestations (men), to see if any good thoughts exist. God within the Imagination, delivers understanding and rewards those who seek God in the midst of all the negative and doubtful thoughts created by man (manifestation).

When it comes to negative thoughts, they have all gone astray, and are considered not worthy, but vile. None of the negative thoughts can be identified with the good of God. The question is, do wicked thoughts have any wisdom? Such thoughts are responsible for consuming the thoughts of manifestations (men).

He said to them, "Why are you afraid, you men of little faith?" Then He got up and rebuked the winds and the sea, and it became perfectly calm.

Matthew 8:26

All men take from the substance of source from which all thoughts, good, bad or indifferent come from. However, men with negative thoughts never call upon the Lord, the Imagination for righteousness. Negative thoughts fear being overcome where they eat their bread; for God is responsible for creating for thoughts that do good, and the demise of all others.

You have placed guilt among the thoughts you have that are lacking, because the Imagination is your haven of all thoughts. Instead, see enlightened thoughts, wonderful thoughts that have manifested from Imagination! When man, God, creates order among his thoughts, the higher consciousness (Jacob) will rejoice, and all enlightened thoughts of God will be glad.

CHAPTER FIFTEEN

PSALM 15

15 Lord, who shall abide in thy tabernacle? who shall dwell in thy holy hill?

² He that walketh uprightly, and worketh righteousness, and speaketh the truth in his heart.

³ He that backbiteth not with his tongue, nor doeth evil to his neighbour, nor taketh up a reproach against his neighbour.

⁴ In whose eyes a vile person is contemned; but he honoureth them that fear the LORD. He that sweareth to his own hurt, and changeth not.

⁵ He that putteth not out his money to usury, nor taketh reward against the innocent. He that doeth these things shall never be moved.

THEME

LEARNING THE TRUTH

POWER IN PSALM

Wisdom; Greater Understanding; Ungodly Words Spoken to You; Unjust or Unfair Judgment

THOUGHT FOR THE PSALM

To know the God within, make your declaration of his existence in him, and he in you.

INTERPRETATION OF EACH VERSE

15 Lord, who shall abide in thy tabernacle? who shall dwell in thy holy hill?

1. God, who remains fixed in my heaven, my subconscious? Who must be the one that keeps their directed attention on me in heaven?

² He that walketh uprightly, and worketh righteousness, and speaketh the truth in his heart.

2. The manifestation that walks with the godly, in thought, and works with Good – God thoughts, and speaks the word of God from his heart or mind.

³ He that backbiteth not with his tongue, nor doeth evil to his neighbour, nor taketh up a reproach against his neighbour.

3. The man that doesn't speak with a forked tongue, who neither creates evil thoughts among his own thoughts nor the thoughts of others, nor blames his other thoughts or the thoughts of others.

⁴ In whose eyes a vile person is condemned; but he honoureth them that fear the LORD. He that sweareth to his own hurt, and changeth not.

4. Whomever condemns or judges a man as abhorrent or foul in action or thought, honor that man also, for that man too is God. The man that curses upon another, is only cursing himself, for God doesn't change.

⁵ He that putteth not out his money to usury, nor taketh reward against the innocent. He that doeth these things shall never be moved.

5. He that neither takes his treasured thoughts and subjects them to heavy burdens, nor take claim from other thoughts or other people for what they have been graced with. This man will not be shaken, for his faith stands strong

ANALYSIS OF THE SCRIPTURE

Is it not God who remains fixed in your heaven, your subconscious? Who must be the one that keeps their directed attention on you in heaven? It is the manifestation that walks with the godly, in thought, and works with Good – God thoughts, and speaks the word of God from his heart or mind.

The man that doesn't speak with a forked tongue, who neither creates evil thoughts among his own thoughts nor the thoughts of others. This man that neither blames his thoughts or the thoughts of others, gets to know where God is.

Whomever condemns or judges a man as abhorrent or foul in action or thought, honor that man also; for that man too is God. The man that curses upon another, is only cursing himself, for God doesn't change.

He that neither takes his treasured thoughts and subjects them to heavy burdens, nor takes claim from other thoughts or other people for what they have been graced with. Such man will not be shaken; for their faith stands strong.

For the word of God is alive and active. Sharper than any double-edged sword, it penetrates even to dividing soul and spirit, joints and marrow; it judges the thoughts and attitudes of the heart.

Hebrews 4:12

CHAPTER SIXTEEN

PSALM 16

ORIGINAL TEXT

16 Preserve me, O God: for in thee do I put my trust.

² O my soul, thou hast said unto the LORD, Thou art my Lord: my goodness extendeth not to thee;

³ But to the saints that are in the earth, and to the excellent, in whom is all my delight.

⁴ Their sorrows shall be multiplied that hasten after another god: their drink offerings of blood will I not offer, nor take up their names into my lips.

⁵ The LORD is the portion of mine inheritance and of my cup: thou maintainest my lot.

⁶ The lines are fallen unto me in pleasant places; yea, I have a goodly heritage.

⁷ I will bless the LORD, who hath given me counsel: my reins also instruct me in the night seasons.

⁸ I have set the LORD always before me: because he is at my right hand, I shall not be moved.

⁹ Therefore my heart is glad, and my glory rejoiceth: my flesh also shall rest in hope.

¹⁰ For thou wilt not leave my soul in hell; neither wilt thou suffer thine Holy One to see corruption.

¹¹ Thou wilt shew me the path of life: in thy presence is fulness of joy; at thy right hand there are pleasures for evermore.

THEME

TRUST, FOR THE INHERITANCE IS YOURS

POWER OF PSALM

Trust, Manifestation, Guidance, Happiness, Counsel, Confidence

THOUGHT FOR THE PSALM

Whatever you imagine with focus and feeling, persisting in the faith of the thing desired, it shall be yours.

INTERPRETATION OF EACH VERSE

16 Preserve me, O God: for in thee do I put my trust.

1. God within me, my wonderful human Imagination, I place my trust.

² O my soul, thou hast said unto the LORD, Thou art my Lord: my goodness extendeth not to thee;

2. My Consciousness is the word of God. My Imagination is my Lord: my goodness is Infinite Wisdom, and there is nothing else.

³ But to the saints that are in the earth, and to the excellent, in whom is all my delight.

3. To the thoughts of blessings below, manifested on earth, the excellent thoughts, I delight in such thoughts.

⁴ Their sorrows shall be multiplied that hasten after another god: their drink offerings of blood will I not offer, nor take up their names into my lips.

4. To anyone that chooses to trust in anything outside of themselves, they have the wrong God; their sorrows shall increase many times over; their offer to partake in their spiritual practice in believing in another god, then God will not acknowledge, nor even recognize the false god.

⁵ The LORD is the portion of mine inheritance and of my cup: thou maintainest my lot.

5. The Imagination is the Kingdom of God all for me to inherit that which I desire. And my emotions directed towards heaven will help me maintain all that is for me.

⁶ The lines are fallen unto me in pleasant places; yea, I have a goodly heritage.

6. Pleasant pathways have come before me, and yes, my rewards are righteous.

⁷ I will bless the LORD, who hath given me counsel: my reins also instruct me in the night seasons.

7. I will reward my Imagination, for God gives me counsel within it. My meditation also instructs me in times of trouble or darkness.

⁸ I have set the LORD always before me: because he is at my right hand, I shall not be moved.

8. I have set my call to Universal Intelligence to guide me, for he guides me righteously, and thus I can't be swayed by anything other.

⁹ Therefore my heart is glad, and my glory rejoiceth: my flesh also shall rest in hope.

9. Therefore, my heart is happy, for my happiness rejoices in praise. My body rests, as surely, I am in the safety of the Lord.

¹⁰ For thou wilt not leave my soul in hell; neither wilt thou suffer thine Holy One to see corruption.

> 10. For God is always with my being including times of suffering. No longer will God see suffering by corruption from me.

¹¹ Thou wilt shew me the path of life: in thy presence is fulness of joy; at thy right hand there are pleasures for evermore.

> 11. God will show me the path of life; in his presence, is fullness of joy, and his truth brings pleasures forever.

ANALYSIS OF THE SCRIPTURE

It is the God within you that you are to trust. For the God in you is your own wonderful human Imagination in action. Knowing how to use your Imagination creates consciousness, and your consciousness is the word of God. Your consciousness may be called whatever name you desire to give it; but know that consciousness is to reflect the goodness of God and that there is nothing else.

It is by your thoughts in heaven above that bring about angels or blessings on earth. For these blessings are loving or what can be termed as excellent thoughts by the Imagination engineer. Beautiful thoughts are what you are to delight in. For anyone to trust in some God outside of themselves, they have the wrong God. In doing so, their sorrows will increase many times over. God will not acknowledge the calls of that person, nor recognize the false god.

The Imagination is the Kingdom of God, and that is the only God that will give you counsel. Counsel will be given to you in both good times and bad times. Fix in your heart your call to the Divine to guide you; for he will guide you righteously. Do not be swayed by any other thoughts.

> *House and wealth are an inheritance from fathers, But a prudent wife is from the LORD.*
>
> *Proverbs 19:14*

In trusting in the Lord, the Law, your heart will be happy, and continue to rejoice in the praise of God. Your mind and body will always be at peace knowing you are in the safety of the Lord. God is always with your being, in both good times and bad. Declare upon yourself that God will no longer see suffering by corruption from you.

CHAPTER SEVENTEEN

PSALM 17

ORIGINAL TEXT

17 Hear the right, O LORD, attend unto my cry, give ear unto my prayer, that goeth not out of feigned lips.

2 Let my sentence come forth from thy presence; let thine eyes behold the things that are equal.

3 Thou hast proved mine heart; thou hast visited me in the night; thou hast tried me, and shalt find nothing; I am purposed that my mouth shall not transgress.

4 Concerning the works of men, by the word of thy lips I have kept me from the paths of the destroyer.

5 Hold up my goings in thy paths, that my footsteps slip not.

6 I have called upon thee, for thou wilt hear me, O God: incline thine ear unto me, and hear my speech.

7 Shew thy marvellous lovingkindness, O thou that savest by thy right hand them which put their trust in thee from those that rise up against them.

8 Keep me as the apple of the eye, hide me under the shadow of thy wings,

9 From the wicked that oppress me, from my deadly enemies, who compass me about.

¹⁰ They are inclosed in their own fat: with their mouth they speak proudly.

¹¹ They have now compassed us in our steps: they have set their eyes bowing down to the earth;

¹² Like as a lion that is greedy of his prey, and as it were a young lion lurking in secret places.

¹³ Arise, O LORD, disappoint him, cast him down: deliver my soul from the wicked, which is thy sword:

¹⁴ From men which are thy hand, O LORD, from men of the world, which have their portion in this life, and whose belly thou fillest with thy hid treasure: they are full of children, and leave the rest of their substance to their babes.

¹⁵ As for me, I will behold thy face in righteousness: I shall be satisfied, when I awake, with thy likeness.

THEME

DIRECTION IN LIFE

POWER OF PSALM:

Feeling Lost; Feeling Lonely; Seeking; Searching; Depression; Despair; Anxiety

THOUGHT FOR THE PSALM

Travel due north and turn to heaven above. You will always find then find yourself on the right path.

INTERPRETATION OF EACH VERSE

17 **Hear the right, O LORD, attend unto my cry, give ear unto my prayer, that goeth not out of feigned lips.**

1. Hear with your right hand, the hand of justice and attend to my call. Listen to my prayer that goes forth, for my words are genuine.

² Let my sentence come forth from thy presence; let thine eyes behold the things that are equal.

2. Let my words speak for me, and let the eyes of the Lord bring to me all that I desire.

³ Thou hast proved mine heart; thou hast visited me in the night; thou hast tried me, and shalt find nothing; I am purposed that my mouth shall not transgress.

3. My Imagination has shown me truth. You have visited me in times of darkness, you have tried my resolve of faith, and you have found nothing. For my purpose is that my mouth will not violate the Law of God.

⁴ Concerning the works of men, by the word of thy lips I have kept me from the paths of the destroyer.

4. Concerning the works of manifestations already created, through faith, and by the word of my mouth, I have been able to avoid the path of the ungodly.

⁵ Hold up my goings in thy paths, that my footsteps slip not.

5. Walk with me on the path of righteousness and help me to avoid doubt and wickedness.

⁶ I have called upon thee, for thou wilt hear me, O God: incline thine ear unto me, and hear my speech.

6. I have called upon you in the hope that you will hear me. Hear me God: make it your mercy to hear my words.

⁷ Shew thy marvellous lovingkindness, O thou that savest by thy right hand them which put their trust in thee from those that rise up against them.

> 7. Imagination, Infinite Intelligence, show your works of marvelous and loving kindness. Save for me, the justice you may bring from that special place of honor for those that place their trust in you. Save me from those negative and doubtful thoughts that choose to rise up against my good thoughts.

⁸ Keep me as the apple of the eye, hide me under the shadow of thy wings,

> 8. Keep me as the honored within your eye, and cloak me with your wisdom and love,

⁹ From the wicked that oppress me, from my deadly enemies, who compass me about.

> 9. Protecting me from the wicked and vain thoughts that oppress me; and from my harmful thoughts who desire to direct my path in life.

¹⁰ They are inclosed in their own fat: with their mouth they speak proudly.

> 10. Such thoughts are enclosed in their own comfort: and with their mouth they are in delight with their own words.

¹¹ They have now compassed us in our steps: they have set their eyes bowing down to the earth;

> 11. Such wicked and doubtful thoughts have directed many of us in our path: for they have set their vision upon me to look only to their manifestation.

¹² Like as a lion that is greedy of his prey, and as it were a young lion lurking in secret places.

> 12. Like a lion greedy for his prey, my negative thoughts lurk in dark places within my mind.

¹³ Arise, O LORD, disappoint him, cast him down: deliver my soul from the wicked, which is thy sword:

13. Awake, and hear me Lord, my Imagination, and disappoint the wicked thoughts. Cast each thought down and deliver my mind from wicked thoughts; which my Imagination is your sword.

¹⁴ From men which are thy hand, O LORD, from men of the world, which have their portion in this life, and whose belly thou fillest with thy hid treasure: they are full of children, and leave the rest of their substance to their babes.

14. From manifestations that come from my Imagination, hear me Imagination. From all of my mind, they take part in my affairs on earth. From my Imagination is your belly that can fill all my desires with hidden treasures of truth and wisdom. My Imagination is full of good young manifestations, and before maturity, they leave an abundance of lovely impressions.

¹⁵ As for me, I will behold thy face in righteousness: I shall be satisfied, when I awake, with thy likeness.

15. As for me, I will hold my face in the direction of righteousness. I will be satisfied when I awaken to see and recognize the likeness of what I once imagined.

ANALYSIS OF THE SCRIPTURE

Here, you are to ask the Lord to hear with his right hand, the hand of justice, and attend to your call. Ask Infinite Intelligence to listen to your prayer that goes forth, for your words are genuine. Let your words speak for you and let the eyes of the Lord bring to you all that you desire.

> *'Do not fear, for I am with you; Do not anxiously look about you, for I am your God I will strengthen you, surely I will help you, Surely I will uphold you with My righteous right hand.'*
>
> Isaiah 41:10

Your Imagination has shown you truth. Infinite Intelligence has visited you in times of darkness. Your own Imagination has tested your resolve in faith, and at times has found nothing. For your true purpose is that your mouth will not violate the Law of God.

Concerning the works of manifestations already created, through faith, and by the word of your mouth, you have been able to avoid the path of the ungodly. Ask the Lord to walk with you on the path of righteousness and help you to avoid doubt and wickedness.

You have called upon the Imagination in the hope that you will be heard. Ask the Universal Mind within you to hear you; and with mercy, to hear the words you speak.

> *Be anxious for nothing, but in everything by prayer and supplication with thanksgiving let your requests be made known to God.*
>
> *Philippians 4:6*

Ask Imagination, Infinite Intelligence, to show His works of marvelous and loving kindness. Save for you, the justice that He may bring from that special place of honor for those that place their trust in Him. Let it be from the special place where those negative and doubtful thoughts choose to rise up against your good thoughts.

Ask for Infinite Mind to keep you as the honored one within His eye and cloak you with His wisdom and love. Declare that you seek protection from the wicked and vain thoughts that oppress you; and from your harmful thoughts who desire to direct your path in life.

Such negative and doubtful thoughts are enclosed in their own comfort: and with their mouth they are in delight with their own words. Such wicked and doubtful thoughts have directed many of us in our path: for they have set their vision upon you to look only to their manifestation.

> *"The wolf and the lamb will graze together, and the lion will eat straw like the ox; and dust will be the serpent's food They will do no evil or harm in all My holy mountain," says the LORD.*
>
> *Isaiah 65:25*

Like a lion greedy for his prey, your negative thoughts lurk in dark places within your mind. Ask for the Imagination to awaken and hear you. Ask for the Lord, your Imagination, to disappoint the wicked thoughts. Ask that such thoughts be cast down and to deliver your mind from wicked thoughts; which is your Imagination, the sword of God.

From manifestations that come from your Imagination, ask to be heard by your Imagination. From all your mind, they take part in your affairs on earth. From your Imagination, is the belly of God that can fill all your desires with hidden treasures of truth and wisdom. Your Imagination is full of good young manifestations, and before maturity, they leave an abundance of lovely impressions.

As for you, you will hold your face in the direction of righteous. You will be satisfied when you awaken to see and recognize the likeness of what you once imagined.

CHAPTER EIGHTEEN

PSALM 18

ORIGINAL TEXT

18 I will love thee, O LORD, my strength.

² The LORD is my rock, and my fortress, and my deliverer; my God, my strength, in whom I will trust; my buckler, and the horn of my salvation, and my high tower.

³ I will call upon the LORD, who is worthy to be praised: so shall I be saved from mine enemies.

⁴ The sorrows of death compassed me, and the floods of ungodly men made me afraid.

⁵ The sorrows of hell compassed me about: the snares of death prevented me.

⁶ In my distress I called upon the LORD, and cried unto my God: he heard my voice out of his temple, and my cry came before him, even into his ears.

⁷ Then the earth shook and trembled; the foundations also of the hills moved and were shaken, because he was wroth.

⁸ There went up a smoke out of his nostrils, and fire out of his mouth devoured: coals were kindled by it.

⁹ He bowed the heavens also, and came down: and darkness was under his feet.

¹⁰ And he rode upon a cherub, and did fly: yea, he did fly upon the wings of the wind.

¹¹ He made darkness his secret place; his pavilion round about him were dark waters and thick clouds of the skies.

¹² At the brightness that was before him his thick clouds passed, hail stones and coals of fire.

¹³ The LORD also thundered in the heavens, and the Highest gave his voice; hail stones and coals of fire.

¹⁴ Yea, he sent out his arrows, and scattered them; and he shot out lightnings, and discomfited them.
¹⁵ Then the channels of waters were seen, and the foundations of the world were discovered at thy rebuke, O LORD, at the blast of the breath of thy nostrils.

¹⁶ He sent from above, he took me, he drew me out of many waters.

¹⁷ He delivered me from my strong enemy, and from them which hated me: for they were too strong for me.

¹⁸ They prevented me in the day of my calamity: but the LORD was my stay.

¹⁹ He brought me forth also into a large place; he delivered me, because he delighted in me.

²⁰ The LORD rewarded me according to my righteousness; according to the cleanness of my hands hath he recompensed me.

²¹ For I have kept the ways of the LORD, and have not wickedly departed from my God.

²² For all his judgments were before me, and I did not put away his statutes from me.

²³ I was also upright before him, and I kept myself from mine iniquity.

²⁴ Therefore hath the LORD recompensed me according to my righteousness, according to the cleanness of my hands in his eyesight.

⁲⁵ With the merciful thou wilt shew thyself merciful; with an upright man thou wilt shew thyself upright;

²⁶ With the pure thou wilt shew thyself pure; and with the froward thou wilt shew thyself froward.

²⁷ For thou wilt save the afflicted people; but wilt bring down high looks.

²⁸ For thou wilt light my candle: the LORD my God will enlighten my darkness.

²⁹ For by thee I have run through a troop; and by my God have I leaped over a wall.

³⁰ As for God, his way is perfect: the word of the LORD is tried: he is a buckler to all those that trust in him.

³¹ For who is God save the LORD? or who is a rock save our God?

³² It is God that girdeth me with strength, and maketh my way perfect.

³³ He maketh my feet like hinds' feet, and setteth me upon my high places.

³⁴ He teacheth my hands to war, so that a bow of steel is broken by mine arms.

³⁵ Thou hast also given me the shield of thy salvation: and thy right hand hath holden me up, and thy gentleness hath made me great.

³⁶ Thou hast enlarged my steps under me, that my feet did not slip.

³⁷ I have pursued mine enemies, and overtaken them: neither did I turn again till they were consumed.

³⁸ I have wounded them that they were not able to rise: they are fallen under my feet.

³⁹ For thou hast girded me with strength unto the battle: thou hast subdued under me those that rose up against me.

⁴⁰ Thou hast also given me the necks of mine enemies; that I might destroy them that hate me.

⁴¹ They cried, but there was none to save them: even unto the LORD, but he answered them not.

⁴² Then did I beat them small as the dust before the wind: I did cast them out as the dirt in the streets.

⁴³ Thou hast delivered me from the strivings of the people; and thou hast made me the head of the heathen: a people whom I have not known shall serve me.

⁴⁴ As soon as they hear of me, they shall obey me: the strangers shall submit themselves unto me.

⁴⁵ The strangers shall fade away, and be afraid out of their close places.

⁴⁶ The LORD liveth; and blessed be my rock; and let the God of my salvation be exalted.

⁴⁷ It is God that avengeth me, and subdueth the people under me.

⁴⁸ He delivereth me from mine enemies: yea, thou liftest me up above those that rise up against me: thou hast delivered me from the violent man.

⁴⁹ Therefore will I give thanks unto thee, O LORD, among the heathen, and sing praises unto thy name.

⁵⁰ Great deliverance giveth he to his king; and sheweth mercy to his anointed, to David, and to his seed for evermore.

THEME

Controlling Your Thoughts

POWER OF PSALM:

Seeking Truth; Refraining from Doubt; Losing Faith

THOUGHT FOR THE PSALM

Walk by faith, and faith alone.

INTERPRETATION OF EACH VERSE

18 I will love thee, O LORD**, my strength.**

1. I will love God, Consciousness, my strength.

² The LORD **is my rock, and my fortress, and my deliverer; my God, my strength, in whom I will trust; my buckler, and the horn of my salvation, and my high tower.**

2. Consciousness is my foundation, and my protection, and my aid; my God, my strength, in whom I will trust; my shield of improper thoughts, and the sound of my salvation, and my heaven.

³ I will call upon the LORD**, who is worthy to be praised: so shall I be saved from mine enemies.**

3. I will call upon Infinite Intelligence, who is worthy to be praised: so will I be saved from thoughts other than Good or God.

⁴ The sorrows of death compassed me, and the floods of ungodly men made me afraid.

4. The ill thoughts of death plot against me, and the lies of ungodly men placed me in fear.

⁵ **The sorrows of hell compassed me about: the snares of death prevented me.**

   5. The ill thoughts of suffering plot against me in many ways: the trapping thoughts of death prevented me from moving forward.

⁶ **In my distress I called upon the LORD, and cried unto my God: he heard my voice out of his temple, and my cry came before him, even into his ears.**

   6. In my distress, I called upon my Conscious awareness, and felt after God: he heard my voice out of my own mind, and my emotions were brought before him, even unto his divine hearing.

⁷ **Then the earth shook and trembled; the foundations also of the hills moved and were shaken, because he was wroth.**

   7. Then the earth moved and vibrated; the same with the base of the hills shifted and shaken, because he was very angry.

⁸ **There went up a smoke out of his nostrils, and fire out of his mouth devoured: coals were kindled by it.**

   8. There went up a black cloud from which I breathe, and intense words like smoke came out of my mouth, overcoming me: negative thoughts fueled the fire.

⁹ **He bowed the heavens also, and came down: and darkness was under his feet.**

   9. He looked down from what I imagined also, and delivered me: and he had a grip on my turmoil.

¹⁰ **And he rode upon a cherub, and did fly: yea, he did fly upon the wings of the wind.**

   10. And as if he came with an order of angels that traveled with him: yes, he did travel upon the wings of the Spirit.

¹¹ **He made darkness his secret place; his pavilion round about him were dark waters and thick clouds of the skies.**

   11. He made the closet, the heaven, his secret place; his temple where he is surrounded by unknown truths and clouded vision.

¹² **At the brightness that was before him his thick clouds passed, hail stones and coals of fire.**

12. In time, a new day will arise. The days of troubled times will have passed, for they were like a storm and a burning fire.

¹³ The LORD also thundered in the heavens, and the Highest gave his voice; hail stones and coals of fire.

13. When change was to come, thunder sounded in the Imagination. The Lord gives his voice unto the desires or prayers; addressing all thoughts with the fire and storm of truth.

¹⁴ Yea, he sent out his arrows, and scattered them; and he shot out lightnings, and discomfited them.

14. Yes, God sent out his arrows upon the negative thoughts, and scattered them wherever they existed, and with bolts of lightning or stabbings, he displaced them from their comforts.

¹⁵ Then the channels of waters were seen, and the foundations of the world were discovered at thy rebuke, O LORD, at the blast of the breath of thy nostrils.

15. Then the channels of truth were seen upon those negative, doubtful and deceitful thoughts, and the foundations of the Imagination were discovered at God's reprimand of such thoughts. Just as simple as a breath from meditation into the Imagination, one could see the power.

¹⁶ He sent from above, he took me, he drew me out of many waters.

16. He sent from heaven, the Imagination, and took me with him, bringing me out of many troubled waters of thought.

¹⁷ He delivered me from my strong enemy, and from them which hated me: for they were too strong for me.

17. He delivered me from my strong enemy, and from those thoughts that hated me: for they were too strong for me to handle on my own.

¹⁸ They prevented me in the day of my calamity: but the LORD was my stay.

18. Such thoughts prevented me in the times of my chaos: but the Imagination was my stay.

¹⁹ **He brought me forth also into a large place; he delivered me, because he delighted in me.**

> 19. The Lord brought me forward into a place beyond my comprehension; he delivered me, because he delighted within my Imagination.

²⁰ **The LORD rewarded me according to my righteousness; according to the cleanness of my hands hath he recompensed me.**

> 20. The Imagination rewarded me according to what I believed to be right; according to the cleanliness of my faith, he returned in kind what I Imagined.

²¹ **For I have kept the ways of the LORD, and have not wickedly departed from my God.**

> 21. For if I kept the faith and belief in my own Imagination, I would not still experience the wicked thoughts remaining within my vision.

²² **For all his judgments were before me, and I did not put away his statutes from me.**

> 22. For the Lord, in all his judgments stood before me, but I did not recognize him. I chose not to put away the statutes that I placed my faith in.

²³ **I was also upright before him, and I kept myself from mine iniquity.**

> 23. I was also up standing upright in the belief that the statute was my God, and believed I kept myself from my wicked thoughts.

²⁴ **Therefore hath the LORD recompensed me according to my righteousness, according to the cleanness of my hands in his eyesight.**

> 24. Thus, the Lord has turned me back to the belief in him, and judged me by the sincerity of my faith in his eyesight.

²⁵ With the merciful thou wilt shew thyself merciful; with an upright man thou wilt shew thyself upright;

> 25. The merciful God will show himself and his mercy upon me; and thus with one that stands affirmed in faith will he show his true self.

²⁶ With the pure thou wilt shew thyself pure; and with the froward thou wilt shew thyself froward.

> 26. With the pure in heart, the Lord, Infinite Intelligence will reveal itself; and from that day on of revelation, and continued faith, he will continue to reveal himself.

²⁷ For thou wilt save the afflicted people; but wilt bring down high looks.

> 27. For the Imagination will save all those that are afflicted by negative thoughts; and will bring down the negative thoughts given the highest regard.

²⁸ For thou wilt light my candle: the LORD my God will enlighten my darkness.

> 28. For the Lord, your Imagination, will light your path: the Lord will provide this light in the darkest of times.

²⁹ For by thee I have run through a troop; and by my God have I leaped over a wall.

> 29. With the help of God, I have been able to go through a gauntlet of negative thoughts; and my own Imagination has given me the ability to overcome a large obstacle.

³⁰ As for God, his way is perfect: the word of the LORD is tried: he is a buckler to all those that trust in him.

> 30. As for God, his way is perfect: the word that comes from the Imagination is tried and true: he is the one that fastens the truth of those that trust in him.

³¹ For who is God save the LORD? or who is a rock save our God?

> 31. For who is God other than yourself? Or, who is the foundation, but your Imagination?

³² It is God that girdeth me with strength, and maketh my way perfect.

32. It is God that circles me with strength, and paves the perfect way.

³³ He maketh my feet like hinds' feet, and setteth me upon my high places.

33. He gives me the lift within my own mind and sets me upon his high place of reward and honor.

³⁴ He teacheth my hands to war, so that a bow of steel is broken by mine arms.

34. He teaches my mind to battle, so that a bow of steel, targeting the most stubborn of negative thoughts can be broken by my strength.

³⁵ Thou hast also given me the shield of thy salvation: and thy right hand hath holden me up, and thy gentleness hath made me great.

35. The Imagination also provides me with a shield that delivers me from the power of missing the mark, or sin. The thought of truth will hold me up, and the gentleness of the Lord's handling of me has made me great.

³⁶ Thou hast enlarged my steps under me, that my feet did not slip.

36. My Imagination has provided me with a foundation in which to stand, and thus I don't doubt in my faith.

³⁷ I have pursued mine enemies, and overtaken them: neither did I turn again till they were consumed.

37. I have pursued my negative thoughts, and have overtaken them: and with my faith, I did not turn away from God, but remained in faith until the thoughts perished.

³⁸ I have wounded them that they were not able to rise: they are fallen under my feet.

38. I have wounded such thoughts, suppressing them from rising up against me: for they fall before me.

³⁹ For thou hast girded me with strength unto the battle: thou hast subdued under me those that rose up against me.

39. For the Lord, Universal Mind, has surrounded me with strength during times of battle: for the Imagination, God in Action has subdued the negative thoughts that were beneath me and those that tried to rise up against me.

⁴⁰ Thou hast also given me the necks of mine enemies; that I might destroy them that hate me.

40. **The Lord has given me the necks of my negative thoughts; in order for me to destroy them that hate me.**

⁴¹ They cried, but there was none to save them: even unto the LORD, but he answered them not.

41. They cried, but nothing could save them: for they cried also unto the Lord, my Imagination, but the Lord did not answer their call.

⁴² Then did I beat them small as the dust before the wind: I did cast them out as the dirt in the streets.

42. Then I dismembered all the negative thoughts into small fragments as the dust before the wind: I threw them out of mind just like dirt into the streets.

⁴³ Thou hast delivered me from the strivings of the people; and thou hast made me the head of the heathen: a people whom I have not known shall serve me.

43. Infinite Intelligence has delivered me from the strivings of the people; and he has made me the head of the negative thoughts that don't acknowledge God: a congregation of thoughts whom I have come to know that they will not serve me well.

⁴⁴ As soon as they hear of me, they shall obey me: the strangers shall submit themselves unto me.

44. As soon as those negative thoughts hear of me, they shall obey me: for the thoughts that I don't even remember will submit themselves unto me.

⁴⁵ The strangers shall fade away, and be afraid out of their close places.

45. The negative thoughts that appear foreign to me will fade away and be scared out of their hidden places within my mind.

⁴⁶ **The LORD liveth; and blessed be my rock; and let the God of my salvation be exalted.**

> 46. The Imagination is alive; and rewarded by my foundational belief in it; and let the God of my deliverance from sin be exalted.

⁴⁷ **It is God that avengeth me, and subdueth the people under me.**

> 47. It is God, my Imagination that will punish for me, and subdue the negative thoughts I have manifested.

⁴⁸ **He delivereth me from mine enemies: yea, thou liftest me up above those that rise up against me: thou hast delivered me from the violent man.**

> 48. He delivers me from my self-created enemies: yes, he lifts me up above those negative thoughts that rise up against me: he has delivered me from the violent manifestation.

⁴⁹ **Therefore will I give thanks unto thee, O LORD, among the heathen, and sing praises unto thy name.**

> 49. Therefore, I will give thanks unto the Lord, for he is to hear me among the heathen. I will sing praises unto his name.

⁵⁰ **Great deliverance giveth he to his king; and sheweth mercy to his anointed, to David, and to his seed for evermore.**

> 50. Great deliverance is given to me by God, the king; and he shows mercy to him that desires God's use of his oily substance that creates manifestation. To David, your son, and to his seed for evermore.

ANALYSIS OF THE SCRIPTURE

You are to love God. Consciousness is your strength. Consciousness is your foundation and your protection. Consciousness is your aid, Imagination is your God and strength, in whom you are to trust. Your Imagination is your shield of improper thoughts, your heaven, and the sound of your salvation.

It is for you to call upon Infinite Intelligence, who is worthy to be praised. Look to Infinite Intelligence to be saved from thoughts other than Good or God. You will be saved from the ill thoughts of death that plot against you; as well as the lies of ungodly manifestations who placed you in fear.

The ill thoughts of suffering plot against you in many ways: the trapping thoughts of death which can prevent you from moving forward. In your distress, you are to call upon your Conscious awareness, and feel after God. He will hear your voice, which comes from your own mind. Your emotions are to be brought before him and allow his divine hearing.

When a change in consciousness occurs, the earth moves and vibrates; the same with the base of the hills that shift and are shaken. This is so, because you, God are very angry; angry enough to change your consciousness for righteousness.

> *I say unto you, that likewise joy shall be in heaven over one sinner that repenteth, more than over ninety and nine just persons, which need no repentance.*
>
> Luke 15:7

There went up a black cloud from which you breathe, and intense words are to come out of your mouth overcoming you: negative thoughts that fueled the fire. For he looked down from what you imagined and delivers you. For God takes a grip on your turmoil.

And as if he came with an order of angels that traveled with him: yes, you will travel upon the wings of the Spirit. He made the closet, the heaven, his secret place; his temple where he is surrounded by unknown truths and clouded vision.

In time, a new day will arise. The days of troubled times have will have passed; for they will be like a storm and a burning fire. When change is to come, thunder sounds in the Imagination. The Lord gives his voice unto your desires or prayers; addressing all thoughts with the fire and storm of truth.

Yes, God sent out his arrows upon the negative thoughts, and scattered them wherever they existed, and with bolts of lightning or stabbings, he displaced them from their comforts. Then the channels of truth are seen upon those negative, doubtful and deceitful thoughts. The foundations of the Imagination are discovered by God's reprimand of such thoughts. Just as simple as a breath from meditation into the Imagination, one can see and feel the power.

He sent from heaven, the Imagination, and takes you with him, bringing you out of many troubled waters of thought. He delivers you from your strong enemy, and from those thoughts that hated you. For they were too strong for you to handle on your own.

Such negative thoughts prevented you from moving forward in the times of chaos: but the Imagination was your stay. The Lord brings you forward into a place beyond your comprehension. He delivers you, because he delights within your Imagination. The Imagination rewards you according to what you believe to be right. According to the sincerity of your faith, he returns in kind what you Imagined.

For if you keep the faith and belief in your own Imagination, you will not continue to experience the wicked thoughts remaining within your vision. For the Lord, in all his judgments stands before you, but do you recognize him? If you chose not to put away the statutes that you placed your faith in, then you will not be rewarded by God; for you have the wrong God.

It is up to you to stand upright and acknowledge your false belief that the statute you worshipped was your God. In doing so by your belief, you falsely believed you've kept yourself from wicked thoughts; but such was not true.

Whoever conceals their sins does not prosper,
but the one who confesses and renounces them finds mercy.

Proverbs 28:13

Thus, the Lord shall turn you back to the belief in him and judge you by the sincerity of your faith in his eyesight. The merciful God will show himself and his mercy upon you; and thus, with one that stands affirmed in faith, will he show his true self.

With the pure in heart, the Lord, Infinite Intelligence, will reveal himself. From that day on of your revelation, and continued faith, he will continue to reveal himself. For the Imagination will save all those that are afflicted by negative thoughts; and will bring down the negative thoughts given the highest regard.

For the Lord, your Imagination, will light your path. The Lord will provide your light in the darkest of times. With the help of God, you will be able to go through a gauntlet of negative thoughts; and your own Imagination will have given you the ability to overcome any large obstacle.

As for God, his way is perfect. The word that comes from the Imagination is tried and true. God is the one that fastens the truth of those that trust in him. For who is God other than yourself? Or, who is the foundation, but your Imagination?

It is God that circles you with strength and paves the perfect way. He gives you the lift within your own mind and sets you upon his high place of reward and honor. He teaches your mind to battle, so that a bow of steel, targeting the most stubborn of negative thoughts can be broken by your strength.

The Imagination also provides you with a shield that delivers you from the power of missing the mark, or sin. The thought of truth will hold you up, and the gentleness of the Lord's handling of you will make you great.

Your Imagination has provided you with a foundation in which to stand, and thus you are not to doubt in your faith. You are to pursue your negative thoughts and have them overtaken with your faith. You are not to turn away from God but remain in faith until the negative thoughts perish.

You can wound such thoughts, suppressing them from rising up against you: for they will all fall before you. For the Lord, Universal Mind, has surrounded you with strength during times of battle: for the Imagination, God in Action has subdued the negative thoughts that were beneath you, and those that tried to rise up against you.

The Lord has given you the necks of your negative thoughts; in order for you to destroy them that hate you. They, your negative thoughts will cry, but nothing will save them. They will also cry unto the Lord, your Imagination, but the Lord will not answer their call.

You shall dismember all the negative thoughts into small fragments as the dust before the wind. You are to throw them out of mind just like dirt swirling in the streets. Infinite Intelligence shall deliver you from the strivings of the people; and he has made you the head of the negative thoughts that don't acknowledge God. As to a congregation of thoughts whom you have come to know, you are to be certain that they will not serve you well.

"Now then, please take your gear, your quiver and your bow, and go out to the field and hunt game for me;

Genesis 27:3

As soon as those negative thoughts hear of you, they shall obey you. For the thoughts that you don't even remember, will submit themselves unto you. The negative thoughts that appear foreign to you will fade away and be scared out of their hidden places within your mind.

The Imagination is alive; and rewarded by your foundational belief in it. Let the God of your deliverance from sin be exalted. It is God, your Imagination that will punish for you, and subdue the negative thoughts you have manifested.

The Lord, your own wonderful human Imagination, delivers you from your self-created enemies. Yes, he lifts you up above those negative thoughts that rise up against you. He shall deliver you from the violent manifestations.

Therefore, you are to give thanks unto the Lord, for he is to hear you among the heathen. You are to sing praises unto his name. Great deliverance is given to you by God, the King. God shows mercy to him that desires God's use of his oily substance that creates manifestation: and unto David, your son, and to his seed for evermore.

Do not be anxious about anything, but in every situation, by prayer and petition, with thanksgiving, present your requests to God. ⁷ And the peace of God, which transcends all understanding, will guard your hearts and your minds in Christ Jesus.

Phillippians 4:6-7

CHAPTER NINETEEN

PSALM 19

ORIGINAL TEXT

19 The heavens declare the glory of God; and the firmament sheweth his handywork.

² Day unto day uttereth speech, and night unto night sheweth knowledge.

³ There is no speech nor language, where their voice is not heard.

⁴ Their line is gone out through all the earth, and their words to the end of the world. In them hath he set a tabernacle for the sun,

⁵ Which is as a bridegroom coming out of his chamber, and rejoiceth as a strong man to run a race.

⁶ His going forth is from the end of the heaven, and his circuit unto the ends of it: and there is nothing hid from the heat thereof.

⁷ The law of the LORD is perfect, converting the soul: the testimony of the LORD is sure, making wise the simple.
⁸ The statutes of the LORD are right, rejoicing the heart: the commandment of the LORD is pure, enlightening the eyes.

⁹ The fear of the LORD is clean, enduring for ever: the judgments of the LORD are true and righteous altogether.

¹⁰ More to be desired are they than gold, yea, than much fine gold: sweeter also than honey and the honeycomb.

¹¹ Moreover by them is thy servant warned: and in keeping of them there is great reward.

¹² Who can understand his errors? cleanse thou me from secret faults.

¹³ Keep back thy servant also from presumptuous sins; let them not have dominion over me: then shall I be upright, and I shall be innocent from the great transgression.

¹⁴ Let the words of my mouth, and the meditation of my heart, be acceptable in thy sight, O LORD, my strength, and my redeemer.

THEME

YOUR THOUGHT – THE HANDYWORK OF GOD

POWER OF PSALM

Need of a Miracle; Understanding of Concepts, Principles, and Problems; Wisdom

THOUGHT FOR THE PSALM

Create a scene within your own mind. Imply that you have what it is you desire. To the degree you are faithful to that state of consciousness, you will witness the unfolding in your own world; the handywork of God.

INTERPRETATION OF EACH VERSE

19 The heavens declare the glory of God; and the firmament sheweth his handywork.

1. The Imagination declares the glory of God; and from the temple is where God shows his handywork. The Imagination is the Glory of God; the place where it is considered his temple and all

of his works are created. The place where creation takes place is above in heaven and manifests below on earth.

² Day unto day uttereth speech, and night unto night sheweth knowledge.

2. Day after day, God speaks, and night after night he shows knowledge. Every day the word of God is spoken. At night is when man receives counsel of wisdom during sleep.

³There is no speech nor language, where their voice is not heard.

3. There is no speech or language where God doesn't hear. There is no thought or word spoken that God does not hear; for he hears all.

⁴ Their line is gone out through all the earth, and their words to the end of the world. In them hath he set a tabernacle for the sun,

4. Their path is traveled all throughout the earth, and such thoughts just the same are carried until the end of time. For all their thoughts, he created a haven for prosperity.

⁵ Which is as a bridegroom coming out of his chamber, and rejoiceth as a strong man to run a race.

5. Out of the subconscious mind comes the manifestation of a particular thought, and rejoices in his new birth, looking to maintain its existence for the period of time given it.

⁶ His going forth is from the end of the heaven, and his circuit unto the ends of it: and there is nothing hid from the heat thereof.

6. Man's thoughts move forward from his Imagination, and such thoughts continue on their path until the desired end; and there is nothing that stands in its way.

⁷The law of the LORD is perfect, converting the soul: the testimony of the LORD is sure, making wise the simple.

7. The law of Infinite Intelligence, your Imagination, is perfect; a law that changes the state of your being. The word of the Law, Universal Law, is certain, providing knowledge or wisdom to the simple person.

⁸ The statutes of the LORD are right, rejoicing the heart: the commandment of the LORD is pure, enlightening the eyes.

8. The statutes of Universal Law are correct, reflecting happiness in the heart. The commandment of the Law is pure, enlightening the eyes of the blind; those that don't see the truth.

⁹ The fear of the LORD is clean, enduring for ever: the judgments of the LORD are true and righteous altogether.

9. The fear of the Law is without blemish, for it is everlasting Law. The judgments of the Law are true and righteous in all.

¹⁰More to be desired are they than gold, yea, than much fine gold: sweeter also than honey and the honeycomb.

10. There is greater a treasure that stems from your desire; more attractive than gold, meaning the material form. The treasure you will find is more desirable than the sweetness of honey and the honeycomb.

¹¹Moreover by them is thy servant warned: and in keeping of them there is great reward.

11. Keeping to the Law of God, man is warned. In doing so, he will be rewarded for his faith.

¹²Who can understand his errors? cleanse thou me from secret faults.

12. Can man find his own faults? Use Universal Law to help you keep righteous, correcting the errors man cannot see.

¹³Keep back thy servant also from presumptuous sins; let them not have dominion over me: then shall I be upright, and I shall be innocent from the great transgression.

13. Hold back the man that continues to miss the mark with his thoughts. Do not let those negative thoughts have control over me. Keeping to the Law, I will be righteous, and I must be innocent from the great violation of the Law.

¹⁴Let the words of my mouth, and the meditation of my heart, be acceptable in thy sight, O LORD, my strength, and my redeemer.

> 14. Let the words of my mouth, and the meditation of my heart, be acceptable in my Imagination. The Law of God is my strength and redeemer.

ANALYSIS OF THE SCRIPTURE

The Imagination declares the glory of God; and from this temple is where God shows his handywork. The temple within man is where you will find the works of God created. This heaven of man is the place above; his own mind. Thus, what is imagined in heaven above, manifests on the earth below.

Day after day, man, is to speak the word of God. Night after night, God shows knowledge to the dreamer. It is at night when man receives counsel of wisdom during his sleep.

There is no speech or language where God doesn't hear. There is no thought or word spoken that God does not hear; for he hears all. The path of the word of God is the path that is traveled all throughout the earth, and any thoughts just the same are carried until the end of time. For all thoughts of man, God has created a haven for prosperity.

Out of the subconscious mind comes the manifestation of that thought created by man, and the new thought rejoices in its new birth, looking to maintain its existence for the period given it. Man's thoughts move forward from his Imagination, and his thoughts continue their path until the desired end; and there is nothing that stands in their way.

> *Mortify therefore your members which are upon the earth; fornication, uncleanness, inordinate affection, evil concupiscence, and covetousness, which is idolatry.*
>
> *Colossians 3:5*

The Law of Infinite Intelligence, your Imagination, is perfect; a law that changes the state of your being. The word of the Law, Universal Law, is certain, providing knowledge or wisdom to the simple person.

The statutes of Universal Law are correct, reflecting happiness in the heart. The commandment of the Law is pure, enlightening the eyes of the blind; those that don't see the truth. The fear of the Law is without blemish, for it is everlasting Law. The judgments of the Law are true and righteous in all.

The one who gets wisdom loves life; the one who cherishes understanding will soon prosper.

Proverbs 19:8

There is greater a treasure that stems from your desire; more attractive than gold; the material form. The treasure you will find in using your Imagination, is more desirable than the sweetness of honey and the honeycomb.

Keeping to the Law of God, man is warned not to waver. For in keeping the faith, he will be rewarded for his faith. Thus, can man find his own faults? This is a challenge to many men. However, if man chooses to use Universal Law to help keep righteous, automatically correcting the errors man cannot see, he will be rewarded in his manifestations.

Stand back, regarding the man that continues to miss the mark with his thoughts. Do not let those negative thoughts have control over you. Keeping to the Law, you will be righteous, and you will be innocent from the great violation of the Law. Let the words of your mouth, and the meditation of your heart, be acceptable in your Imagination. The Law of God is your strength and redeemer.

CHAPTER TWENTY

PSALM 20

ORIGINAL TEXT

20 The LORD hear thee in the day of trouble; the name of the God of Jacob defend thee;

² Send thee help from the sanctuary, and strengthen thee out of Zion;

³ Remember all thy offerings, and accept thy burnt sacrifice; Selah.

⁴ Grant thee according to thine own heart, and fulfil all thy counsel.

⁵ We will rejoice in thy salvation, and in the name of our God we will set up our banners: the LORD fulfil all thy petitions.

⁶ Now know I that the LORD saveth his anointed; he will hear him from his holy heaven with the saving strength of his right hand.

⁷ Some trust in chariots, and some in horses: but we will remember the name of the LORD our God.

⁸ They are brought down and fallen: but we are risen and stand upright.

⁹ Save, LORD: let the king hear us when we call.

THEME

UNDERSTANDING PRAYER WITHIN SELF

POWER OF PSALM

Troubled Times; Belief, Trust

THOUGHT FOR THE PSALM

Prayer is desire, and desire is prayer. Focus on what it is that you want, and don't just see it in your mind's eye, but feel as though you already possess that which you desire or pray for.

INTERPRETATION OF EACH VERSE

²⁰The LORD hear thee in the day of trouble; the name of the God of Jacob defend thee;

1. God, hear my call in the time of trouble. Have the supplanter defend me.

² Send thee help from the sanctuary, and strengthen thee out of Zion;

2. Send me help from the place of safety. Give me strength out of heaven.

³ Remember all thy offerings, and accept thy burnt sacrifice; Selah.

3. Remember all the thoughts I have already created, and accept my suffering for your help. Selah: (Selah – this is foundational truth that is where God answers from; truth that is self-evident.)

⁴ Grant thee according to thine own heart, and fulfil all thy counsel.

4. Grant me your counsel upon my open heart.

⁵ We will rejoice in thy salvation, and in the name of our God we will set up our banners: the LORD fulfil all thy petitions.

5. We will rejoice in my salvation, and in the name of our God, we will display his name. The Imagination fulfills all my desires.

⁶ Now know I that the LORD saveth his anointed; he will hear him from his holy heaven with the saving strength of his right hand.

6. Know that the Law saves the chosen; he will hear him from his temple with the understanding of truth.

⁷ Some trust in chariots, and some in horses: but we will remember the name of the LORD our God.

7. Some trust in objects, and some trust in animals: but we will remember it is all Imagination, our God.

⁸ They are brought down and fallen: but we are risen, and stand upright.

8. Negative thoughts don't survive: but we are gods, risen and stand upright.

⁹ Save, LORD: let the king hear us when we call.

9. Understand the Law: let the ruler of mind hear when called.

ANALYSIS OF THE SCRIPTURE

It is for you to make declarations to God using your own human Imagination. Declare: God, hear my call in the time of trouble. Have the Imagination defend me. Send me help from the place of safety. Give me strength out of heaven. Remember all the thoughts I have already created and accept my suffering for your help. Selah

> *"Afterward Jesus findeth him in the temple, and said unto him, Behold, thou art made whole: sin no more, lest a worse thing come unto thee".*
>
> *John 5:14*

Grant me your counsel upon my open heart. We, my loving thoughts, will rejoice in my salvation, and in the name of our God, we will display your name. The Imagination fulfills all my desires. Know that the Law saves the chosen. For you know he will hear you from his temple with the understanding of truth.

Some trust in objects, and some trust in animals: but we will remember that your Imagination, is the Law of your God. Negative and doubtful thoughts don't survive; for we are gods. We have risen and stand upright. Understand the Law: let the ruler of mind hear when called.

CHAPTER TWENTY-ONE

PSALM 21

ORIGINAL TEXT

21 The king shall joy in thy strength, O LORD; and in thy salvation how greatly shall he rejoice!

² Thou hast given him his heart's desire, and hast not withholden the request of his lips. Selah.

³ For thou preventest him with the blessings of goodness: thou settest a crown of pure gold on his head.

⁴ He asked life of thee, and thou gavest it him, even length of days for ever and ever.

⁵ His glory is great in thy salvation: honour and majesty hast thou laid upon him.

⁶ For thou hast made him most blessed for ever: thou hast made him exceeding glad with thy countenance.

⁷ For the king trusteth in the LORD, and through the mercy of the most High he shall not be moved.

⁸ Thine hand shall find out all thine enemies: thy right hand shall find out those that hate thee.

⁹ Thou shalt make them as a fiery oven in the time of thine anger: the LORD shall swallow them up in his wrath, and the fire shall devour them.

¹⁰ Their fruit shalt thou destroy from the earth, and their seed from among the children of men.

¹¹ For they intended evil against thee: they imagined a mischievous device, which they are not able to perform.

¹² Therefore shalt thou make them turn their back, when thou shalt make ready thine arrows upon thy strings against the face of them.

¹³ Be thou exalted, LORD, in thine own strength: so will we sing and praise thy power.

THEME

The Strength of God is Within Man

POWER OF PSALM

Salvation; Rightful Thinking; Strength; Evil Actions; Hatred; Anger; Praise

THOUGHT FOR THE PSALM

Salvation is in the one that seeks to master the use of his own Imagination.

INTERPRETATION OF EACH VERSE

21 **The king shall joy in thy strength, O LORD; and in thy salvation how greatly shall he rejoice!**

1. The ruler of mind shall enjoy his strength, in Imagination; and knowing this to be your salvation, you will be happy!

² Thou hast given him his heart's desire, and hast not withholden the request of his lips. Selah.

2. God within man, his Imagination, has given him his heart's desire, and has not withheld any request of desire spoken by the ruler.

³ For thou preventest him with the blessings of goodness: thou settest a crown of pure gold on his head.

3. For you are the only one that can prevent the blessings of God: you are responsible for setting the thoughts correctly upon your own temple of mind.

⁴ He asked life of thee, and thou gavest it him, even length of days for ever and ever.

4. Man imagines the life of his thoughts and gave manifestation each and every time; and will do so forever.

⁵ His glory is great in thy salvation: honour and majesty hast thou laid upon him.

5. God's glory is wonderful in the salvation of man. Honor and majesty have been bestowed upon man in such salvation.

⁶ For thou hast made him most blessed for ever: thou hast made him exceeding glad with thy countenance.

6. God has made man the most blessed forever. He has created excessive joy of expression within man.

⁷ For the king trusteth in the LORD, and through the mercy of the most High he shall not be moved.

7. For the ruler of his thoughts is to trust in the Imagination, the Law of Mind. And through the mercy of God, Infinite Intelligence, man will not be diverted from his desired path.

⁸ Thine hand shall find out all thine enemies: thy right hand shall find out those that hate thee.

    8. The right hand of God will find all of man's enemies. The right hand of God will find out those that hate man; meaning hate God.

⁹ Thou shalt make them as a fiery oven in the time of thine anger: the LORD shall swallow them up in his wrath, and the fire shall devour them.

    9. You will make for your negative thoughts, a burning flame in the period where they create anger or hatred within you. The Law of God, your Imagination, will with rightful thinking, swallow them up in your anger of them. The punishment of your new desire will make them perish.

¹⁰ Their fruit shalt thou destroy from the earth, and their seed from among the children of men.

    10. The negative thoughts that you create must be destroyed from this earth, and any offspring of those negative thoughts shall not continue to exist either.

¹¹ For they intended evil against thee: they imagined a mischievous device, which they are not able to perform.

    11. Negative thoughts intend evil against you, and their manifestation seeks only to express mischievous harm which they are not able to perform, but your vessel or vehicle of body can.

¹² Therefore shalt thou make them turn their back, when thou shalt make ready thine arrows upon thy strings against the face of them.

    12. Therefore, you will have to make them turn their back so they cannot see you, as you prepare their demise with deadly arrows of new thoughts that will soon face them head on.

¹³ Be thou exalted, LORD, in thine own strength: so will we sing and praise thy power.

13. Be strong with praise in the Law, the Imagination, in your own strength. In doing so, man can sing and praise his power; the power of the God within every man.

ANALYSIS OF THE SCRIPTURE

You, the ruler of mind, shall enjoy your strength, in Imagination. Knowing Imagination to be your salvation, you will be happy! God within man, his Imagination, has given you his heart's desire, and has not withheld any request of desire spoken by you, the ruler of your own thoughts. Selah.

"But those who hope in the Lord will renew their strength. They will soar on wings like eagles; they will run and not grow weary, they will walk and not be faint".

Isaiah 40:31

For you are the only one that can prevent the blessings of God. You are responsible for setting the thoughts correctly upon your own temple of mind. It is you that imagines life into your thoughts, and God gives manifestation to all your thoughts, and will do so forever.

God's glory is wonderful in the salvation of man. Honor and majesty have been bestowed upon you in such salvation. God has made you the most blessed forever. He has created excessive joy of expression within you, if you seek it. You, the ruler of your thoughts, are to trust in the Imagination, the Law of God. Through the mercy of God, Infinite Intelligence, you will not be diverted from your desired path.

"Neither is there salvation in any other: for there is none other name under heaven given among men, whereby we must be saved".

Acts 4:12

The right hand of God will find all your enemies. The right hand represents the truth of God, and he will find out those thoughts that bring about hate in you; meaning hate in God. You will make for your negative thoughts, a burning flame. This means, a new truth; a new and wonderful desire in the place where they create anger or hatred within you. The Law of God, your Imagination with rightful thinking, will swallow them up in his anger of them. The punishment will be expressed through your new desire and make them perish.

The negative thoughts that you create must be destroyed from this earth, and any offspring of those negative thoughts shall not continue to exist either. Negative thoughts intend evil against you, and their manifestation seek only to express mischievous harm. It is a harm that your thoughts cannot personally perform, but your vessel or vehicle of body can. Your thoughts need your body to carry out the actions you desire.

Therefore, you will have to make your negative thoughts turn their back so they cannot see you. You are to prepare their demise with deadly arrows of new thoughts that will soon face them head on. Be strong with praise in the Law, the Imagination, in your own strength. In doing so, you too can sing and praise his power; the power of the God within every man.

PSALM 22

ORIGINAL TEXT

22 My God, my God, why hast thou forsaken me? why art thou so far from helping me, and from the words of my roaring?

² O my God, I cry in the day time, but thou hearest not; and in the night season, and am not silent.

³ But thou art holy, O thou that inhabitest the praises of Israel.

⁴ Our fathers trusted in thee: they trusted, and thou didst deliver them.

⁵ They cried unto thee, and were delivered: they trusted in thee, and were not confounded.

⁶ But I am a worm, and no man; a reproach of men, and despised of the people.

⁷ All they that see me laugh me to scorn: they shoot out the lip, they shake the head, saying,

⁸ He trusted on the LORD that he would deliver him: let him deliver him, seeing he delighted in him.

⁹ But thou art he that took me out of the womb: thou didst make me hope when I was upon my mother's breasts.

¹⁰ I was cast upon thee from the womb: thou art my God from my mother's belly.

¹¹ Be not far from me; for trouble is near; for there is none to help.

¹² Many bulls have compassed me: strong bulls of Bashan have beset me round.

¹³ They gaped upon me with their mouths, as a ravening and a roaring lion.

¹⁴ I am poured out like water, and all my bones are out of joint: my heart is like wax; it is melted in the midst of my bowels.

¹⁵ My strength is dried up like a potsherd; and my tongue cleaveth to my jaws; and thou hast brought me into the dust of death.

¹⁶ For dogs have compassed me: the assembly of the wicked have inclosed me: they pierced my hands and my feet.

¹⁷ I may tell all my bones: they look and stare upon me.

¹⁸ They part my garments among them, and cast lots upon my vesture.

¹⁹ But be not thou far from me, O LORD: O my strength, haste thee to help me.

²⁰ Deliver my soul from the sword; my darling from the power of the dog.

²¹ Save me from the lion's mouth: for thou hast heard me from the horns of the unicorns.

²² I will declare thy name unto my brethren: in the midst of the congregation will I praise thee.

²³ Ye that fear the LORD, praise him; all ye the seed of Jacob, glorify him; and fear him, all ye the seed of Israel.

²⁴ For he hath not despised nor abhorred the affliction of the afflicted; neither hath he hid his face from him; but when he cried unto him, he heard.

²⁵ My praise shall be of thee in the great congregation: I will pay my vows before them that fear him.

²⁶ The meek shall eat and be satisfied: they shall praise the LORD that seek him: your heart shall live for ever.

²⁷ All the ends of the world shall remember and turn unto the LORD: and all the kindreds of the nations shall worship before thee.

²⁸ For the kingdom is the LORD's: and he is the governor among the nations.

²⁹ All they that be fat upon earth shall eat and worship: all they that go down to the dust shall bow before him: and none can keep alive his own soul.

³⁰ A seed shall serve him; it shall be accounted to the Lord for a generation.

³¹ They shall come, and shall declare his righteousness unto a people that shall be born, that he hath done this.

THEME

God Never Turns His Back, But Instructs How He Hears

POWER OF PSALM

Being Ignored; Plea Falling on Deaf Ears; Meditation Instruction; Delivery of Your Thoughts; When Mocked; When Laughed At; Plots Against You; Tired and Weak; Feeling of Nowhere to Turn; Disruption in Life

THOUGHT FOR THE PSALM

God always hears. God always responds to those that seek him. God works through you, in you and as you.

INTERPRETATION OF EACH VERSE

22 My God, my God, why hast thou forsaken me? why art thou so far from helping me, and from the words of my roaring?

1. My Imagination, Law of God, why have you turned away from me? Why are you not helping me as I scream or shout for help from you?

² O my God, I cry in the day time, but thou hearest not; and in the night season, and am not silent.

2. Imagination, Infinite Intelligence, I cry to you throughout my good times about my desires, but you don't seem to hear me. During times of chaos and confusion, I still cry, but you don't seem to hear me. When night before sleep comes, I don't meditate to hear you, but instead still cry.

³ But thou art holy, O thou that inhabitest the praises of Israel.

3. But you are the one, the one that takes dwells in the praises of those that know their Imagination; know God.

⁴ Our fathers trusted in thee: they trusted, and thou didst deliver them.

4. Our negative manifestations of the past trusted in me, just me alone, and you did not deliver such thoughts.

⁵ They cried unto thee, and were delivered: they trusted in thee, and were not confounded.

5. The good thoughts I have desired in my Imagination were delivered. Trust was placed in their manifestation, and those thoughts were not cursed.

⁶ But I am a worm, and no man; a reproach of men, and despised of the people.

6. The conception I have of myself is a worm of the dust living in confusion, and no manifestation; a reflection of my many thoughts, do I currently look down on.

⁷**All they that see me laugh me to scorn: they shoot out the lip, they shake the head, saying,**

7. All the thoughts that see me, laugh and dismiss my other thoughts. They talk through the conscious mind and look at me with doubt, telling me,

⁸**He trusted on the LORD that he would deliver him: let him deliver him, seeing he delighted in him.**

8. I trusted in the Lord, my Imagination in that he would deliver me from them. They mock and tell me let the Lord deliver me, all to see what delight I had in him.

⁹**But thou art he that took me out of the womb: thou didst make me hope when I was upon my mother's breasts.**

9. But I tell my thoughts, it is not you who created me, you didn't make me hope when I was in need of nourishment; hearing the word of God.

¹⁰**I was cast upon thee from the womb: thou art my God from my mother's belly.**

10. I was cast upon this earth from Universal Intelligence, God, and you are my God from your image of me; your Imagination of me.

¹¹**Be not far from me; for trouble is near; for there is none to help.**

11. Father, God, be not far from me; for trouble is with me, and I of myself is no help.

¹²**Many bulls have compassed me: strong bulls of Bashan have beset me round.**

12. Many breaths of negative thought have plotted against me: strong thoughts of Bashan have surrounded me.

¹³**They gaped upon me with their mouths, as a ravening and a roaring lion.**

13. Such thoughts stand and watch me with their mouths open as in the gawking of a raven and that of a roaring lion.

¹⁴ I am poured out like water, and all my bones are out of joint: my heart is like wax; it is melted in the midst of my bowels.

14. The truth in what I believe is poured out. The bones of my body, my health is not in sync. My heart is hardened and melted in the midst of my last hope.

¹⁵ My strength is dried up like a potsherd; and my tongue cleaveth to my jaws; and thou hast brought me into the dust of death.

15. My strength is dried up like an ancient relic. My tongue no longer moves in my mouth freely and you have brought me into the dust of death, but by my own Imagination.

¹⁶ For dogs have compassed me: the assembly of the wicked have inclosed me: they pierced my hands and my feet.

16. For my manifestations have plotted against me. The congregation of the wicked thoughts have encircled me. Such thoughts have immobilized me.

¹⁷ I may tell all my bones: they look and stare upon me.

17. I may tell my own creations of such wicked things, and they just look and stare upon me.

¹⁸ They part my garments among them, and cast lots upon my vesture.

18. As a congregation, such wicked thoughts partake in the division of my being and cast disruptions upon this robe of flesh I wear.

¹⁹ But be not thou far from me, O LORD: O my strength, haste thee to help me.

19. Not far from me is my Imagination. That is my strength, and with swiftness you come to my help.

²⁰ Deliver my soul from the sword; my darling from the power of the dog.

20. Deliver me from my thoughts that will lead to my death; my weapon of choice and power of the ungodly.

²¹ Save me from the lion's mouth: for thou hast heard me from the horns of the unicorns.

21. Save me from roar that lead me to the jaws of death; for you have heard me from the temple of the divine power that nurtures all living things.

²² I will declare thy name unto my brethren: in the midst of the congregation will I praise thee.

22. I will declare myself as the man of God unto all of my negative thoughts; in the midst of their congregation, I will praise the Lord.

²³ Ye that fear the LORD, praise him; all ye the seed of Jacob, glorify him; and fear him, all ye the seed of Israel.

23. All of you that feel after the Lord, praise him. All of you are seeds of higher consciousness, thus glorify him. Feel after him, all of you that are seeds that know God.

²⁴ For he hath not despised nor abhorred the affliction of the afflicted; neither hath he hid his face from him; but when he cried unto him, he heard.

24. For the man that has neither despised nor detested the affliction of the afflicted thoughts; neither had has hid his face from God, God heard his call.

²⁵ My praise shall be of thee in the great congregation: I will pay my vows before them that fear him.

25. My praise shall be of God in the congregation of my thoughts. I am bound to act accordingly towards the thoughts that feel after him.

²⁶ The meek shall eat and be satisfied: they shall praise the LORD that seek him: your heart shall live for ever.

26. Those that have been afflicted, with patience, shall eat and be satisfied. They shall praise the Imagination, Infinite Intelligence within me, that seek him. Your heart shall live forever.

²⁷ **All the ends of the world shall remember and turn unto the LORD: and all the kindreds of the nations shall worship before thee.**

> 27. Everyone in the world will come to remember and turn to the Lord, the Imagination. All the thoughts that stem from initial thoughts will worship before God, their Father.

²⁸ **For the kingdom is the LORD's: and he is the governor among the nations.**

> 28. For the kingdom of heaven is the abode of the Lord. He is the ruler of all thoughts.

²⁹ **All they that be fat upon earth shall eat and worship: all they that go down to the dust shall bow before him: and none can keep alive his own soul.**

> 29. All those loving thoughts manifested that have feasted upon the earth, too shall eat and worship. All those negative thoughts that go down to the dust shall bow before God; and no one will keep such negative manifestations alive in their soul.

³⁰ **A seed shall serve him; it shall be accounted to the Lord for a generation.**

> 30. A manifestation (thought) shall serve God. Like sheep, it will be accounted for by God for a lifetime.

³¹ **They shall come, and shall declare his righteousness unto a people that shall be born, that he hath done this.**

> 31. The thoughts will come and will declare the goodness of God to all thoughts that shall be born of the Imagination, tell them that God is their creator.

ANALYSIS OF THE SCRIPTURE

As for this Psalm, Imagination, Law of God, why have you turned away from me? Why are you not helping me as I scream or shout for help from you?

Many people may question God as to why he turned his back on them, or never hears their cry? Many men look for help and continue to plead and scream the name of God; with no response. Man can claim that they call upon God in good times and bad, and still claim that they are not heard.

At night, man is to meditate when the activity of day busied by the conscious mind is at rest; making the subconscious mind more susceptible to suggestion. Since many men don't meditate, they find themselves continuing to plead and ask for guidance or counsel of God.

"What is the outcome then? I will pray with the spirit and I will pray with the mind also; I will sing with the spirit and I will sing with the mind also".

1 Corinthians 14:15

But you are holy. For you are the one that is to take in the praises from knowing God. The thoughts present themselves to you on your screen of space right before your eyes, were given life thorough your Imagination.

The thoughts you have desired in your Imagination are always delivered; manifestation. Trust was placed in their manifestation by you, and those thoughts were not confused. For if they were, you would not be able to identify the results with clarity. The conception man may have of himself as a worm of the dust living in confusion without the desired manifestation; is nothing more than a reflection of his many thoughts that he currently looks down upon.

All the negative thoughts that one may see, you must laugh and dismiss all those thoughts including similar thoughts. They talk through the conscious mind and look at you with doubt. Those thoughts tell you that they know you trusted in the Lord, your Imagination; and know you believed that God would deliver you from them. They mock and laugh, and tell you to let the Lord deliver you, all to see what delight you had in him.

But it is for you to tell your thoughts, that it was neither them that created you, nor did they make you hope when you needed nourishment; hearing the word of God. You were cast upon this earth from Universal Intelligence, God, and you are the God from your image of self; your Imagination of God. Father, God, is not far from you. In times of trouble, he is with you and you know that you yourself, working by yourself is not the answer; for the God within you is the answer to all your problems.

Many breaths of negative thought have plotted against you: strong thoughts of the most horrific kind have surrounded you. Such thoughts stand and watch you with their mouths open as in the gawking of a raven and that of a roaring lion.

The truth in what you believe is poured out. The bones of your body, your health is not in sync. Your heart is hardened and melted in the midst of your last hope. Your strength is dried up like an ancient relic. Your tongue no longer moves in your mouth freely and God has brought you into the dust of death; but by your own Imagination.

For many of your manifestations have plotted against you. The congregation of the wicked thoughts have encircled you. Such thoughts have immobilized you. It is for you to tell your own creations of God. For your creations are the ones who remind you of such wicked things; knowing that they just look and stare at you upon your conviction of their actions.

As a congregation, such wicked thoughts partake in the division of your being and cast disruptions upon the robe of flesh you wear. Not far from you is my Imagination. That is your strength, and with swiftness, it will come to your help.

Ask for deliverance within yourself, for your negative thoughts will lead to your death; for your Imagination is the weapon of choice and power of the ungodly. Ask to be saved from a roar that leads you to the jaws of death; for the Lord hears you from the temple of the divine power that nurtures all living things.

You are to declare of yourself, as a man of God, that you will give unto God, all your negative thoughts. You will do so in the midst of their congregation of negativity, and you are to continue to praise the Lord. All of you that feel after the Lord, praise him. All of you are seeds of higher consciousness, thus glorify him. Feel after him, all of you that are seeds that know God.

For the man that has neither despised nor detested the affliction of the afflicted thoughts. You are not to hide your face from God, God hears all calls.

Your praise shall be of God in the congregation of all your thoughts. You are bound to act accordingly towards the thoughts that feel after God. Those that have been afflicted, with patience, shall eat and be satisfied. They shall praise the Imagination, Infinite Intelligence within you, that seek him. Your heart shall live forever.

Everyone in the world will come to remember and turn to the Lord, the Imagination. All the thoughts that stem from initial thoughts will worship before God, their Father. For the kingdom of heaven is the abode of the Lord. He is the ruler of all thoughts.

All those loving thoughts manifested that have feasted upon the earth, too shall eat and worship in the reward of God. All those negative thoughts that will go down to the dust shall bow before God; and no one will keep such negative manifestations alive in their soul.

A manifestation (thought) shall serve God. Like sheep, it will be accounted for by God for a lifetime. The thoughts will all come, and one day declare the goodness of God. All thoughts that shall be born of the Imagination, it will be you that tell them that God is their creator.

CHAPTER TWENTY-THREE

PSALM 23

ORIGINAL TEXT

23 The LORD is my shepherd; I shall not want.

² He maketh me to lie down in green pastures: he leadeth me beside the still waters.

³ He restoreth my soul: he leadeth me in the paths of righteousness for his name's sake.

⁴ Yea, though I walk through the valley of the shadow of death, I will fear no evil: for thou art with me; thy rod and thy staff they comfort me.

⁵ Thou preparest a table before me in the presence of mine enemies: thou anointest my head with oil; my cup runneth over.

⁶ Surely goodness and mercy shall follow me all the days of my life: and I will dwell in the house of the LORD for ever.

THEME

GUIDANCE

POWER OF PSALM

Bring Joy to Heart; Rescue; Satisfaction; Peace of Mind; Being Ignored; Plea Falling on Deaf Ears; Meditation Instruction; Delivery of Your Thoughts; When Mocked; When Laughed At; Plots Against You; Tired and Weak; Feeling of Nowhere to Turn; Disruption in Life

THOUGHT FOR THE PSALM

Let your shepherd be your guide. You will never go wrong. In fact, so well do your sheep (your thoughts) know your voice, they have never failed to respond to your call. The "I AM" is you, and with you at all times. In knowing this, there will never be an instance where your sheep will fail to find you.

INTERPRETATION OF EACH VERSE

23 **The LORD is my shepherd; I shall not want.**

1. The Imagination, Universal Mind, is my shepherd, and I must not want of anything.

² He maketh me to lie down in green pastures: he leadeth me beside the still waters.

2. He makes me lie down within the wonderful field of abundance in my own mind: he leads me in meditation to the truth.

³ He restoreth my soul: he leadeth me in the paths of righteousness for his name's sake.

3. He restores my mind: he leads me in the path of righteousness in the name of God.

⁴ **Yea, though I walk through the valley of the shadow of death, I will fear no evil: for thou art with me; thy rod and thy staff they comfort me.**

    4. Yes, though I walk through this world of death and decay, I will fear no evil thoughts: for Infinite Intelligence, Universal Mind, is with me; my thought and affirmation comfort me.

⁵ **Thou preparest a table before me in the presence of mine enemies: thou anointest my head with oil; my cup runneth over.**

    5. Universal Mind, Infinite Intelligence prepares a space before me in the presence of my negative thoughts, which creates negative thinking: Universal Mind will fill my consciousness; my welcoming of abundance overflows.

⁶ **Surely goodness and mercy shall follow me all the days of my life: and I will dwell in the house of the LORD for ever.**

    6. Surely goodness and mercy will follow me all the days of my life: and I will dwell in my Imagination, the house of the Lord forever.

ANALYSIS OF THE SCRIPTURE:

The Imagination is your shepherd, and there is nothing on earth that you should long for. You are the creator responsible for all things on earth; all through your thinking. Your conscious use of your Imagination shall always be your guidance.

Whatever you think about in life, there is always more than enough. Place whatever you think about in the field of your mind (green pastures, like rolling hills of farmland). The field is your fertile place for manifestation, and all manifestations are born into that field. The Lord, the Imagination, leads you in counsel through meditation. God restores your path in the field and leads you down the path of truth.

Declare: Yes, though I walk through this world of death and decay, I will fear no evil thoughts: for Infinite Intelligence, Universal Mind, is with me; my thought and affirmation comfort me. You are to remember this world is only a shadow.

Declare: Universal Mind, Infinite Intelligence prepares a space before me in the presence of my negative thoughts, which creates negative thinking: Universal Mind will fill my consciousness; and my welcoming of abundance overflows.

Fear no harm, for God is always with you, and in him is the truth in which you walk. In facing times that seem to be utterly filled with trouble and confusion, opposition and conflict, you will succeed in obtaining all your desires. Surely, goodness and mercy will follow you all the days of your life; and you will dwell in the house of the Lord forever.

FURTHER UNDERSTANDING

I

The Lord is my Shepherd; I shall not want

Your knowing, your consciousness or what can be called your awareness of being, is your "Lord and shepherd." Your consciousness is the "I AM" in all scriptures.

Therefore, in reading this verse, that which "I AM" aware of being (good, bad, indifferent thoughts) are the sheep that follow you. So, if I am a successful engineer, then it is because my thoughts were concentrated on being a successful engineer. Each thought came into manifestation and played their role in creating my reality.

It was the *congregation* of positive thoughts that reflected a successful engineer to came to pass. Not one thought "sheep" was lost in the herding of those thoughts. The subconscious mind heard the voice of my conscious mind call unto my flock; for I am the Shepherd of thoughts reflecting engineering.

The "I AM" is God. The "I AM" is you. Thus, you are the great Shepherd. Your awareness of being, is the Shepherd who has never lost a sheep or anything in its existence that "I AM" aware of being. Thus, anything in your existence has been, is and will always be accounted for.

Consciousness you may ask? Consciousness is the voice in the distance that calls to you, the one experiencing a world of chaos, confusion, calamity, lack and folly. That voice is always calling all that I AM, (you) are conscious of being. You know yourself very well, and thus when the call is made, your thoughts (your sheep), know your voice. Knowing that this is true, your thoughts have never failed to respond to your call. And never consider yourself lost, for there will never be time when that which you are convinced I AM will never fail to find you. For your thoughts will always find you and keep right in step with you.

You are conscious of all those thoughts, and you attach those thoughts to you, the "I AM", by acknowledging that you are aware of all of those horrible things. With your awareness, those same negative thoughts follow you and create additional manifestations (children in scripture) that relate to all of the horrors. All of those thoughts can be manifested by you either consciously or unconsciously.

As the Shepherd, you can command good, bad or indifferent thoughts. Positive thoughts will manifest positive results. Thus, negative thoughts manifest negative results, and those results will follow you wherever you think to lead them or perceive them to lead you. Think poverty, you get poverty. Think health, wealth and abundance, you get health, wealth and abundance. Not sometimes, but all the time.

> *So shall my word be that goeth forth out of my mouth: it shall not return unto me void, but it shall accomplish that which I please, and it shall prosper in the thing whereto I sent it.*
>
> *Isaiah 55:11*

Whatever you give attention, you will get the results of intention, whether you are conscious of it or not. Negative or positive thoughts, the sheep, know your voice very well; the voice of the Shepherd is always heard. Those sheep feel your energy (your attention).

I AM, (meaning you are, the statement(s) you declare to yourself) the open passageway for all that I AM to walk through. Your awareness of being is Lord and Shepherd of your life.

Additionally, as for the statement "I shall not want," has confused many people around the world. Reading that statement repeatedly on its face says, "I must not want", meaning I must not want the Shepherd?

On the contrary, it means that "I shall (shall meaning must) never be in want or in need of proof of that which you are aware of being. You want to be healed of an ailment? You don't need immediate proof that you will be healed. Impress upon your subconscious mind that you are healed, and your thoughts (sheep) of healing will follow you and heal your body: coupled with faith. See it, and the Imagination will make way for you to become healed.

II

He maketh me to lie down in green pastures.

Your awareness of being intensifies all that you are aware of being. This means that all that you are aware of yourself being, is already in existence, or will eventually come into existence due to your belief.

This statement is telling you that there is an abundance of that which you are ("I AM") conscious of being to manifest within the field your mind. Whatever you think about in life, there is always more than enough space in the field of manifestation.

Place whatever you think about in the field of your mind (green pastures, like rolling hills of farmland). The field is your fertile place for manifestation, and all manifestations are born unto that field. The Lord, the Imagination, leads you in counsel through meditation. God restores your path in the field and leads you down the path of truth.

> *"Then He will give you rain for the seed which you will sow in the ground, and bread from the yield of the ground, and it will be rich and plenteous; on that day your livestock will graze in a roomy pasture".*
>
> Isaiah 30:23

No matter what your religion, what your race, creed or color, it makes no difference. It is all about whatever the man (manifestation) is conscious of being (your imaginative thoughts), he will find it eternally projecting from him or herself into the world in which they exist. The Lord's measure (meaning the imaginative conception you have of yourself, be it rich, poor, healthy or whatever you've admired) is always molded, fashioned and overflowing. The Lord's measure is man's conception of himself.

III

He leadeth me beside the still waters

There is no need to try earning what it is you desire. The blessings of God are not wages. There is no need to work by the sweat of your brow, or even fight for that which you desire. Be still in meditation and listen to Infinite Intelligence provide you counsel. In meditation, being quiet to hear instruction for your thoughts, is the same as a shepherd that leads his flock to the still waters (meditation for truth) in which to drink from the source of life.

IV

He restoreth my soul; he leadeth me in the paths of righteousness for his name's sake.

Here, we are restoring the mind to consciousness of what we truly are; referring to the actual Spirit we all are. Your Imagination is the "I AM", the Supreme, the Lord, and he leads you down the path of righteousness in his name.

> *"Come to me, all who labor and are heavy laden, and I will give you rest. Take my yoke upon you, and learn from me, for I am gentle and lowly in heart, and you ill find rest in your souls. For my yoke is easy, and my burden is light".*
> *Matthew 11:28-30*

This Psalm, as do all others, reflect the restoration of your memory. You are to know that you are the I AM the Lord, and beside you, there is no God. For the world is all God, so how can there be anything other than God? Acknowledging this, the Kingdom of God is restored.

The Kingdom of heaven was dismantled the day you took it upon yourself to believe in a God, objects or forces apart from yourself. However, your acknowledgement of the power of God that you are, your awareness, your memory is restored. In knowing this, it is up to you to make righteous use of this knowledge. You can do this by becoming aware of being that which you pray or in other words, desire to be.

V

Yea, though I walk through the valley of the shadow of death, I will fear no evil; for thou art with me; thy rod and thy staff they comfort me.

Yes, though you walk through this place on earth, in this world among Caesar's governments, changing opinions, politics, chaos, confusion and distractions, you perceive death and decay. You are to fear no harm to become of you.

> *'Do not fear, for I am with you; Do not anxiously look about you, for I am your God I will strengthen you, surely I will help you, Surely I will uphold you with My righteous right hand.'*
>
> *Isaiah 41:10*

You will fear no evil, for you have found awareness or consciousness to be that which creates all the chaos and confusion; your own thinking. In yourself, you are to restore the consciousness of your being. You can, no matter what confusion or distractions you are now conscious of being. Changing the way you think. will reflect your own nobleness.

VI

Thou prepares a table before me in the presence of mine enemies; thou annointest my head with oil; my cup runneth over.

Universal Mind, Infinite Intelligence prepares a space before you in the field of your negative thoughts. Universal Mind will fill your consciousness, and your welcoming of abundance shall overflow.

In facing times that seem to be utterly filled with trouble and confusion, opposition and conflict, you will succeed in obtaining all your desires.

VII

Surely goodness and mercy shall follow me all the days of my life; and I will dwell in the house of the Lord forever.

Because you are now conscious of being good and merciful, signs of goodness and mercy are forced to follow you all the days of your life. It is up to you to continue to dwell in the house (or consciousness) of Being, the house of God (good) forever.

> *Mountains quake because of Him And the hills dissolve; Indeed the earth is upheaved by His presence, The world and all the inhabitants in it*
>
> *Nahum1:5*

In Summary

Now you understand this blueprint quoted in scripture. Say this verse to yourself and aloud to remember you are the power. Now you must declare what it is you want in life. Declare the person you wish to be and then assume as if it already happened; with feeling. Go about your business, and in its appointed time, you will manifest your declarations.

CHAPTER TWENTY-FOUR

PSALM 24

ORIGINAL TEXT

24 The earth is the LORD's, and the fulness thereof; the world, and they that dwell therein.

² For he hath founded it upon the seas, and established it upon the floods.

³ Who shall ascend into the hill of the LORD? or who shall stand in his holy place?

⁴ He that hath clean hands, and a pure heart; who hath not lifted up his soul unto vanity, nor sworn deceitfully.

⁵ He shall receive the blessing from the LORD, and righteousness from the God of his salvation.

⁶ This is the generation of them that seek him, that seek thy face, O Jacob. Selah.

⁷ Lift up your heads, O ye gates; and be ye lift up, ye everlasting doors; and the King of glory shall come in.

⁸ Who is this King of glory? The LORD strong and mighty, the LORD mighty in battle.

⁹ Lift up your heads, O ye gates; even lift them up, ye everlasting doors; and the King of glory shall come in.
¹⁰ Who is this King of glory? The LORD of hosts, he is the King of glory. Selah.

THEME

Power of your Rulership

POWER OF PSALM

Need Prayer Answered; Organizing Thoughts; Clear Thinking; Understanding

THOUGHT FOR THE PSALM

Be mindful of each thought. If you give thoughts feeling, then they are certain to manifest.

INTERPRETATION OF EACH VERSE

24 The earth is the LORD's, and the fulness thereof; the world, and they that dwell therein.

1. The earth is a product of Imagination, and all its plentitude. It reflects your world and all your thoughts dwell within it.

² For he hath founded it upon the seas, and established it upon the floods.

2. For your thoughts have been brought from the body of the temple, and the thoughts concentrated upon most are the floods of thoughts that have manifested on earth.

³ Who shall ascend into the hill of the LORD? or who shall stand in his holy place?

3. Who will ascend into the temple of the Lord? Or, who shall meditate within their own mind?

⁴ He that hath clean hands, and a pure heart; who hath not lifted up his soul unto vanity, nor sworn deceitfully.

4. Earnest seekers of the Law, Infinite Intelligence, God, who have not traded their soul regarding solely the thought of their perceived selves, nor lie as to their true being.

⁵ He shall receive the blessing from the LORD**, and righteousness from the God of his salvation.**

5. You will receive reward from your Imagination. And, you will receive goodness from your Imagination, which is your salvation, your savior.

⁶ This is the generation of them that seek him, that seek thy face, O Jacob. Selah.

6. The wonderful and loving thoughts are those that seek the Lord, for he is higher consciousness, Infinite Intelligence. Selah (Selah – this is foundational truth, the axiom, wherein this true statement is self-evident.)

⁷ Lift up your heads, O ye gates; and be ye lift up, ye everlasting doors; and the King of glory shall come in.

7. Seek the kingdom, your heaven above, and open the doors of your Imagination. Upon their opening, the glory of God will you enter.

⁸ Who is this King of glory? The LORD **strong and mighty, the L**ORD **mighty in battle.**

8. Who is the ruler of glory? Your Imagination is the strong and mighty, and it is the higher consciousness, the Universal Mind, that is the greatest in all your battles.

⁹ Lift up your heads, O ye gates; even lift them up, ye everlasting doors; and the King of glory shall come in.

9. Seek the kingdom, your heaven above, and open the doors of your Imagination. Upon their opening, the glory of God will you enter.

¹⁰ Who is this King of glory? The LORD **of hosts, he is the King of glory. Selah.**

10. Who is the ruler of the Imagination that brings glory? The Lord of hosts, he is the ruler of glory.

ANALYSIS OF THE SCRIPTURE

Earnest seekers of the Law, God, will find the truth.

> *"All flesh that moved on the earth perished, birds and cattle and beasts and every swarming thing that swarms upon the earth, and all mankind; of all that was on the dry land, all in whose nostrils was the breath of the spirit of life, died. Thus He blotted out every living thing that was upon the face of the land, from man to animals to creeping things and to birds of the sky, and they were blotted out from the earth; and only Noah was left, together with those that were with him in the ark".*
>
> *Genesis 7:21-23*

What you see on earth is a product of your Imagination, and all its multitude of manifestations. What you see reflects your world and all your thoughts that dwell within it. It is because of your thoughts that bring about cause and effect of your actions. It is from your holy temple above, your own mind where God resides. This is the place where your congregation of thoughts are impressed upon the subconscious mind and are manifested in abundance on earth.

The question is, who will decide to ascend above and use the Imagination? Or, who will be the one that will meditate within their own mind? For those that do meditate through their ascension, will receive the blessings promised by God.

Earnest seekers of the Law of God, Infinite Intelligence, and who have not traded their minds to worship their own vanity or entertain lies, will attain the kingdom. You will receive blessings from the Lord, as well as his goodness; for your Imagination is your salvation which is deemed in scripture as your savior. The wonderful and loving thoughts are those that seek the Lord, for he is Higher Consciousness, Infinite Intelligence. Selah (Selah – this is foundational truth, the axiom, wherein this true statement is self-evident.)

Seek the kingdom, your heaven above, and open the doors of your Imagination. Upon their opening, the glory of God will you enter.

Emphasis is added and repeated in the remaining verses:

Who is the ruler of glory? Your Imagination is the strong and mighty, and it is the Higher Consciousness, the Universal Mind, that is the greatest in all your battles. Again, seek the kingdom, your heaven above, and open the doors of your Imagination. Upon their opening, the glory of God will you enter.

Keep this in mind.

CHAPTER TWENTY-FIVE

PSALM 25

ORIGINAL TEXT

25 Unto thee, O LORD, do I lift up my soul.

² O my God, I trust in thee: let me not be ashamed, let not mine enemies triumph over me.

³ Yea, let none that wait on thee be ashamed: let them be ashamed which transgress without cause.

⁴ Shew me thy ways, O LORD; teach me thy paths.

⁵ Lead me in thy truth, and teach me: for thou art the God of my salvation; on thee do I wait all the day.

⁶ Remember, O LORD, thy tender mercies and thy loving-kindnesses; for they have been ever of old.

⁷ Remember not the sins of my youth, nor my transgressions: according to thy mercy remember thou me for thy goodness' sake, O LORD.

⁸ Good and upright is the LORD: therefore will he teach sinners in the way.

⁹ The meek will he guide in judgment: and the meek will he teach his way.

¹⁰ All the paths of the LORD are mercy and truth unto such as keep his covenant and his testimonies.

¹¹ For thy name's sake, O LORD, pardon mine iniquity; for it is great.

¹² What man is he that feareth the LORD? him shall he teach in the way that he shall choose.

¹³ His soul shall dwell at ease; and his seed shall inherit the earth.

¹⁴ The secret of the LORD is with them that fear him; and he will shew them his covenant.

¹⁵ Mine eyes are ever toward the LORD; for he shall pluck my feet out of the net.

¹⁶ Turn thee unto me, and have mercy upon me; for I am desolate and afflicted.

¹⁷ The troubles of my heart are enlarged: O bring thou me out of my distresses.

¹⁸ Look upon mine affliction and my pain; and forgive all my sins.

¹⁹ Consider mine enemies; for they are many; and they hate me with cruel hatred.

²⁰ O keep my soul, and deliver me: let me not be ashamed; for I put my trust in thee.

²¹ Let integrity and uprightness preserve me; for I wait on thee.

²² Redeem Israel, O God, out of all his troubles.

THEME

Enemies

POWER OF PSALM:

Enemies; Looking for Answers; Will to Overcome; Learning

THOUGHT FOR THE PSALM

When you pray, never bow your head, but look upward.

INTERPRETATION OF EACH VERSE

25 **Unto thee, O LORD, do I lift up my soul.**

1. My Imagination, I lift my head up for the answer to my being.

² O my God, I trust in thee: let me not be ashamed, let not mine enemies triumph over me.

2. The Law of God, I trust. My Imagination will not allow me to be ashamed. My negative thoughts will not win over me.

³ Yea, let none that wait on thee be ashamed: let them be ashamed which transgress without cause.

3. Yes, I will not be ashamed in my thoughts as I wait upon the Lord to answer my prayers. As for those thoughts that miss the mark, shall they be ashamed.

⁴ Shew me thy ways, O LORD; teach me thy paths.

4. Show me the way Imagination, Universal Mind. Teach me the paths I may take leading to God.

⁵ Lead me in thy truth, and teach me: for thou art the God of my salvation; on thee do I wait all the day.

5. Lead me to the truth and teach me. For I am the God of my salvation and my Lord, I wait upon day and night.

⁶ Remember, O LORD, thy tender mercies and thy loving kindnesses; for they have been ever of old.

6. Remember, the Imagination, the temple of God is where his mercy resides with loving kindness. His mercy is timeless, as it is infinite.

⁷ Remember not the sins of my youth, nor my transgressions: according to thy mercy remember thou me for thy goodness' sake, O LORD.

7. It is not for me to concentrate on my initial thoughts that miss the mark, nor the ones that are missing the mark currently. According to the mercy of God, I am to only remember the goodness of my Imagination for where I am to prosper.

⁸ Good and upright is the LORD: therefore will he teach sinners in the way.

8. With goodness and steadfastness is the Lord God; the Infinite Intelligence within man. Knowing this, will Universal Intelligence teach man who has missed the mark, the proper path to his Kingdom.

⁹ The meek will he guide in judgment: and the meek will he teach his way.

9. The man who is submissive in his thoughts, deficient in his spirit, will God guide him in judgment also. For the man who seeks courage or spirit in his thinking, will be taught the way of God.

¹⁰ All the paths of the LORD are mercy and truth unto such as keep his covenant and his testimonies.

10. There are many paths to God, and all paths have mercy and truth; keeping the covenant of God and all the testimonies spoken of in scripture.

¹¹ **For thy name's sake, O LORD, pardon mine iniquity; for it is great.**

11. In the name of your own Imagination, set aside your wicked thoughts, for they are great in number.

¹² **What man is he that feareth the LORD? him shall he teach in the way that he shall choose.**

12. What is a man that believes in something other than the Lord; other than God being himself. For those that believe in something other, shall be taught in the way chosen from man's own chaotic Imagination.

¹³ **His soul shall dwell at ease; and his seed shall inherit the earth.**

13. Your being shall be at ease; knowing that the seed planted in your Imagination, will bring about an identical harvest upon the earth.

¹⁴ **The secret of the LORD is with them that fear him; and he will shew them his covenant.**

14. The secret of Imagining, of Consciousness, of Infinite Intelligence, is with those you seek another god; and God will also show him through thought his covenant in which God resides.

¹⁵ **Mine eyes are ever toward the LORD; for he shall pluck my feet out of the net.**

15. My eyes are to always seek the temple of God; for he will untangle the web of steps I have tread.

¹⁶ **Turn thee unto me, and have mercy upon me; for I am desolate and afflicted.**

16. Turn to your own mind, for your Imagination will have mercy upon you; even though now you are feeling abandoned and afflicted.

¹⁷ **The troubles of my heart are enlarged: O bring thou me out of my distresses.**

17. My troubles of the heart are overwhelming. The Imagination will hear and bring me out of my distress.

¹⁸ Look upon mine affliction and my pain; and forgive all my sins.

> 18. It is I that must look upon my own affliction and pain; for the Imagination doesn't live in the past, thus all your sins, times of missing the mark, are forgiven.

¹⁹ Consider mine enemies; for they are many; and they hate me with cruel hatred.

> 19. I must consider my negative thoughts, for there are many. They speak of worry and cruel hatred of me.

²⁰ O keep my soul, and deliver me: let me not be ashamed; for I put my trust in thee.

> 20. Hear my being, Imagination, and deliver me. No longer shall I be ashamed of my negative thoughts, for I place my trust in God.

²¹ Let integrity and uprightness preserve me; for I wait on thee.

> 21. Allow for honesty and goodness to preserve me; for I will wait for the healing of God.

²² Redeem Israel, O God, out of all his troubles.

> 22. Redeem Enlightenment, God the Father, and bring me out of all my troubles.

ANALYSIS OF THE SCRIPTURE

It is for you to affirm that:

In my Imagination, I lift my head up for the answer to my being. The Law of God, I trust. My Imagination will not allow me to be ashamed. My negative thoughts will not win over me. Yes, I will not be ashamed in my thoughts as I wait upon the Lord to answer my prayers. As for those thoughts that miss the mark, they shall be ashamed.

Show me the way Imagination, Universal Mind. Teach me the paths I may take leading to God. Lead me to the truth. For I am the God of my salvation and my Lord, whom I wait upon day and night.

Remember, the Imagination, the temple of God is where his mercy resides with loving-kindness. His mercy is timeless, as it is infinite. It is not for me to concentrate on my initial thoughts that miss the mark, nor the ones that are missing the mark currently. According to the mercy of God, I am to only remember the goodness of my Imagination for where I am to prosper.

With goodness and steadfastness is the Lord God; the Infinite Intelligence within man. Knowing this, will Universal Intelligence teach every man who has missed the mark, the proper path to his Kingdom.

"The fear of the LORD is the instruction for wisdom, And before honor comes humility".

Proverbs 15:33

The man who is submissive in his thoughts, deficient in his spirit, will have God guide him in judgment also. For the man who seeks courage or spirit in his thinking, will be taught the way of God. There are many paths to God, and all paths have mercy and truth; keeping the covenant of God and all the testimonies spoken of in scripture.

In the name of your own Imagination, set aside your wicked thoughts, for they are great in number. What is a man that believes in something other than the Lord; other than God being himself? For those that believe in something other the God within themselves, shall be taught in a way chosen apart from man's own chaotic Imagination.

Your being shall be at ease; knowing that the seed planted in your Imagination will bring about an identical harvest upon the earth. The secret of Imagining, of Consciousness, of Infinite Intelligence, is even with those who seek another god; but God will also show him through the misguided thought, his covenant in which God resides. One is to confess in missing the mark and he too will be shown the way.

My eyes are to always seek the temple of God; for he will untangle the web of steps I have tread. Turn to your own mind, for your Imagination will have mercy upon you; even though now you are feeling abandoned and afflicted. Even though troubles of the heart are overwhelming, the Imagination will hear and bring you out of your distress.

> *"So now, our God, listen to the prayer of Your servant and to his supplications, and for Your sake, O Lord, let Your face shine on Your desolate sanctuary."*
>
> *Daniel 9:17*

Declare that: It is I that must look upon my own affliction and pain; for the Imagination doesn't live in the past. Thus, all your sins, times of missing the mark, are forgiven. I must consider my negative thoughts, for there are many. They speak of worry and cruel hatred of me.

Hear my being, Imagination, and deliver me. No longer shall I be ashamed of my negative thoughts, for I place my trust in God. Allow for honesty and goodness to preserve me; for I will wait for the healing of God. Redeem Enlightenment, God the Father, and bring me out of all my troubles.

CHAPTER TWENTY-SIX

PSALM 26

ORIGINAL TEXT

26 Judge me, O LORD; for I have walked in mine integrity: I have trusted also in the LORD; therefore I shall not slide.

² Examine me, O LORD, and prove me; try my reins and my heart.

³ For thy lovingkindness is before mine eyes: and I have walked in thy truth.

⁴ I have not sat with vain persons, neither will I go in with dissemblers.

⁵ I have hated the congregation of evil doers; and will not sit with the wicked.

⁶ I will wash mine hands in innocency: so will I compass thine altar, O LORD:

⁷ That I may publish with the voice of thanksgiving, and tell of all thy wondrous works.

⁸ LORD, I have loved the habitation of thy house, and the place where thine honour dwelleth.

⁹ Gather not my soul with sinners, nor my life with bloody men:

¹⁰ In whose hands is mischief, and their right hand is full of bribes.

¹¹ But as for me, I will walk in mine integrity: redeem me, and be merciful unto me.

¹² My foot standeth in an even place: in the congregations will I bless the LORD.

THEME

CONFIDENCE AND HONESTY

POWER OF PSALM

Doubt; Test of Mental Strength; Fearless; Unwavering Passion; Testing Resolve; Honesty

THOUGHT FOR THE PSALM

Do not wither in your thoughts.

INTERPRETATION OF EACH VERSE

26 Judge me, O LORD; for I have walked in mine integrity: I have trusted also in the LORD; therefore I shall not slide.

1. Consider my thoughts, Imagination. For I have traveled in honesty. I have trusted in the Lord, my Imagination, therefore, I must not doubt.

² **Examine me, O LORD, and prove me; try my reins and my heart.**

2. Look at me, Universal Mind, and test me as my heart and passion do not waiver.

³ For thy loving-kindness is before mine eyes: and I have walked in thy truth.

 3. For your mercy stands before me; and I have walked in your truth.

⁴ I have not sat with vain persons, neither will I go in with dissemblers.

 4. I have neither sat in the seat of conceited thoughts, nor will I go and hide myself under a false pretense.

⁵ I have hated the congregation of evil doers; and will not sit with the wicked.

 5. I have hated my negative thoughts that influence evil actions, and I will not sit with such wicked thoughts.

⁶ I will wash mine hands in innocency: so will I compass thine altar, O LORD:

 6. I claim my innocence, and will let the altar of God direct me; the altar of my Imagination.

⁷ That I may publish with the voice of thanksgiving, and tell of all thy wondrous works.

 7. I can tell the world with my voice of praise about all your wonderful works of glory.

⁸ LORD, I have loved the habitation of thy house, and the place where thine honour dwelleth.

 8. God in action, I treasure your actions from above; the place where you dwell.

⁹ Gather not my soul with sinners, nor my life with bloody men:

 9. Do not place my being with thoughts that miss the mark, nor with wicked manifestations.

¹⁰ In whose hands is mischief, and their right hand is full of bribes.

    10. For in their hands is mischief, and their so-called hand of truth are lies.

¹¹ But as for me, I will walk in mine integrity: redeem me, and be merciful unto me.

    11. However, as for me, I will walk with honesty. Take me back and be merciful unto me in my thoughts.

¹² My foot standeth in an even place: in the congregations will I bless the LORD.

    12. My thoughts stand together, but while in the congregation of negative thoughts, I will continue to bless the Lord.

ANALYSIS OF THE SCRIPTURE

In these passages, the request is being made to have one's thoughts considered by God. Here, we find: Consider my thoughts, Imagination. For I have traveled in honesty. I have trusted in the Lord, my Imagination, therefore, I must not doubt. Look at me, Universal Mind, and test me as my heart and passion do not waiver. For your mercy stands before me; and I have walked in your truth.

> *"Therefore, we regard the message of the prophets as confirmed beyond doubt, and you will do well to pay attention to it, as to a lamp that is shining in a gloomy place, until the day dawns and the morning star rises in your hearts".*
>
> *2 Peter 1:19*

I have neither sat in the seat of conceited thoughts, nor will I go and hide myself under a false pretense. I have hated my negative thoughts that influence evil actions, and I will not sit with such wicked thoughts.

I claim my innocence and will let the altar of God direct me; the altar of my Imagination. I can tell the world with my voice of praise about all your wonderful works of glory. God in action, I treasure your actions from above; the place where you dwell.

> *"Keep far from a false charge, and do not kill the innocent or the righteous, for I will not acquit the guilty."*
>
> *Exodus 23:7*

Do not place my being with thoughts that miss the mark, nor with wicked manifestations. For in their hands is mischief, and their so-called hand of truth are lies. However, as for me, I will walk with honesty. Take me back and be merciful unto me in my thoughts. My thoughts stand together, but while in the congregation of negative thoughts, I will continue to bless the Lord.

CHAPTER TWENTY-SEVEN

PSALM 27

ORIGINAL TEXT

27 The LORD is my light and my salvation; whom shall I fear? the LORD is the strength of my life; of whom shall I be afraid?

² When the wicked, even mine enemies and my foes, came upon me to eat up my flesh, they stumbled and fell.

³ Though an host should encamp against me, my heart shall not fear: though war should rise against me, in this will I be confident.

⁴ One thing have I desired of the LORD, that will I seek after; that I may dwell in the house of the LORD all the days of my life, to behold the beauty of the LORD, and to enquire in his temple.

⁵ For in the time of trouble he shall hide me in his pavilion: in the secret of his tabernacle shall he hide me; he shall set me up upon a rock.

⁶ And now shall mine head be lifted up above mine enemies round about me: therefore will I offer in his tabernacle sacrifices of joy; I will sing, yea, I will sing praises unto the LORD.

⁷ Hear, O LORD, when I cry with my voice: have mercy also upon me, and answer me.

⁸ When thou saidst, Seek ye my face; my heart said unto thee, Thy face, LORD, will I seek.

⁹ Hide not thy face far from me; put not thy servant away in anger: thou hast been my help; leave me not, neither forsake me, O God of my salvation.

¹⁰ When my father and my mother forsake me, then the LORD will take me up.

¹¹ Teach me thy way, O LORD, and lead me in a plain path, because of mine enemies.

¹² Deliver me not over unto the will of mine enemies: for false witnesses are risen up against me, and such as breathe out cruelty.

¹³ I had fainted, unless I had believed to see the goodness of the LORD in the land of the living.

¹⁴ Wait on the LORD: be of good courage, and he shall strengthen thine heart: wait, I say, on the LORD.

THEME

PROTECTION

POWER OF PSALM

Solace; Fear; Strength; Peace of Mind

THOUGHT FOR THE PSALM

Faith overcomes fear and gives you strength to move forward.

INTERPRETATION OF EACH VERSE

27 The LORD is my light and my salvation; whom shall I fear? the LORD is the strength of my life; of whom shall I be afraid?

1. The Imagination is my truth and savior; whom other shall I believe in? The Imagination is the strength of my life; of whom other shall I place my faith in?

² **When the wicked, even mine enemies and my foes, came upon me to eat up my flesh, they stumbled and fell.**

2. When the wicked, my negative thoughts, came upon me to devour my flesh, they stumbled and fell.

³ **Though an host should encamp against me, my heart shall not fear: though war should rise against me, in this will I be confident.**

3. Even if a negative thought should take route inside me, my heart shall not have faith in any other god. The negative thought will rise against me, in God I will be confident.

⁴ **One thing have I desired of the LORD, that will I seek after; that I may dwell in the house of the LORD all the days of my life, to behold the beauty of the LORD, and to enquire in his temple.**

4. If there is anything I desire of God, that I am able to seek after him. My pleasure is to dwell within my own Imagination, God in action, for the rest of my life. To praise the wonders of my Imagination, I will seek counsel in his temple.

⁵ **For in the time of trouble he shall hide me in his pavilion: in the secret of his tabernacle shall he hide me; he shall set me up upon a rock.**

5. For in time of trouble, I will hide in his temple: the secret of his tabernacle is where he will secret me. He will create a foundation for me to stand upright.

⁶ **And now shall mine head be lifted up above mine enemies round about me: therefore will I offer in his tabernacle sacrifices of joy; I will sing, yea, I will sing praises unto the LORD.**

6. And now, my head may look up into my Imagination, above my enemies that surround me. Therefore, I will offer my presence in his tabernacle sacrifices of joy. I will sing. Yes, I will sing praises unto the Lord.

⁷ **Hear, O LORD, when I cry with my voice: have mercy also upon me, and answer me.**

7. Listen to me Imagination as I feel for you with my voice. Have mercy upon me and answer my call.

⁸ **When thou saidst, Seek ye my face; my heart said unto thee, Thy face, LORD, will I seek.**

8. When you said, you seek my face, my heart says to you, my face, face of Imagination I will seek.

⁹ **Hide not thy face far from me; put not thy servant away in anger: thou hast been my help; leave me not, neither forsake me, O God of my salvation.**

9. Don't hide your face far from me. Don't stifle my Imagination because of anger. You have been my help. Don't leave me, nor abandon me, Lord, my savior.

¹⁰ **When my father and my mother forsake me, then the LORD will take me up.**

10. When my conscious mind and subconscious mind have apparently abandoned me, the Lord will set me straight.

¹¹ **Teach me thy way, O LORD, and lead me in a plain path, because of mine enemies.**

11. Teach me thy way, O LORD, and lead me in a plain path that I can follow where my enemies have created obstacles otherwise.

¹² **Deliver me not over unto the will of mine enemies: for false witnesses are risen up against me, and such as breathe out cruelty.**

12. Do not deliver me unto the congregation of negative thoughts: for liars will rise up against me, and spew hatred through their breath.

¹³ **I had fainted, unless I had believed to see the goodness of the LORD in the land of the living.**

13. I had doubted, unless I actually believed to see goodness in my thoughts in the land of the existing manifestations.

¹⁴ **Wait on the LORD: be of good courage, and he shall strengthen thine heart: wait, I say, on the LORD.**

14. Wait on the desires placed in Imagination. Have courage, and God will strengthen your heart. Wait for the coming of the Lord; his delivery.

ANALYSIS OF THE SCRIPTURE

The Imagination is your truth and savior; whom other shall you believe in? The Imagination is the strength of your life; of whom other shall you place your faith in? When the wicked, your negative thoughts came upon you to devour your flesh, they stumbled and fell. Even if a negative thought should take route inside you, your heart shall not have faith in any other god. The negative thought will rise against you; however, in God you must be confident.

> *"The LORD is my strength and song, And He has become my salvation; This is my God, and I will praise Him; My father's God, and I will extol Him.*
>
> *Exodus 15:2*

If there is anything to be desired of God, is the ability to able to seek after him. Your pleasure is to dwell within your own Imagination, God in action, for the rest of your life. To praise the wonders of your Imagination, you are to seek counsel in his temple.

For in time of trouble, you will hide in his temple: the secret of his tabernacle is where he will secret you. He will create a foundation for you to stand upright.

And now, your head may look up into your Imagination, above your enemies that surround you. Therefore, you will offer your presence in his tabernacle sacrifices of joy. You will sing. Yes, you will sing praises unto the Lord.

Listen to your Imagination as you feel for God with your voice. He will have mercy upon you and answer your call. When God said, you seek his face, his heart says to you, your face, is the face of Imagination that you will seek.

Don't hide your face far from him. Don't stifle your Imagination because of anger. God has been your help. He will neither leave, nor abandon you, for the Lord is your savior. When my conscious mind and subconscious mind have apparently abandoned me, the Lord will set me straight.

Who say to a tree, 'You are my father,' And to a stone, 'You gave me birth.' For they have turned their back to Me, And not their face; But in the time of their trouble they will say, 'Arise and save us.'

Jeremiah 2:27-28

Ask the Lord to teach you the way. For the LORD will lead you to a plain path that you can follow. He will create a clear path even where your enemies have created obstacles otherwise. Ask not to be delivered unto the congregation of negative thoughts: for liars will rise up against you, and spew hatred through their breath.

Acknowledge you had once doubted, confessing that you actually believed to see goodness in your negative thoughts in the land of the existing manifestations. Wait on the desires placed in your Imagination. Have courage, and God will strengthen your heart. Wait for the coming of the Lord; for the delivery of your desires are sure to come and they won't be late.

SPECIAL NOTE

Knowing the Lord, the Infinite Intelligence within you, is your own wonderful human Imagination is the key to having vision. Knowing that you have this vision, you can see the measure of all things. In reading this Psalm, you can come to realize that you are protected from all harms, evils or whatever else you have imagined being in fear of. Such thoughts of evil are considered sin; for you have missed the mark in knowing your true self to even think in such manner.

This Psalm confirms that you should not be afraid of anyone or anything, and that you are to use the power of Infinite Intelligence within you to solve all your problems. If there is any doubt to these words of the Psalms, think of disciple Andrew, a representative of the twelve faculties of mind. He represents strength. It is the strength of your faith within, in the God within you, that you shall fear nothing; for all is possible unto you.

Thus, any unprofitable thoughts such as thoughts of wickedness, do not exist but in your mind. Your enemies, foes and those that you believe can do you harm, also represent your imaginative thoughts that work to consume your flesh just from your way of thinking. Although as it says in this Psalm, knowing the power of the Lord and believing in him with total faith, all those sinful (missing the mark) thoughts, all those bad things will stumble and fall.

Clearly, this Psalm declares that negative thoughts will do their very best, for they are living thoughts, to find a home within you; within your heart and mind. However, through declaration of your faith and praise, you are to reject fear of them entering your mind and heart; for they are an unwanted intrusion.

In understanding this Psalm, the person that faces challenges or trouble of any kind, goes into their own Imagination, the secret tabernacle that every man possesses, and sets his desires. Desires can be complex or as simple as the desire to be free from such challenges and harm. No indication is ever made through any of the Psalms that you are to believe in anything outside of yourself for the answer to your troubles. Your Imagination is God in action. God answers all desires through your Imagination.

Sing with praise to the soul, your subconscious mind. For Infinite Intelligence reminds you that there is never a need to look down upon yourself. The Universal Mind within you, rests in the tabernacle of your mind. God hears your sacrifices of joy and feels your heart in all your inquiries. It is for you to say yes that you know your prayers are not going to be answered, but the fact that they are already answered. Sing praises unto the Lord, unto your own Imagination; only to bring about the manifestation of all your desires.

Remember, in times of trouble, turmoil, the most challenging of times, go within self and ask of your Father. Mercy will be given unto you, and your answers to your prayers, or in other words your desires will come to pass. For when you ask for the Lord to show himself, let your heart express the face of God through your own loving feeling. In your Imagination, the Lord will act and relieve you of all the troubles that plague you.

Ask of the Lord not to be handed over or to take part in the pit of bad thoughts. If you are not careful, bad thoughts will certainly rise up against you. And if such happens, you can expect through your breath, will come cruelty, evil and harm; intended or not.

Wait on the Lord. Wait on your Imagination. Hold steadfast with good courage, and he will strengthen your heart. He will fulfill your desires. Scripture tells you in this Psalm, wait on the Lord; wait on the declaration you made within your own wonderful human Imagination.

CHAPTER TWENTY-EIGHT

PSALM 28

ORIGINAL TEXT

28 Unto thee will I cry, O LORD my rock; be not silent to me: lest, if thou be silent to me, I become like them that go down into the pit.

² Hear the voice of my supplications, when I cry unto thee, when I lift up my hands toward thy holy oracle.

³ Draw me not away with the wicked, and with the workers of iniquity, which speak peace to their neighbours, but mischief is in their hearts.

⁴ Give them according to their deeds, and according to the wickedness of their endeavours: give them after the work of their hands; render to them their desert.

⁵ Because they regard not the works of the LORD, nor the operation of his hands, he shall destroy them, and not build them up.

⁶ Blessed be the LORD, because he hath heard the voice of my supplications.

⁷ The LORD is my strength and my shield; my heart trusted in him, and I am helped: therefore my heart greatly rejoiceth; and with my song will I praise him.

⁸ The LORD is their strength, and he is the saving strength of his anointed.

⁹ Save thy people, and bless thine inheritance: feed them also, and lift them up for ever.

THEME

The Working Congregation of Wicked Thoughts

POWER OF PSALM

Hearing the Voice of Prayers; Deliverance from Wicked Thoughts;

THOUGHT FOR THE PSALM

Give praised day and night to the Absolute, the Father, and as you travel, know that you will receive deliverance from negative and doubtful thoughts that collectively rise up against you.

INTERPRETATION OF EACH VERSE

28 Unto thee will I cry, O LORD my rock; be not silent to me: lest, if thou be silent to me, I become like them that go down into the pit.

1. Unto you I will cry, hear me Lord. My Imagination, my foundation, do not return my desires unto me void. If you are silent, I will feel like those that suffer in a place of emptiness.

² Hear the voice of my supplications, when I cry unto thee, when I lift up my hands toward thy holy oracle.

2. Hear my voice of my prayers unto my Imagination as I feel for you. I lift my hands upward to receive the answers from Infinite Intelligence.

³ Draw me not away with the wicked, and with the workers of iniquity, which speak peace to their neighbours, but mischief is in their hearts.

3. Do not place me in the company of the wicked, nor complete actions of the wicked thoughts; for they speak peace to their neighbors in congregation, but it is mischief from which they work from.

⁴ Give them according to their deeds, and according to the wickedness of their endeavours: give them after the work of their hands; render to them their desert.

4. Give such thoughts what are due them for their deeds, and according to their wickedness of their actions, place them in isolation for them to perish.

⁵ Because they regard not the works of the LORD, nor the operation of his hands, he shall destroy them, and not build them up.

5. Because they don't respect the works of the Lord, nor the operation of creation of righteousness, he will destroy the negative thoughts; never building them up.

⁶ Blessed be the LORD, because he hath heard the voice of my supplications.

6. Rewarded is the Law of God, my Imagination, because the Law hears the voice of my prayers.

⁷ The LORD is my strength and my shield; my heart trusted in him, and I am helped: therefore my heart greatly rejoiceth; and with my song will I praise him.

7. The Imagination is my strength and my shield. I trust in it with my heart, and it helps me in times of troubled thoughts. Therefore, my heart rejoices and with happiness, I will praise him.

⁸ The LORD is their strength, and he is the saving strength of his anointed.

8. The Imagination is their strength, and it is the saving grace of the awakened man.

⁹ Save thy people, and bless thine inheritance: feed them also, and lift them up for ever.

9. Hold on to the good thoughts and receive the blessings that come with them. Continue thinking or expressing loving and righteous thoughts, and they will reward you forever.

ANALYSIS OF THE SCRIPTURE

Unto your Imagination you must cry; for that is asking the Lord to hear you. Your Imagination, your foundation, does not return your desires unto you void. If you are silent and not take action upon your own self, it will feel like those that suffer in a place of emptiness who do the same.

Ask for the voice of your prayers, your desires to be heard, using your own wonderful Imagination with emotion or feeling. When asking, you may lift your hands upward as if to receive the answers from Infinite Intelligence.

Do not place yourself in the company of wicked thoughts, nor complete actions of wicked thoughts; for they speak peace to their neighbors in congregation of other wicked thoughts. Remember, it is mischief from which they work from.

Let your Imagination, God, give such thoughts what are due them for their deeds. According to their wickedness of their actions, place them in isolation for them to perish. Because wicked thoughts don't respect the works of the Lord, nor the operation of creation of righteousness, your favor of God will destroy the negative thoughts; never building them up again.

Rewarded is the adherence to the Law of God, your Imagination. Your Imagination will always hear the voice of your prayers. The Imagination is your strength and your shield. You are to trust in it with all your heart, and it will help you in times of troubled thoughts. Therefore, your heart must rejoice, and with happiness, you are to praise him.

> *"Then He will also say to those on His left, 'Depart from Me, accursed ones, into the eternal fire which has been prepared for the devil and his angels;*
>
> *Matthew 25:41*

The Imagination is your strength, and it is the saving grace of the awakened man. Hold on to the good thoughts and receive the blessings that come with them. Continue thinking or expressing loving and righteous thoughts, and they will reward you forever.

CHAPTER TWENTY-NINE

PSALM 29

ORIGINAL TEXT

29 Give unto the LORD, O ye mighty, give unto the LORD glory and strength.

² Give unto the LORD the glory due unto his name; worship the LORD in the beauty of holiness.

³ The voice of the LORD is upon the waters: the God of glory thundereth: the LORD is upon many waters.

⁴ The voice of the LORD is powerful; the voice of the LORD is full of majesty.

⁵ The voice of the LORD breaketh the cedars; yea, the LORD breaketh the cedars of Lebanon.

⁶ He maketh them also to skip like a calf; Lebanon and Sirion like a young unicorn.

⁷ The voice of the LORD divideth the flames of fire.

⁸ The voice of the LORD shaketh the wilderness; the LORD shaketh the wilderness of Kadesh.

⁹ The voice of the LORD maketh the hinds to calve, and discovereth the forests: and in his temple doth every one speak of his glory.

¹⁰ The LORD sitteth upon the flood; yea, the LORD sitteth King for ever.

¹¹ The LORD will give strength unto his people; the LORD will bless his people with peace.

THEME

STRENGTH OF THE WORD OF THE LAW (LORD)

POWER OF PSALM

Strength; Solid Faith; Corruptible Thoughts; Alien Thoughts

THOUGHT FOR THE PSALM

Wearing the armor of God is to understand the Word of the Law.

INTERPRETATION OF EACH VERSE

29 **Give unto the LORD, O ye mighty, give unto the LORD glory and strength.**

1. Give yourself to the Law. Hear this, for this is your power. Give yourself to the Law with your praises and all your strength.

² Give unto the LORD the glory due unto his name; worship the LORD in the beauty of holiness.

2. Give yourself to the Law, praises unto God; celebrate your Imagination in the beauty of its wholeness.

³ The voice of the LORD is upon the waters: the God of glory thundereth: the LORD is upon many waters.

3. The word of the Law is the truth. The power of the Law is thunderous. Again, the Law is the truth.

⁴ The voice of the LORD is powerful; the voice of the LORD is full of majesty.

> 4. The word of the Law is powerful. The word of the Law is the authority of all.

⁵ The voice of the LORD breaketh the cedars; yea, the LORD breaketh the cedars of Lebanon.

> 5. The word of the Law can break the hardest of substances. Yes, the Law can break through the durability of an incorruptible mind.

⁶ He maketh them also to skip like a calf; Lebanon and Sirion like a young unicorn.

> 6. The Law makes incorruptible thoughts fall over themselves. Such thoughts are exposed and labeled.

⁷ The voice of the LORD divideth the flames of fire.

> 7. The word of the Law ignites its strengths in many ways.

⁸ The voice of the LORD shaketh the wilderness; the LORD shaketh the wilderness of Kadesh.

> 8. The word of the Law disrupts whatever thoughts that have lost their way. The Law of the lost place of thought is also recognized.

⁹ The voice of the LORD maketh the hinds to calve, and discovereth the forests: and in his temple doth every one speak of his glory.

> 9. The word of the Law raises itself up and discovers the multitude of thoughts. In the mind of man, do all thoughts express his power.

¹⁰ The LORD sitteth upon the flood; yea, the LORD sitteth King for ever.

> 10. The Law is atop of all truths. Yes, the Law sits on his throne in the temple of the Imagination forever.

¹¹ The LORD will give strength unto his people; the LORD will bless his people with peace.

> 11. The Law will provide strength to all thoughts. The Law will reward good thoughts with peace.

ANALYSIS OF THE SCRIPTURE

Give yourself to the Law, the Law which is the Lord. Hear this, for this is your power. Give yourself to the Law with your praises and all your strength. Give yourself to the Law, praises unto God; celebrate your Imagination in the beauty of its wholeness.

The word of the Law is the truth. The power of the Law is thunderous. Again, the Law is the truth. The word of the Law is powerful. The word of the Law is the authority of all. The word of the Law is God.

The word of the Law can break the hardest of substances. Yes, the Law can break through the durability of an incorruptible mind. The Law makes incorruptible thoughts fall over themselves. Such thoughts are exposed and labeled.

And He said to them, "Where is your faith?" They were fearful and amazed, saying to one another, "Who then is this, that He commands even the winds and the water, and they obey Him?"

Luke 8:25

The word of the Law ignites its strengths in many ways. The word of the Law disrupts whatever thoughts that have lost their way. The Law of the lost place of thought is also recognized.

The word of the Law raises itself up and discovers the multitude of thoughts. In the mind of man, do all thoughts express his holy power. The Law is atop of all truths. Yes, the Law sits upon the throne in the temple of the Imagination forever. The Law will provide strength to all thoughts. The Law will reward good thoughts with peace.

CHAPTER THIRTY

PSALM 30

Original Text

30 I will extol thee, O LORD; for thou hast lifted me up, and hast not made my foes to rejoice over me.

² O LORD my God, I cried unto thee, and thou hast healed me.

³ O LORD, thou hast brought up my soul from the grave: thou hast kept me alive, that I should not go down to the pit.

⁴ Sing unto the LORD, O ye saints of his, and give thanks at the remembrance of his holiness.

⁵ For his anger endureth but a moment; in his favour is life: weeping may endure for a night, but joy cometh in the morning.

⁶ And in my prosperity I said, I shall never be moved.

⁷ LORD, by thy favour thou hast made my mountain to stand strong: thou didst hide thy face, and I was troubled.

⁸ I cried to thee, O LORD; and unto the LORD I made supplication.

⁹ What profit is there in my blood, when I go down to the pit? Shall the dust praise thee? shall it declare thy truth?

¹⁰ Hear, O LORD, and have mercy upon me: LORD, be thou my helper.

¹¹ Thou hast turned for me my mourning into dancing: thou hast put off my sackcloth, and girded me with gladness;

¹² To the end that my glory may sing praise to thee, and not be silent. O LORD my God, I will give thanks unto thee for ever.

THEME

Handling Your Foes

POWER OF PSALM

Fighting; Arguments; Disapproval of Something; Anger; Torment; Feeling of Suffering

THOUGHT FOR THE PSALM

You will always be in awe and receive more than you expected when the Lord handles your enemies.

INTERPRETATION OF EACH VERSE

30 I will extol thee, O LORD; for thou hast lifted me up, and hast not made my foes to rejoice over me.

1. I will praise you, hear me Imagination; for you have lifted me up, and have not let my enemies have dominion over me.

² O LORD my God, I cried unto thee, and thou hast healed me.

2. Imagination, my God, hear me. I cry unto you, and through Imagination, I am healed.

³ O LORD, thou hast brought up my soul from the grave: thou hast kept me alive, that I should not go down to the pit.

3. Hear me Imagination, for you have brought my being of thought up from the grave. You have kept my desires alive, and have not sent them into the abyss.

⁴Sing unto the LORD**, O ye saints of his, and give thanks at the remembrance of his holiness.**

    4. Praise the Imagination, and hear your good thoughts. Give thanks and remember from where they come from.

⁵For his anger endureth but a moment; in his favour is life: weeping may endure for a night, but joy cometh in the morning.

    5. Angry thoughts last for a short period of time. Such thoughts of anger exist because you gave the thought of anger life. You may cry over the anger at dark moment and time of the anger, but a brighter day is ahead.

⁶And in my prosperity I said, I shall never be moved.

    6. And in my thought of prosperity, I declared I would never doubt what was to come.

⁷LORD**, by thy favour thou hast made my mountain to stand strong: thou didst hide thy face, and I was troubled.**

    7. Imagination, by your favor, you have made my foundation stand strong. You did not hide your face from me even though I was troubled.

⁸I cried to thee, O LORD**; and unto the L**ORD **I made supplication.**

    8. I voiced myself to you. Hear me Infinite Intelligence. Unto you I declare my desires to you humbly.

⁹What profit is there in my blood, when I go down to the pit? Shall the dust praise thee? shall it declare thy truth?

    9. What do I stand to gain from congregating with negative, deceitful and ungodly thoughts in the place of darkness?

¹⁰Hear, O LORD**, and have mercy upon me: L**ORD**, be thou my helper.**

    10. Hear me Imagination. Have mercy upon me. Universal Mind, always be my helper.

¹¹ Thou hast turned for me my mourning into dancing: thou hast put off my sackcloth, and girded me with gladness;

> 11. You have turned days of wonder, into times of happiness. You have removed my burdens, and filled my heart with gladness.

¹² To the end that my glory may sing praise to thee, and not be silent. O LORD my God, I will give thanks unto thee for ever.

> 12. All the days of my life, I choose to sing praises to you; for I do not elect to be silent. Imagination, God in action, I will give thanks unto you forever.

ANALYSIS OF THE SCRIPTURE

Acknowledge that you will praise your Imagination. Know that it will lift you up, and upon your calling to the heaven above, it will not let your enemies have dominion over you.

Imagination, Infinite Intelligence, Universal Mind, is God, and he always hears you if you recognize him. Call unto the heaven above. Declare whatever it is, you are healed.

Call upon him, for he will lift you from the grave of negative and wicked thoughts. He will keep your desires alive, and your desires will not go unheard.

> *"The officers also shall speak to the people, saying, 'Who is the man that has built a new house and has not dedicated it? Let him depart and return to his house, otherwise he might die in the battle and another man would dedicate it.*
>
> *Deuteronomy 20:5*

Praise the Imagination and hear your good thoughts. Give thanks and remember from where they come from. For angry thoughts last for a short period of time. Such thoughts of anger exist, because you gave the thought of anger life. You may cry over the anger in dark moments, but a brighter day will come forth before you.

And in your thought of prosperity, you are to declare that you will never doubt what is to come. Imagination, by favor, has made your foundation stand strong. He will not hide his face in times of trouble. Voice yourself unto him. Ask Infinite Intelligence to hear you from within you. Declare your desires unto the universe within you.

So, what do you stand to gain from congregating with negative, deceitful and ungodly thoughts in the place of darkness? Nothing! Ask your Imagination, the Lord to have mercy upon you for thinking such thoughts: ask that he always be your helper.

Acknowledge that he can turn days of wonder into times of happiness for you. Know that he can remove your burdens and fill your heart with gladness.

Know that all the days, for the rest of your life, you choose to sing praises to him. Declare unto the Universal Mind, God within you that you will not elect to be silent. You know that Imagination is God in action, and there is no other. You will give thanks to him forever.

CHAPTER THIRTY-ONE

PSALM 31

ORIGINAL TEXT

31 In thee, O LORD, do I put my trust; let me never be ashamed: deliver me in thy righteousness.

² Bow down thine ear to me; deliver me speedily: be thou my strong rock, for an house of defence to save me.

³ For thou art my rock and my fortress; therefore for thy name's sake lead me, and guide me.

⁴ Pull me out of the net that they have laid privily for me: for thou art my strength.

⁵ Into thine hand I commit my spirit: thou hast redeemed me, O LORD God of truth.

⁶ I have hated them that regard lying vanities: but I trust in the LORD.

⁷ I will be glad and rejoice in thy mercy: for thou hast considered my trouble; thou hast known my soul in adversities;

⁸ And hast not shut me up into the hand of the enemy: thou hast set my feet in a large room.

⁹ Have mercy upon me, O LORD, for I am in trouble: mine eye is consumed with grief, yea, my soul and my belly.

¹⁰ For my life is spent with grief, and my years with sighing: my strength faileth because of mine iniquity, and my bones are consumed.

¹¹ I was a reproach among all mine enemies, but especially among my neighbours, and a fear to mine acquaintance: they that did see me without fled from me.

¹² I am forgotten as a dead man out of mind: I am like a broken vessel.

¹³ For I have heard the slander of many: fear was on every side: while they took counsel together against me, they devised to take away my life.

¹⁴ But I trusted in thee, O LORD: I said, Thou art my God.

¹⁵ My times are in thy hand: deliver me from the hand of mine enemies, and from them that persecute me.

¹⁶ Make thy face to shine upon thy servant: save me for thy mercies' sake.

¹⁷ Let me not be ashamed, O LORD; for I have called upon thee: let the wicked be ashamed, and let them be silent in the grave.

¹⁸ Let the lying lips be put to silence; which speak grievous things proudly and contemptuously against the righteous.

¹⁹ Oh how great is thy goodness, which thou hast laid up for them that fear thee; which thou hast wrought for them that trust in thee before the sons of men!

²⁰ Thou shalt hide them in the secret of thy presence from the pride of man: thou shalt keep them secretly in a pavilion from the strife of tongues.

²¹ Blessed be the LORD: for he hath shewed me his marvellous kindness in a strong city.

²² For I said in my haste, I am cut off from before thine eyes: nevertheless thou heardest the voice of my supplications when I cried unto thee.

²³ O love the LORD, all ye his saints: for the LORD preserveth the faithful, and plentifully rewardeth the proud doer.

²⁴ Be of good courage, and he shall strengthen your heart, all ye that hope in the LORD.

THEME

REDEMPTION

POWER OF PSALM

Forgiveness; Apology Needed; Need to Confess;

THOUGHT FOR THE PSALM

God, the redeemer is to become one with the redeemed. When Jesus spoke to his Father, he declared: "Thou hast redeemed me,". However, remember, Jesus has already confessed in the 10th Chapter of John, "I and the Father are one." The redeemer and the redeemed are really one.

INTERPRETATION OF EACH VERSE

31 In thee, O LORD, do I put my trust; let me never be ashamed: deliver me in thy righteousness.

1. In Universal Intelligence I place my trust. I am never to be ashamed, for God will provide me with goodness.

² Bow down thine ear to me; deliver me speedily: be thou my strong rock, for an house of defence to save me.

2. Universal Intelligence, God within, listen to my call, and quickly give me the answers I seek. Be my foundation, for the tabernacle where you reside in my mind is my defense; the place I create my own thoughts.

³ For thou art my rock and my fortress; therefore for thy name's sake lead me, and guide me.

3. Universal Intelligence, you are my foundation and my protection. Therefore, in my name whom I ask, lead and guide me in the right the direction.

⁴ Pull me out of the net that they have laid privily for me: for thou art my strength.

4. Release me from the web of negative, ungodly thoughts I am ensnared in. You are my strength.

⁵Into thine hand I commit my spirit: thou hast redeemed me, O LORD God of truth.

5. Into the hand of righteousness, I commit my spirit. You have redeemed me. Hear me, God, my Imagination of truth.

⁶I have hated them that regard lying vanities: but I trust in the LORD.

6. I have hated those thoughts that lie about the way I am. I trust in my Imagination.

⁷I will be glad and rejoice in thy mercy: for thou hast considered my trouble; thou hast known my soul in adversities;

7. I will be glad and rejoice in the mercy of my Imagination, God in action. Infinite Intelligence, you have considered my troubled thoughts. You have known the adversities that my subconscious mind encounters.

⁸And hast not shut me up into the hand of the enemy: thou hast set my feet in a large room.

8. With your mercy, you have not cast me into the pit of my negative thoughts. You have given me space to once again stand on my own in righteousness.

⁹Have mercy upon me, O LORD, for I am in trouble: mine eye is consumed with grief, yea, my soul and my belly.

9. Have mercy upon me Infinite Intelligence, for my thoughts trouble me. I find myself in a state of worry. Yes, in both my subconscious mind and in my heart.

¹⁰For my life is spent with grief, and my years with sighing: my strength faileth because of mine iniquity, and my bones are consumed.

10. For my life is spent with grief, and my years with worry. I do not possess the strength because of my wicked thoughts that are deep down in my soul.

MIND SCIENCE OF THE PSALMS · 201

¹¹ **I was a reproach among all mine enemies, but especially among my neighbours, and a fear to mine acquaintance: they that did see me without fled from me.**

> 11. I was disapproved by all my negative thoughts, but especially among those thoughts that were closest to me. My closest thoughts remained distant from me because of their fear in just looking at what I have become.

¹² **I am forgotten as a dead man out of mind: I am like a broken vessel.**

> 12. I am forgotten as the man of negative thoughts with no hope of revival. I am like vessel that no longer functions because of my thoughts.

¹³ **For I have heard the slander of many: fear was on every side: while they took counsel together against me, they devised to take away my life.**

> 13. For I have heard the false and defamatory statements made about my thoughts. Such slander surrounded me; while they, the negative thoughts themselves took counsel in congregation against me. They plotted to take away my life of good forever.

¹⁴ **But I trusted in thee, O LORD: I said, Thou art my God.**

> 14. But I trusted in my Imagination, hearing you God. I declared; my Imagination is my God.

¹⁵ **My times are in thy hand: deliver me from the hand of mine enemies, and from them that persecute me.**

> 15. My experience of life is now in your hands. Deliver me from the ways of my wicked thoughts and those thoughts that persecute me in the things I do and say.

¹⁶ **Make thy face to shine upon thy servant: save me for thy mercies' sake.**

> 16. Make your face to shine upon my subconscious mind. Do this for me for the sake of your mercy.

¹⁷ Let me not be ashamed, O LORD; for I have called upon thee: let the wicked be ashamed, and let them be silent in the grave.

> 17. I will not be ashamed, for the Imagination, I called upon you. Let the wicked be ashamed and upon their death, may they remain silent in their grave.

¹⁸ Let the lying lips be put to silence; which speak grievous things proudly and contemptuously against the righteous.

> 18. Let the lying lips be put to silence; which speak complaints with pride and contempt against the goodness of God.

¹⁹ Oh how great is thy goodness, which thou hast laid up for them that fear thee; which thou hast wrought for them that trust in thee before the sons of men!

> 19. Praise! Oh, how great is your goodness, a place you have prepared that negative thoughts fear to tread. You have provided the place of reward for those that trust in you and stand before the sons of all manifestations!

²⁰ Thou shalt hide them in the secret of thy presence from the pride of man: thou shalt keep them secretly in a pavilion from the strife of tongues.

> 20. You must hide those thoughts of goodness in the secret of my presence; presence from the pride of men. You are to keep the thoughts of goodness in the secret pavilion within your own mind away from those men with poisonous tongues.

²¹ Blessed be the LORD: for he hath shewed me his marvellous kindness in a strong city.

> 21. Rewarded is the Imagination that has shown me his marvelous kindness in a collection of great positive thoughts.

²² For I said in my haste, I am cut off from before thine eyes: nevertheless thou heardest the voice of my supplications when I cried unto thee.

> 22. For I said in great swiftness, I am not one to see with my physical eyes. Nevertheless, you heard my humble voice when I called unto the Infinite Intelligence within me.

²³ O love the LORD, all ye his saints: for the LORD preserveth the faithful, and plentifully rewardeth the proud doer.

23. Love the Imagination. Love all your good thoughts, for the Imagination will preserve the desired thoughts of those who are faithful. He will reward you plentifully; those that are proud in holding to the faith.

²⁴ Be of good courage, and he shall strengthen your heart, all ye that hope in the LORD.

24. Be strong, and God will strengthen your heart; the hearts of all those that place their hope in the Lord.

ANALYSIS OF THE SCRIPTURE

In Universal Intelligence, you are to place your trust. You are to never to be ashamed, for God will provide you with goodness. Ask Universal Intelligence, Brahma, Jesus, Allah, the God within, to listen to your call, and quickly give you the answers you seek. Ask the Lord to be your foundation; for the tabernacle where he resides in your mind is your defense; the place you create your own thoughts.

Universal Intelligence, is your foundation and protection. Therefore, in your name, you are to ask Infinite Intelligence to lead and guide you in the right the direction. You are to ask God to release you from the web of negative, ungodly thoughts you find yourself ensnared in. God within you, is your strength.

And He has said to me, "My grace is sufficient for you, for power is perfected in weakness " Most gladly, therefore, I will rather boast about my weaknesses, so that the power of Christ may dwell in me.

2 Corinthians 12:9

Into the hand of righteousness, you commit your spirit. Know that God has redeemed you. Ask for him to hear you; for God, is your Imagination of truth. You are to hate those thoughts that lie about the way you are. You are to trust in your Imagination.

You are to be glad and rejoice in the mercy of your own Imagination; God in action. Infinite Intelligence, is the source to consider your troubled thoughts. You, through experience, will know the adversities that subconscious mind encounters.

With the mercy of God, you believing in him, will never be cast into the pit of your negative thoughts. You have been given space to once again stand on your own in righteousness.

Ask for mercy upon Infinite Intelligence, for when your thoughts trouble you. This is to be done when you find yourself in a state of worry. Yes, this is to be true in both your subconscious mind and in your heart.

> *The angel who has redeemed me from all evil, Bless the lads; And may my name live on in them, And the names of my fathers Abraham and Isaac; And may they grow into a multitude in the midst of the earth."*
>
> *Genesis 48:16*

For when your life is spent with grief, and your years with worry, you will feel as though you don't possess the strength because of your wicked thoughts that reside deep down in your soul.

At times, you will find yourself disapproved by all your negative thoughts, and especially among those thoughts that were dearest to you. In fact, your dearest good thoughts remained distant from you because of their fear in just looking at what you have become.

You may declare that you are forgotten, as does a man of negative thoughts with no hope of revival. You are like a vessel that no longer functions because of your thoughts.

For you have heard the false and defamatory statements made about your thoughts. Such slander may give you the feeling as though they surrounded you. Caution, as those same negative thoughts themselves took counsel in congregation against you, only to overrule you. They continue to plot in order to take away your life of good forever.

You are to trust in your Imagination, for that is the hearing of God. You are to declare; your Imagination is your God. Your experience of life is now in the hands of God. Ask for deliverance from the God within you, from the ways of your wicked thoughts and those thoughts that persecute you in the things you do and say.

Look for the face of God to shine upon your subconscious mind. Ask for the mercy that comes with the love that God gives. You are not to be ashamed, for the Imagination when in need, is to be called upon. Let the wicked thoughts be ashamed, and upon their death, may they remain silent in their grave.

Let the lying lips be put to silence; which speak complaints with pride and contempt against the goodness of God. Praise! Oh, how great is the goodness of God, the place that has been prepared: a place that negative thoughts fear to tread. Know that you have been provided the place of reward, a reward for those that trust in him, and stand before the sons of all manifestations!

> *Thus says the LORD, the Redeemer of Israel and its Holy One, To the despised One, To the One abhorred by the nation, To the Servant of rulers, "Kings will see and arise, Princes will also bow down, Because of the LORD who is faithful, the Holy One of Israel who has chosen You."*
>
> *Isaiah 49:7*

You must hide those thoughts of goodness in the secret of your own presence; presence from the pride of men. You are to keep the thoughts of goodness in the secret pavilion within your own mind, away from those men with poisonous tongues.

Rewarded is the Imagination that has shown you his marvelous kindness in a collection of great positive thoughts. For you are to say in great swiftness, you are not one to see with your physical eyes. Nevertheless, God is to hear your humble voice when you call unto the Infinite Intelligence within you.

Love the Imagination. Love all your good thoughts, for the Imagination will preserve the desired thoughts of those who are faithful. He will reward you plentifully; those that are proud in holding to the faith. Be strong, and God will strengthen your heart; the hearts of all those that place their hope in the Lord.

CHAPTER THIRTY-TWO

PSALM 32

Original Text

32 Blessed is he whose transgression is forgiven, whose sin is covered.

² Blessed is the man unto whom the LORD imputeth not iniquity, and in whose spirit there is no guile.

³ When I kept silence, my bones waxed old through my roaring all the day long.

⁴ For day and night thy hand was heavy upon me: my moisture is turned into the drought of summer. Selah.

⁵ I acknowledge my sin unto thee, and mine iniquity have I not hid. I said, I will confess my transgressions unto the LORD; and thou forgavest the iniquity of my sin. Selah.

⁶ For this shall every one that is godly pray unto thee in a time when thou mayest be found: surely in the floods of great waters they shall not come nigh unto him.

⁷ Thou art my hiding place; thou shalt preserve me from trouble; thou shalt compass me about with songs of deliverance. Selah.

⁸ I will instruct thee and teach thee in the way which thou shalt go: I will guide thee with mine eye.

⁹ Be ye not as the horse, or as the mule, which have no understanding: whose mouth must be held in with bit and bridle, lest they come near unto thee.

¹⁰ Many sorrows shall be to the wicked: but he that trusteth in the LORD, mercy shall compass him about.

¹¹ Be glad in the LORD, and rejoice, ye righteous: and shout for joy, all ye that are upright in heart.

THEME

YOUR SINS FORGIVEN

POWER OF PSALM

Vision; Direction; Sin; Renewal of Mind; Broken Laws; Guidance; Forgiveness; Deliverance; Teaching

THOUGHT FOR THE PSALM

"Sin" is not something that is evil, deplorable, shameful or a sign of something demeaning. In fact, to "Sin" is to miss the Mark. All sins are forgiven, for one needs to learn to forgive themselves.

INTERPRETATION OF EACH VERSE

32 Blessed is he whose transgression is forgiven, whose sin is covered.

1. Rewarded are even those that violated laws, for even their sins (missing the mark) are covered with mercy in the eyes of God.

² Blessed is the man unto whom the LORD imputeth not iniquity, and in whose spirit there is no guile.

2. Rewarded is the man that is not responsible for embracing wickedness nor deceitfulness.

³ When I kept silence, my bones waxed old through my roaring all the day long.

3. When I meditated, my old ways have become no more. My soul is renewed with courage; all through solid faith, all day long.

⁴ For day and night thy hand was heavy upon me: my moisture is turned into the drought of summer. Selah.

4. Because, all the day long, the burden of the ungodly was upon me: the anointing of my being experienced drought. Selah

⁵ I acknowledge my sin unto thee, and mine iniquity have I not hid. I said, I will confess my transgressions unto the LORD; and thou forgavest the iniquity of my sin. Selah. (Selah – this is foundational truth, the axiom, wherein this true statement is self-evident.)

5. I acknowledge missing the mark unto God, my Imagination, and my wicked thoughts I do not hide. I said, I will confess my law breaking unto my Imagination; and God forgave my wickedness, which are my thoughts missing the mark. Selah. (Selah – this is foundational truth, the axiom, wherein this true statement is self-evident.)

⁶ For this shall every one that is godly pray unto thee in a time when thou mayest be found: surely in the floods of great waters they shall not come nigh unto him.

6. Understanding this, every one that seeks goodness will pray (desire) unto the human Imagination at any time; the place where God can be found. Among the many truths within the Imagination, negative thoughts will not come near the temple of God.

⁷ Thou art my hiding place; thou shalt preserve me from trouble; thou shalt compass me about with songs of deliverance. Selah.

7. Man is God's hiding place; man's human Imagination. There, in Imagination, God will preserve me from trouble; for God will direct me with scriptures and Psalms of deliverance. Selah. (Selah – this is foundational truth, the axiom, wherein this true statement is self-evident.)

⁸ **I will instruct thee and teach thee in the way which thou shalt go: I will guide thee with mine eye.**

8. God will instruct you and teach you in the direction you must travel. God will guide you through his vision.

⁹ **Be ye not as the horse, or as the mule, which have no understanding: whose mouth must be held in with bit and bridle, lest they come near unto thee.**

9. Do not become like the beast, the horse or mule, that is forced to hold his tongue due to a lack of knowledge; as he is also stifled (educated) because of the bit and bridle.

¹⁰ **Many sorrows shall be to the wicked: but he that trusteth in the LORD, mercy shall compass him about.**

10. Many sorrows will fall upon the wicked thoughts of man. But those that trust in his own Imagination, Infinite Intelligence, God's mercy will give him guidance.

¹¹ **Be glad in the LORD, and rejoice, ye righteous: and shout for joy, all ye that are upright in heart.**

11. Be glad in the Law of God, the Imagination, and rejoice. Be righteous and shout for joy in the praise of God and let him know you are firm in your faith within your heart.

ANALYSIS OF THE SCRIPTURE

Rewarded are even those that violated laws, meaning your sins. Sin only means to miss the mark in that which you desire. In the eyes of God, you are covered by his mercy. Rewarded is the man that is no longer responsible for embracing wickedness nor deceitfulness.

When you meditate, your old ways will cease to exist. Your subconscious mind is renewed with courage; all through solid faith, all day long. You will have experienced each and every day, the burden of the ungodly thoughts upon you. Continuing to let the burden run through you, you will exhaust yourself. You will not experience salvation without faith. Selah. (Selah – this is foundational truth, the axiom, wherein this true statement is self-evident.)

Acknowledge to God, your own Imagination, that you have been missing the mark. Expose your wicked thoughts unto the Lord. Tell the Lord, you confess your law breaking unto your Imagination; and God will forgive your wickedness. (Selah – this is foundational truth, the axiom, wherein this true statement is self-evident.)

Understanding this, every one that seeks goodness must pray (meaning desire) unto the human Imagination at all times; the place where God can be found. Among the many truths within the Imagination, negative thoughts will not come near the temple of God. They will no longer trouble you.

"Take My yoke upon you and learn from Me, for I am gentle and humble in heart, and you will find rest for your souls."

Matthew 11:29

Man is God's hiding place; man's human Imagination. There, in Imagination, God will preserve you from trouble; for God will direct you with scriptures and Psalms of deliverance. Selah. (Selah – this is foundational truth, the axiom, wherein this true statement is self-evident.)

God will instruct you and teach you in the direction you must travel. God will guide you through his vision. Thus, do not become like the beast, the horse or mule, that is forced to hold his tongue due to a lack of knowledge; as he is also stifled (mis-educated) because of the bit and bridle.

Many sorrows will fall upon the wicked thoughts of man. But when you trust in your own Imagination, Infinite Intelligence, God's mercy will give you guidance. Therefore, be glad in the Law of God, the Imagination, and rejoice. Be righteous and shout for joy in the praise of God and let him know you are firm in your faith within your heart.

CHAPTER THIRTY-THREE

PSALM 33

Original Text

33 Rejoice in the LORD, O ye righteous: for praise is comely for the upright.

² Praise the LORD with harp: sing unto him with the psaltery and an instrument of ten strings.

³ Sing unto him a new song; play skilfully with a loud noise.

⁴ For the word of the LORD is right; and all his works are done in truth.

⁵ He loveth righteousness and judgment: the earth is full of the goodness of the LORD.

⁶ By the word of the LORD were the heavens made; and all the host of them by the breath of his mouth.

⁷ He gathereth the waters of the sea together as an heap: he layeth up the depth in storehouses.

⁸ Let all the earth fear the LORD: let all the inhabitants of the world stand in awe of him.

⁹ For he spake, and it was done; he commanded, and it stood fast.

¹⁰ The LORD bringeth the counsel of the heathen to nought: he maketh the devices of the people of none effect.

¹¹ The counsel of the LORD standeth for ever, the thoughts of his heart to all generations.

¹² Blessed is the nation whose God is the LORD; and the people whom he hath chosen for his own inheritance.

¹³ The LORD looketh from heaven; he beholdeth all the sons of men.

¹⁴ From the place of his habitation he looketh upon all the inhabitants of the earth.

¹⁵ He fashioneth their hearts alike; he considereth all their works.

¹⁶ There is no king saved by the multitude of an host: a mighty man is not delivered by much strength.

¹⁷ An horse is a vain thing for safety: neither shall he deliver any by his great strength.

¹⁸ Behold, the eye of the LORD is upon them that fear him, upon them that hope in his mercy;

¹⁹ To deliver their soul from death, and to keep them alive in famine.

²⁰ Our soul waiteth for the LORD: he is our help and our shield.

²¹ For our heart shall rejoice in him, because we have trusted in his holy name.

²² Let thy mercy, O LORD, be upon us, according as we hope in thee.

THEME

REJOICE AND PRAISE

POWER OF PSALM

Changing Your Vibration; Keeping in Tune with Righteousness; Collective Thoughts; Creating Thoughts; Manifesting Your Creation; Counsel of the Lord; Understanding the Abode of God

THOUGHT FOR THE PSALM

Give praise to all your thoughts. Your thoughts are to be loving and righteous; for giving thanks to the Father, is giving thanks to the power you have in the Imagination.

INTERPRETATION OF EACH VERSE

33 Rejoice in the LORD, O ye righteous: for praise is comely for the upright.

1. Rejoice in the Imagination. Hear, those that choose to be righteous with God; for praise will be given unto you by God.

² Praise the LORD with harp: sing unto him with the psaltery and an instrument of ten strings.

2. Praise the Imagination with vibration: sing unto God as in the days of old and an instrument of different cords.

³ Sing unto him a new song; play skilfully with a loud noise.

3. Sing unto God a new song; sing it with precision as to what you want. Make your tune be heard. (Sing unto your subconscious mind a new song; play that new tune with skill, loud enough where nothing else can be heard within your Imagination.)

⁴ For the word of the LORD is right; and all his works are done in truth.

4. For the thought of the Law is right; all the works of God are done in truth.

⁵ He loveth righteousness and judgment: the earth is full of the goodness of the LORD.

5. The Lord loves those that seeks goodness and judgment in him. The earth is full of the creation of God.

⁶ By the word of the LORD were the heavens made; and all the host of them by the breath of his mouth.

6. Through the thought of God, was your Imagination made; and all the host of thoughts within it, are created by your breath.

⁷ He gathereth the waters of the sea together as an heap: he layeth up the depth in storehouses.

7. Imagination collects all of your thoughts, created with emotion and impressed in your subconscious mind, and sees all, and records all.

⁸ Let all the earth fear the LORD: let all the inhabitants of the world stand in awe of him.

8. Let all of the manifestations upon the earth fear the Law. Let all the manifestations of the earth watch his works in amazement.

⁹ For he spake, and it was done; he commanded, and it stood fast.

9. For he thought, and it was done. He declared, and it came into existence.

¹⁰ The LORD bringeth the counsel of the heathen to nought: he maketh the devices of the people of none effect.

10. The Lord gives counsel to those that fail to acknowledge him. The Lord creates ways that are not readily comprehensible.

¹¹ **The counsel of the LORD standeth for ever, the thoughts of his heart to all generations.**

> 11. When the Lord speaks, his words of counsel lasts forever. The thoughts of the subconscious mind apply all the thoughts of mind.

¹² **Blessed is the nation whose God is the LORD; and the people whom he hath chosen for his own inheritance.**

> 12. Rewarded are the thoughts that praise God (Imagination) as Lord. And the people whom have righteous thoughts, he has chosen to receive the inheritance of all the beautiful things God has to offer.

¹³ **The LORD looketh from heaven; he beholdeth all the sons of men.**

> 13. The Lord sees from the Imagination. He looks upon all sons of men.

¹⁴ **From the place of his habitation he looketh upon all the inhabitants of the earth.**

> 14. From the temple of the human Imagination, the Lord see all manifestations on earth.

¹⁵ **He fashioneth their hearts alike; he considereth all their works.**

> 15. He occupies the minds of all men. He considers the thoughts of all.

¹⁶ **There is no king saved by the multitude of an host: a mighty man is not delivered by much strength.**

> 16. There is no one ruler of one thought, of the many thoughts within the Imagination of man. The only ruler is man that created all of his own thoughts.

¹⁷ **An horse is a vain thing for safety: neither shall he deliver any by his great strength.**

17. Believing in something other than your Imagination, such as a beast or another man for safety, God will not respond to your desires, nor address desires of man with his might.

¹⁸ Behold, the eye of the LORD is upon them that fear him, upon them that hope in his mercy;

18. Listen, the Lord oversees all those thoughts that fear him. Upon those thoughts, mercy is contemplated.

¹⁹ To deliver their soul from death, and to keep them alive in famine.

19. For man seeks to have his subconscious mind delivered from the thoughts of wickedness, and to keep such negative thoughts at bay through starvation.

²⁰ Our soul waiteth for the LORD: he is our help and our shield.

20. Our subconscious mind waits upon the Lord. He is our help and our shield.

²¹ For our heart shall rejoice in him, because we have trusted in his holy name.

21. For our subconscious mind will rejoice in him, because we have trusted in his holy name.

²² Let thy mercy, O LORD, be upon us, according as we hope in thee.

22. Let his mercy, that of the Lord God, be upon us, according to his law we hope in him.

ANALYSIS OF THE SCRIPTURE

Rejoice in the Imagination. Hear those that choose to be righteous with God; for praise will be given unto you by God. Praise the Imagination with vibration. Sing unto God as you did with the thoughts you once created. Those are the days of the old.

Sing as if you were playing an instrument of different cords. Sing unto God a new song and sing it with precision as to what you desire. Make your tune be heard. (Sing unto your subconscious mind a new song; play that new tune with skill, loud enough where nothing else can be heard within your Imagination.)

For the thought of the Law of God is right, for all the works of God are done in truth. The Lord loves that seeks goodness and judgment in him. The earth is full of the creation of God. It was through the thought of God, that your Imagination was made; including the host of thoughts within it. All such thoughts are created by your breath.

Imagination collects all your thoughts, created with emotion and impressed upon your subconscious mind. Thus, God sees all, and records all. Let all the manifestations upon the earth fear the Law. Let all the manifestations of the earth watch his works in amazement. For he thought, and it was done. He declared, and it came into existence.

Then Hannah prayed and said, "My heart exults in the LORD; My horn is exalted in the LORD, My mouth speaks boldly against my enemies, Because I rejoice in Your salvation.

1 Samuel 2:1

The Lord also gives counsel to those that fail to acknowledge him. The Lord creates ways that are not readily comprehensible. When the Lord speaks, his words of counsel lasts forever. The thoughts of the subconscious mind apply to all the thoughts of mind.

Rewarded are the thoughts that praise God (Imagination) as Lord. And the people whom have righteous thoughts, he has chosen to receive the inheritance of all the beautiful things God has to offer. The Lord sees from the Imagination. He looks upon all sons of men.

From the temple of the human Imagination, the Lord see all manifestations on earth. He occupies the minds of all men. He considers the thoughts of all. There is no one ruler of one thought, of the many thoughts within the Imagination of man. The only ruler is man that created all his own thoughts.

Believing in something other than your Imagination, such as a beast or another man for safety is not the answer. God will not respond to your desires, nor address desires of man with his might. Listen, the Lord oversees all those thoughts that fear him. Upon those thoughts, mercy is contemplated.

For man seeks to have his subconscious mind delivered from the thoughts of wickedness, and to keep such negative thoughts at bay through starvation. Your subconscious mind waits upon the Lord. He is your help and your shield.

For your subconscious mind will rejoice in him, because you have trusted in his holy name. Let his mercy, that of the Lord God, be upon you according to his law. You are to hope in him.

CHAPTER THIRTY-FOUR

PSALM 34

34 I will bless the LORD at all times: his praise shall continually be in my mouth.

² My soul shall make her boast in the LORD: the humble shall hear thereof, and be glad.

³ O magnify the LORD with me, and let us exalt his name together.

⁴ I sought the LORD, and he heard me, and delivered me from all my fears.

⁵ They looked unto him, and were lightened: and their faces were not ashamed.

⁶ This poor man cried, and the LORD heard him, and saved him out of all his troubles.

⁷ The angel of the LORD encampeth round about them that fear him, and delivereth them.

⁸ O taste and see that the LORD is good: blessed is the man that trusteth in him.

⁹ O fear the LORD, ye his saints: for there is no want to them that fear him.

¹⁰ The young lions do lack, and suffer hunger: but they that seek the LORD shall not want any good thing.

¹¹ Come, ye children, hearken unto me: I will teach you the fear of the LORD.

¹² What man is he that desireth life, and loveth many days, that he may see good?

¹³ Keep thy tongue from evil, and thy lips from speaking guile.

¹⁴ Depart from evil, and do good; seek peace, and pursue it.

¹⁵ The eyes of the LORD are upon the righteous, and his ears are open unto their cry.

¹⁶ The face of the LORD is against them that do evil, to cut off the remembrance of them from the earth.

¹⁷ The righteous cry, and the LORD heareth, and delivereth them out of all their troubles.

¹⁸ The LORD is nigh unto them that are of a broken heart; and saveth such as be of a contrite spirit.

¹⁹ Many are the afflictions of the righteous: but the LORD delivereth him out of them all.

²⁰ He keepeth all his bones: not one of them is broken.

²¹ Evil shall slay the wicked: and they that hate the righteous shall be desolate.

²² The LORD redeemeth the soul of his servants: and none of them that trust in him shall be desolate.

THEME

CORRECTING YOUR THOUGHTS

POWER OF PSALM

Need a Conclusion; Resolution in a Legal Case; Sadness; Keeping Tongue in Check

THOUGHT FOR THE PSALM

Anything is possible once you correct your thoughts.

INTERPRETATION OF EACH VERSE

34 I will bless the LORD at all times: his praise shall continually be in my mouth.

1. I will love my Imagination at all times. The praise of Universal Mind, God, will always be my thought.

² My soul shall make her boast in the LORD: the humble shall hear thereof, and be glad.

2. My subconscious mind will pride itself excessively from my thoughts. God hears all thoughts, particularly humble thoughts, and is most happy.

³ O magnify the LORD with me, and let us exalt his name together.

3. Listen created thoughts, tremendously praise with me, and let us exalt his name with recognition together.

⁴ I sought the LORD, and he heard me, and delivered me from all my fears.

4. I called upon my subconscious mind, and the Lord heard me. He delivered me through my Imagination, of all my fears.

⁵ They looked unto him, and were lightened: and their faces were not ashamed.

5. Those thoughts adhered to the calling of the Imagination, and removed of burden. Their faces were not hidden, but revealed.

⁶ This poor man cried, and the LORD heard him, and saved him out of all his troubles.

6. The thought of the burdened man was heard by God, and God within man saved him of his troubles.

⁷ The angel of the LORD encampeth round about them that fear him, and delivereth them.

7. The loving thoughts within the Imagination take refuge in places that fear the power of the Lord, and delivers them with proper guidance in manifestation.

⁸ O taste and see that the LORD is good: blessed is the man that trusteth in him.

8. Use your senses and determine that your Imagination is good. Rewarded is the man that trusts in his own human Imagination.

⁹ O fear the LORD, ye his saints: for there is no want to them that fear him.

9. Those thoughts that respect the Law, Law of God, those are saints. For there are no need for thoughts to exist that don't fear the Lord.

¹⁰ The young lions do lack, and suffer hunger: but they that seek the LORD shall not want any good thing.

10. New thoughts are young, for they are in their infancy. They suffer from hunger, hunger for your focus and concentration. Thoughts that seek goodness, the Lord shall provide, and they will not starve.

¹¹ Come, ye children, hearken unto me: I will teach you the fear of the LORD.

11. Come, all new thoughts, and adhere to me. I will teach you the fear of the Lord.

¹² **What man is he that desireth life, and loveth many days, that he may see good?**

> 12. What thought manifestation deserves to remain in existence? What thought manifestation loves the many days of his existence and that desires to see good?

¹³ **Keep thy tongue from evil, and thy lips from speaking guile.**

> 13. Keep the negative thoughts from the tongue, from evil, from the lips that speak wickedness.

¹⁴ **Depart from evil, and do good; seek peace, and pursue it.**

> 14. Cast away evil thoughts, and do good. Seek peace in your mind and pursue it with faith.

¹⁵ **The eyes of the LORD are upon the righteous, and his ears are open unto their cry.**

> 15. The vision of the Imagination is to be upon the righteous. His ears are open to the calling of the desire.

¹⁶ **The face of the LORD is against them that do evil, to cut off the remembrance of them from the earth.**

> 16. Imagination is not for evil doers. Cast away the remembrance of such thoughts from the earth.

¹⁷ **The righteous cry, and the LORD heareth, and delivereth them out of all their troubles.**

> 17. Thoughts of goodness are heard by the Law. The Lord delivers the thoughts of goodness out of their troubles.

¹⁸ **The LORD is nigh unto them that are of a broken heart; and saveth such as be of a contrite spirit.**

> 18. The Lord, the human Imagination is close at hand to those suffering from a broken heart. The Lord recognizes one with a feeling of repentance; changing the way one thinks.

¹⁹ **Many are the afflictions of the righteous: but the LORD delivereth him out of them all.**

19. Many thoughts have been afflicted by bad thoughts, however, the Lord, the Imagination can deliver you out of such troubled thoughts.

[20] He keepeth all his bones: not one of them is broken.

20. He keeps his thought convictions of the righteous firm upright and none are left alone.

[21] Evil shall slay the wicked: and they that hate the righteous shall be desolate.

21. Evil thoughts consume themselves. They that hate the good thoughts, the ungodly thoughts will perish.

[22] The LORD redeemeth the soul of his servants: and none of them that trust in him shall be desolate.

22. The Lord takes back the consciousness of the good thoughts: and none of them that trust in him will perish.

ANALYSIS OF THE SCRIPTURE

Love your Imagination at all times. The praise of Universal Mind, God, should always be your thought. Your subconscious mind should pride itself excessively from your thoughts of goodness. God hears all thoughts, particularly humble thoughts. God loves joyous thoughts.

Have your wonderfully created thoughts praise God along with you. Exalt his name with recognition together. Call upon your subconscious mind, and the Lord shall hear you. He will deliver you, through your own Imagination, of all your fears.

Your thoughts are to adhere to the calling of the Imagination, and God will remove your burdens. Faces of your thoughts are not to be hidden, but in fact, they are to be revealed to the Lord. The thought of the burdened man will be heard by God, and God within man will save you of your troubles.

The loving thoughts within the Imagination take refuge in places that fear the power of the Lord and delivers them with proper guidance in manifestation. Use your senses and determine that your Imagination is good. Rewarded is the man that trusts in his own human Imagination.

> *"Then Peter opened his mouth and said: 'In truth I perceive that God shows no partiality. But in every nation whoever fears Him and works righteousness is accepted by Him.'"*
>
> *Acts 10:34-35*

Those thoughts that respect the Law, Law of God, are your saints of goodness. For there are no need for thoughts to exist that don't fear the Lord. As for new thoughts that are young, they are in their infancy. They suffer from hunger, hunger for your focus and concentration. Young thoughts that seek goodness, the Lord shall provide, and they will not starve.

Have all new thoughts adhere to you. You are to teach them the fear of the Lord. What thought manifestation deserves to remain in existence? What thought manifestation loves the many days of his existence and that desires to see good?

To see what kind of manifestations are spoken of, keep the negative thoughts from your tongue; from evil; from your lips that speak wickedness. Cast away evil thoughts and do good. Seek peace in your mind and pursue peace with faith.

The vision of the Imagination is to be upon the righteous. The ears of God are open to the calling of desire. Imagination is not for evil doers. Cast away the remembrance of such thoughts from the earth. For thoughts of goodness are heard by the Law. It is the Lord that delivers the thoughts of goodness out of their troubles.

The Lord, the human Imagination is close at hand to those suffering from a broken heart. The Lord recognizes you with a feeling of repentance; changing the way you think. Many thoughts have been afflicted by bad thoughts, however, the Lord, can deliver you out of such troubled thoughts. He who keeps his thought convictions of the righteous firm and upright, will find none of his good thoughts left alone.

Evil thoughts consume themselves. They that hate the good thoughts, will find that the ungodly thoughts will perish. The Lord takes back the consciousness of the good thoughts: and none of them that trust in him will perish.

CHAPTER THIRTY-FIVE

PSALM 35

ORIGINAL TEXT

35 Plead my cause, O LORD, with them that strive with me: fight against them that fight against me.

² Take hold of shield and buckler, and stand up for mine help.

³ Draw out also the spear, and stop the way against them that persecute me: say unto my soul, I am thy salvation.

⁴ Let them be confounded and put to shame that seek after my soul: let them be turned back and brought to confusion that devise my hurt.

⁵ Let them be as chaff before the wind: and let the angel of the LORD chase them.

⁶ Let their way be dark and slippery: and let the angel of the LORD persecute them.

⁷ For without cause have they hid for me their net in a pit, which without cause they have digged for my soul.

⁸ Let destruction come upon him at unawares; and let his net that he hath hid catch himself: into that very destruction let him fall.

⁹ And my soul shall be joyful in the LORD: it shall rejoice in his salvation.

¹⁰ All my bones shall say, LORD, who is like unto thee, which deliverest the poor from him that is too strong for him, yea, the poor and the needy from him that spoileth him?

¹¹ False witnesses did rise up; they laid to my charge things that I knew not.

¹² They rewarded me evil for good to the spoiling of my soul.

¹³ But as for me, when they were sick, my clothing was sackcloth: I humbled my soul with fasting; and my prayer returned into mine own bosom.

¹⁴ I behaved myself as though he had been my friend or brother: I bowed down heavily, as one that mourneth for his mother.

¹⁵ But in mine adversity they rejoiced, and gathered themselves together: yea, the abjects gathered themselves together against me, and I knew it not; they did tear me, and ceased not:

¹⁶ With hypocritical mockers in feasts, they gnashed upon me with their teeth.

¹⁷ Lord, how long wilt thou look on? rescue my soul from their destructions, my darling from the lions.

¹⁸ I will give thee thanks in the great congregation: I will praise thee among much people.

¹⁹ Let not them that are mine enemies wrongfully rejoice over me: neither let them wink with the eye that hate me without a cause.

²⁰ For they speak not peace: but they devise deceitful matters against them that are quiet in the land.

²¹ Yea, they opened their mouth wide against me, and said, Aha, aha, our eye hath seen it.

²² This thou hast seen, O Lord: keep not silence: O Lord, be not far from me.

²³ Stir up thyself, and awake to my judgment, even unto my cause, my God and my Lord.

²⁴ Judge me, O Lord my God, according to thy righteousness; and let them not rejoice over me.

²⁵ Let them not say in their hearts, Ah, so would we have it: let them not say, We have swallowed him up.

²⁶ Let them be ashamed and brought to confusion together that rejoice at mine hurt: let them be clothed with shame and dishonour that magnify themselves against me.

²⁷ Let them shout for joy, and be glad, that favour my righteous cause: yea, let them say continually, Let the LORD be magnified, which hath pleasure in the prosperity of his servant.

²⁸ And my tongue shall speak of thy righteousness and of thy praise all the day long.

THEME

WORKING THROUGH THE CONFLICT OF YOUR THOUGHTS

POWER OF PSALM

Looking to be Heard; Lack of Confidence; Build Esteem; Enlightenment

THOUGHT FOR THE PSALM

No longer is there a need to fight anyone or anything. Correct the conflict of your thoughts and a resolution will always appear.

INTERPRETATION OF EACH VERSE

35 Plead my cause, O LORD, with them that strive with me: fight against them that fight against me.

1. Hear my desires Infinite Intelligence. Favor those thoughts that strive with me, and fight against those negative, deceitful and doubtful thoughts that fight against me.

² Take hold of shield and buckler and stand up for mine help.

2. Stand before the negative thoughts with the armor of God and help me.

³ Draw out also the spear and stop the way against them that persecute me: say unto my soul, I am thy salvation.

3. Stop such negative thoughts that revolt against me, in their tracks with precision. Declare unto my subconscious mind, I am your salvation.

⁴ Let them be confounded and put to shame that seek after my soul: let them be turned back and brought to confusion that devise my hurt.

4. Let those negative thoughts be confused and put those thoughts to shame that seek my subconscious mind. Turn them away and place them into confusion those that desire to persecute me.

⁵ Let them be as chaff before the wind: and let the angel of the LORD chase them.

5. Treat those negative thoughts like debris before the wind. Let the holy spirit of my Imagination chase them away.

⁶ Let their way be dark and slippery: and let the angel of the LORD persecute them.

6. Place a veil over my negative thoughts and make their way impossible to persecute me. Let the holy spirit of my Imagination persecute them.

⁷ For without cause have they hid for me their net in a pit, which without cause they have digged for my soul.

7. With no reason, the wicked thoughts hide from me, waiting for me to fall into their evil pit. Without cause, they have worked to penetrate my subconscious mind.

⁸ Let destruction come upon him at unawares; and let his net that he hath hid catch himself: into that very destruction let him fall.

8. Let destruction come to any single negative thought that fixes their attention upon me. Let their net hidden for me to tread upon catch itself and self-destruct.

⁹ And my soul shall be joyful in the LORD: it shall rejoice in his salvation.

9. And my subconscious mind shall consist of loving thoughts projected by my Imagination. My Imagination shall rejoice in my salvation.

¹⁰ All my bones shall say, LORD, who is like unto thee, which deliverest the poor from him that is too strong for him, yea, the poor and the needy from him that spoileth him?

10. All my fixed thoughts within my Imagination, expressing their love unto God, are fixed thoughts that will deliver those that lack understanding and principles that are too strong to grasp. Yes, those thoughts that lack and need understanding that are delivering the spoils of men.

¹¹ False witnesses did rise up; they laid to my charge things that I knew not.

11. Lying thoughts have revolted against me. They presented to me things that appeared true to me.

¹² They rewarded me evil for good to the spoiling of my soul.

12. Such thoughts have rewarded me with evil as if it were good; only to spoil the thoughts within my subconscious mind.

¹³ But as for me, when they were sick, my clothing was sackcloth: I humbled my soul with fasting; and my prayer returned into mine own bosom.

13. But as for me, when those negative thoughts were without direction, without fuel for nourishment, my ways were a burden upon them. I humbled my subconscious mind and withheld nourishment for any negative thought; and my loving desire returned unto me within my Imagination.

¹⁴ I behaved myself as though he had been my friend or brother: I bowed down heavily, as one that mourneth for his mother.

> 14. I behaved as though such negative thoughts were like family. I would grieve for them when things did not appear right in what they intended for me.

¹⁵ But in mine adversity they rejoiced, and gathered themselves together: yea, the abjects gathered themselves together against me, and I knew it not; they did tear me, and ceased not:

> 15. But being deceived, in my adversity against the loving thoughts I should have tended to, the wicked thoughts rejoiced and gathered, creating strength; eliminating their sickness. Yes, those wicked obstacles congregated against me, and I did not recognize it. They ripped into my thoughts of goodness and were relentless in their fervor against them.

¹⁶ With hypocritical mockers in feasts, they gnashed upon me with their teeth.

> 16. With negative thoughts that display false appearances of virtue, thriving on mocking me, they grind their teeth into my thoughts of goodness.

¹⁷ Lord, how long wilt thou look on? rescue my soul from their destructions, my darling from the lions.

> 17. Infinite Intelligence, how long will you look on upon the negative thoughts I am creating? Clear my subconscious mind from their destructions; rescue my goodness from the lions.

¹⁸ I will give thee thanks in the great congregation: I will praise thee among much people.

> 18. Upon your rescue, Infinite Intelligence, I will give you thanks in the great multitude of loving thoughts. I will praise you among many of my thoughts.

¹⁹ Let not them that are mine enemies wrongfully rejoice over me: neither let them wink with the eye that hate me without a cause.

19. Don't let my enemies wrongfully rejoice over me. Neither let them give me a nod of their existence that hate me without cause.

[20] For they speak not peace: but they devise deceitful matters against them that are quiet in the land.

20. Wicked thoughts do not speak of peace, but they devise deceitful matters against those thoughts that have not yet matured.

[21] Yea, they opened their mouth wide against me, and said, Aha, aha, our eye hath seen it.

21. Yes, such wicked thoughts speak loudly against me. However, in triumph, the eyes of goodness can see.

[22] This thou hast seen, O LORD: keep not silence: O Lord, be not far from me.

22. Imagination, Universal Mind, Lord within me, you have seen what has taken place among those negative thoughts. Do not be silent and stay close to me.

[23] Stir up thyself, and awake to my judgment, even unto my cause, my God and my Lord.

23. I must stir myself up and awake to my cause, and even the kind of thoughts I am creating; for my thoughts are to be of God, my Lord.

[24] Judge me, O LORD my God, according to thy righteousness; and let them not rejoice over me.

24. Judge me, through my Imagination, my God, according to my thinking of goodness; and let those that fail in your judgment, let them not rejoice over me.

[25] Let them not say in their hearts, Ah, so would we have it: let them not say, We have swallowed him up.

25. Don't let negative thoughts say in their hearts, that they have control over me. Don't let them say that they have consumed me upon their will.

²⁶ **Let them be ashamed and brought to confusion together that rejoice at mine hurt: let them be clothed with shame and dishonour that magnify themselves against me.**

>26. Bring shame and confusion upon my wicked thoughts that choose to bring me hurt. Clothe them with shame and dishonor that choose to enlarge themselves against me.

²⁷ **Let them shout for joy, and be glad, that favour my righteous cause: yea, let them say continually, Let the LORD be magnified, which hath pleasure in the prosperity of his servant.**

>27. Let my loving thoughts shout for joy, and be glad, that favor my righteous cause. Yes, let them continually express themselves that the Imagination is supreme, which has pleasure in the prosperity of the subconscious mind.

²⁸ **And my tongue shall speak of thy righteousness and of thy praise all the day long.**

>28. And my tongue shall speak of thy righteousness and of the praise of God all day long.

ANALYSIS OF THE SCRIPTURE

Ask that your desires be heard by Infinite Intelligence; your Higher Self. Ask Infinite Intelligence to favor those good thoughts that strive within you. Ask that it will help fight against those negative, deceitful and doubtful thoughts that fight against you.

Ask Infinite Intelligence to stand before the negative thoughts with the armor of God and help you. For you are to desire that negative thoughts that rise up against you, are stopped in their tracks with precision. Know that Infinite Intelligence is your salvation.

Ask the Lord, the Absolute, to let those negative thoughts within your mind, be confused and put to shame; for they seek control of your subconscious mind. Ask that they be turned away, and to place them into confusion; those thoughts that desire to persecute you.

Treat those negative thoughts like debris before the wind. Let the holy spirit of your Imagination chase them away. Declare that a veil be placed over your negative thoughts and make their way impossible to persecute you. Let the holy spirit of your Imagination persecute them.

With no reason, the wicked thoughts hide from you, waiting for you to fall into their evil pit. Without cause, they have worked to penetrate your subconscious mind. Let destruction come to any single negative thought that fixes their attention upon you. Let their net hidden for you to tread upon, catch themselves and self-destruct.

Your subconscious mind shall consist of loving thoughts projected by your Imagination. Your Imagination shall rejoice in your salvation. All your fixed thoughts within your Imagination, expressing their love unto God, are the fixed thoughts that will deliver those that lack understanding and principles that are too strong to grasp. Yes, those thoughts will deliver and address the spoils of men.

Lying thoughts have risen up against you. They have presented things that appeared true to you. Such thoughts have rewarded you with evil, as if such thoughts were good; only to spoil the thoughts within your subconscious mind.

But as for you, when those negative thoughts were without direction, without fuel for nourishment, your ways were a burden upon them. Humble your subconscious mind and withhold nourishment from any negative thoughts. Let your loving desires return unto you from your Imagination.

You have behaved as though such negative thoughts were like family. You would grieve for them when things did not appear right in what they intended for you.

But being deceived, in adversity to the loving thoughts you should have tended to, the wicked thoughts rejoiced and gathered. In doing so, they are the ones responsible for creating strength and eliminating their sickness. Yes, those wicked obstacles congregated against you, and you did not recognize them. They ripped into your thoughts of goodness and were relentless in their fervor against them.

With negative thoughts that display false appearances of virtue, they thrive on mocking you, as they grind their teeth into your thoughts of goodness.

Ask Infinite Intelligence, how long will you look on upon the negative thoughts you are creating? Clear your subconscious mind from their destructions. Have Infinite Intelligence rescue your goodness from the lions. Upon your rescue, from Infinite Intelligence, you will give you thanks in the great multitude of loving thoughts. You are to praise Infinite Intelligence among many of your thoughts.

"The lion roars and the wildcat snarls, but the teeth of strong lions will be broken".

Job 4:10

Don't let your enemies wrongfully rejoice over you. Neither let those thoughts give you a nod of their existence, for they hate you without cause. Wicked thoughts do not speak of peace, but they devise deceitful ways against those thoughts that have not yet matured.

Yes, such wicked thoughts speak loudly against you. However, in triumph, the eyes of goodness can see. Imagination, Universal Mind, Lord within me, has seen what has taken place among those negative thoughts within you. Declare that Infinite Intelligence refrain from silence, and to stay close to you.

You must stir yourself up and awake to your cause; including the kind thoughts you are creating. For your thoughts are to be of God, your Lord. Be judged, through your Imagination, your God, according to your thinking of goodness. As to those thoughts that fail in your judgment, let them not rejoice over you.

Don't let negative thoughts say in their hearts, that they have control over you. Don't let them say that they have consumed you upon their will. Ask Infinite Intelligence to bring shame and confusion upon your wicked thoughts that choose to bring you hurt. Clothe them with shame and dishonor that choose to enlarge themselves against you.

Let your loving thoughts shout for joy and be glad that favor your righteous cause. Yes, let them continually express themselves indicating that the Imagination is supreme. Such thoughts make pleasure in the prosperity of the subconscious mind. And be sure that your tongue will speak of righteousness and of the praise of God all day long.

CHAPTER THIRTY-SIX

PSALM 36

ORIGINAL TEXT

36 The transgression of the wicked saith within my heart, that there is no fear of God before his eyes.

² For he flattereth himself in his own eyes, until his iniquity be found to be hateful.

³ The words of his mouth are iniquity and deceit: he hath left off to be wise, and to do good.

⁴ He deviseth mischief upon his bed; he setteth himself in a way that is not good; he abhorreth not evil.

⁵ Thy mercy, O LORD, is in the heavens; and thy faithfulness reacheth unto the clouds.

⁶ Thy righteousness is like the great mountains; thy judgments are a great deep: O LORD, thou preservest man and beast.

⁷ How excellent is thy lovingkindness, O God! therefore the children of men put their trust under the shadow of thy wings.

⁸ They shall be abundantly satisfied with the fatness of thy house; and thou shalt make them drink of the river of thy pleasures.

⁹ For with thee is the fountain of life: in thy light shall we see light.

¹⁰ O continue thy lovingkindness unto them that know thee; and thy righteousness to the upright in heart.

¹¹ Let not the foot of pride come against me, and let not the hand of the wicked remove me.

¹² There are the workers of iniquity fallen: they are cast down, and shall not be able to rise.

THEME:

THOUGHTS FEARLESS OF GOD

POWER OF PSALM:

Plotting Against You; Cease Wicked Thoughts; Mischievous Thoughts

THOUGHT FOR THE PSALM

Your mind is the domain of spirit; your domain for harvesting the seeds that you sow. In your domain is where you will find your practical power of Imagination. Your domain is your estate; estate of mind.

It is for you to remember that you are the heir of your estate. Thus, in order to assert your heirship and possess the abundance you desire, you must use this estate rightly. Power over those thoughts that are brazen enough to have you contemplate evil must be overcome by your practical power of Imagination.

It is you that has the power over situations and circumstances by which such thoughts have created on your screen of space. To banish such thoughts, you only need to use the great resources of mind to harvest the crop of victory over such thoughts.

You don't have to sacrifice anything, except the loss of your limitations or weaknesses you've imposed upon yourself. Your estate clothes you in the armor of God, which includes the power within yourself, and puts the scepter of truth in your hands.

INTERPRETATION OF EACH VERSE

36 **The transgression of the wicked saith within my heart, that there is no fear of God before his eyes.**

1. The plot of the wicked thoughts tell me in my mind, that there is no fear of God in what they desire me to do. Fear of God is dismissed.

²For he flattereth himself in his own eyes, until his iniquity be found to be hateful.

2. For man flatters himself in his own eyes, until he discovers that his thoughts are wicked.

³The words of his mouth are iniquity and deceit: he hath left off to be wise, and to do good.

3. The words of his mouth are wicked and full of lies: he has forgotten his wisdom and that he is to do good.

⁴He deviseth mischief upon his bed; he setteth himself in a way that is not good; he abhorreth not evil.

4. Man calculates and calibrates mischief upon his bed; he places himself in the position that is not good; he hates good but desires evil.

⁵Thy mercy, O LORD, is in the heavens; and thy faithfulness reacheth unto the clouds.

5. The mercy of the Lord in the Imagination; and your faithfulness will reach unto the clouds of mind where heaven can be found.

⁶Thy righteousness is like the great mountains; thy judgments are a great deep: O LORD, thou preservest man and beast.

6. Doing what is right, goodness can be equated to great mountains; your judgments are great in depth; Hear Lord, Imagination, for it is God that saves man and all else man thinks about.

⁷How excellent is thy lovingkindness, O God! therefore the children of men put their trust under the shadow of thy wings.

7. Praise be to God for his loving kindness! Therefore, the great manifested thoughts of man are to be preserved and protected by God.

⁸ They shall be abundantly satisfied with the fatness of thy house; and thou shalt make them drink of the river of thy pleasures.

8. For the great thoughts of man will be abundantly satisfied with the comforts of the heaven; and God, Imagination will make them drink from the river of man's great desires.

⁹ For with thee is the fountain of life: in thy light shall we see light.

9. For Universal Mind, Infinite Intelligence is the fountain of life: in thy truth, we will see the truth.

¹⁰ O continue thy lovingkindness unto them that know thee; and thy righteousness to the upright in heart.

10. Continue Lord, to deliver loving kindness unto those thoughts that know you; and knowing that their righteousness stands affirmed in mind.

¹¹ Let not the foot of pride come against me, and let not the hand of the wicked remove me.

11. Do not let the steps of my pride come against me and halt the hand of the wicked thoughts that try to remove me from goodness.

¹² There are the workers of iniquity fallen: they are cast down, and shall not be able to rise.

12. Workers of the wicked fall: they are cast down and will not be able to rise.

ANALYSIS OF THE SCRIPTURE

Wicked thoughts plot, and tell you in your mind, that there is no need to fear of God in what they desire you to do. The negative thoughts claim action while being fearless. Man tends to flatter himself within his own senses and continues to do so until he discovers that his thoughts are wicked.

The words of your mouth are wicked and full of lies. This is because you have forgotten your own wisdom and that you are to do good. Man can find himself capable of the ability to calculate and calibrate mischief upon his bed; for he places himself in a position that is not good. He may find himself with reason to hate good, and desire evil.

> *"The good man out of the good treasure of his heart brings forth what is good; and the evil man out of the evil treasure brings forth what is evil; for his mouth speaks from that which fills his heart."*
>
> *Luke 6:45*

The mercy of the Lord is in the Imagination, and your faithfulness will reach unto the clouds of your mind where heaven can be found. Doing what is right, goodness can be equated to great mountains. Your judgments are great in depth. When asking for the hearing of the Lord, the Imagination, you will discover that it is God that saves man, and all else man thinks about.

Praise be to God for his loving kindness! The great and good manifested thoughts of man are to be preserved and protected by God. For the great thoughts of man will be abundantly satisfied with the comforts of heaven; and God, Imagination will make them drink from the river of man's great desires.

Universal Mind, Infinite Intelligence is the fountain of life. In his truth, you will see the truth. The Lord will always continue to deliver loving kindness unto those thoughts that know you; and you know that your righteousness thoughts stand affirmed in your mind.

Do not let the steps of your pride come against you. Halt the hand of the wicked thoughts that try to remove you from goodness. Workers of the wicked shall fall, for they are cast down and will never rise again.

CHAPTER THIRTY-SEVEN

PSALM 37

ORIGINAL TEXT

37 Fret not thyself because of evildoers, neither be thou envious against the workers of iniquity.

²For they shall soon be cut down like the grass, and wither as the green herb.

³Trust in the LORD, and do good; so shalt thou dwell in the land, and verily thou shalt be fed.

⁴Delight thyself also in the LORD: and he shall give thee the desires of thine heart.

⁵Commit thy way unto the LORD; trust also in him; and he shall bring it to pass.

⁶And he shall bring forth thy righteousness as the light, and thy judgment as the noonday.

⁷Rest in the LORD, and wait patiently for him: fret not thyself because of him who prospereth in his way, because of the man who bringeth wicked devices to pass.

⁸Cease from anger, and forsake wrath: fret not thyself in any wise to do evil.

⁹For evildoers shall be cut off: but those that wait upon the LORD, they shall inherit the earth.

¹⁰For yet a little while, and the wicked shall not be: yea, thou shalt diligently consider his place, and it shall not be.

¹¹ But the meek shall inherit the earth; and shall delight themselves in the abundance of peace.

¹² The wicked plotteth against the just, and gnasheth upon him with his teeth.

¹³ The LORD shall laugh at him: for he seeth that his day is coming.

¹⁴ The wicked have drawn out the sword, and have bent their bow, to cast down the poor and needy, and to slay such as be of upright conversation.

¹⁵ Their sword shall enter into their own heart, and their bows shall be broken.

¹⁶ A little that a righteous man hath is better than the riches of many wicked.

¹⁷ For the arms of the wicked shall be broken: but the LORD upholdeth the righteous.

¹⁸ The LORD knoweth the days of the upright: and their inheritance shall be for ever.

¹⁹ They shall not be ashamed in the evil time: and in the days of famine they shall be satisfied.

²⁰ But the wicked shall perish, and the enemies of the LORD shall be as the fat of lambs: they shall consume; into smoke shall they consume away.

²¹ The wicked borroweth, and payeth not again: but the righteous sheweth mercy, and giveth.

²² For such as be blessed of him shall inherit the earth; and they that be cursed of him shall be cut off.

²³ The steps of a good man are ordered by the LORD: and he delighteth in his way.
²⁴ Though he fall, he shall not be utterly cast down: for the LORD upholdeth him with his hand.

²⁵ I have been young, and now am old; yet have I not seen the righteous forsaken, nor his seed begging bread.

²⁶ He is ever merciful, and lendeth; and his seed is blessed.

²⁷ Depart from evil, and do good; and dwell for evermore.

²⁸ For the LORD loveth judgment, and forsaketh not his saints; they are preserved for ever: but the seed of the wicked shall be cut off.

²⁹ The righteous shall inherit the land, and dwell therein for ever.

³⁰ The mouth of the righteous speaketh wisdom, and his tongue talketh of judgment.

³¹ The law of his God is in his heart; none of his steps shall slide.

³² The wicked watcheth the righteous, and seeketh to slay him.

³³ The LORD will not leave him in his hand, nor condemn him when he is judged.

³⁴ Wait on the LORD, and keep his way, and he shall exalt thee to inherit the land: when the wicked are cut off, thou shalt see it.

³⁵ I have seen the wicked in great power, and spreading himself like a green bay tree.

³⁶ Yet he passed away, and, lo, he was not: yea, I sought him, but he could not be found.

³⁷ Mark the perfect man, and behold the upright: for the end of that man is peace.

³⁸ But the transgressors shall be destroyed together: the end of the wicked shall be cut off.

³⁹ But the salvation of the righteous is of the LORD: he is their strength in the time of trouble.

⁴⁰ And the LORD shall help them, and deliver them: he shall deliver them from the wicked, and save them, because they trust in him.

THEME

Commit to the Imagination – Don't Fret Evil Thoughts

POWER OF PSALM

Evil Thoughts; Deliverance; Discipline

THOUGHT FOR THE PSALM

The perception of evil thoughts, circumstances, situations or actions all come from thoughts within your own being. It is your "Objective Mind" or what is called the "Conscious Mind" (dealing with your outward manifestations), that uses your five senses (Satan, Devil) that deal with the impressions made inwardly upon the "Subjective Mind" or what is called the "Subconscious Mind" (dealing with your inner thought impressions in which it will manifest). The Conscious Mind is responsible for being the guardian of the Subconscious Mind; though also making impressions upon the Subconscious Mind. For what you think can eventually become what you believe.

INTERPRETATION OF EACH VERSE

37 **Fret not thyself because of evildoers, neither be thou envious against the workers of iniquity.**

1. Don't fear your evil thoughts, neither be envious against the workers of wickedness.

² For they shall soon be cut down like the grass, and wither as the green herb.

2. For they will soon be cut down like the grass, and wither away as the truth is seen in the green of a plant.

³ Trust in the LORD, and do good; so shalt thou dwell in the land, and verily thou shalt be fed.

3. Trust in the Imagination, and do good. You must dwell in the land of the mind, and verily you will be fed.

⁴Delight thyself also in the LORD: and he shall give thee the desires of thine heart.

4. Give praise for the workings of the mind, God in action, and he shall give you all the desires of your heart.

⁵Commit thy way unto the LORD; trust also in him; and he shall bring it to pass.

5. Make a commitment unto your Imagination; trust in him and he shall bring your desire to pass.

⁶And he shall bring forth thy righteousness as the light, and thy judgment as the noonday.

6. And he shall bring forth your righteousness you seek in your witness of the truth, and your judgment can be seen clearly.

⁷Rest in the LORD, and wait patiently for him: fret not thyself because of him who prospereth in his way, because of the man who bringeth wicked devices to pass.

7. Rest in the Imagination, and wait patiently for him: don't worry yourself because despite those who choose not to prosper in the way to the Lord, is the manifestation that bringeth wickedness to come forth.

⁸Cease from anger, and forsake wrath: fret not thyself in any wise to do evil.

8. Stop your anger, and turn away from the wrath of the wicked: don't worry yourself, for they choose to do evil.

⁹For evildoers shall be cut off: but those that wait upon the LORD, they shall inherit the earth.

9. Those thoughts that do evil, will be cut off: but those that wait upon the Lord, shall inherit the earth.

¹⁰ **For yet a little while, and the wicked shall not be: yea, thou shalt diligently consider his place, and it shall not be.**

    10. Wait a little while, and in the time of God, the time of harvest, the wicked thoughts shall be no longer: yes, you must diligently recognize their place in your mind, but in time, they shall no longer be.

¹¹ **But the meek shall inherit the earth; and shall delight themselves in the abundance of peace.**

    11. But the patient without resentment will inherit the earth; and shall delight themselves in the abundance of peace.

¹² **The wicked plotteth against the just, and gnasheth upon him with his teeth.**

    12. The wicked thoughts plot against the righteous thoughts, and grind upon the mind with their teeth.

¹³ **The LORD shall laugh at him: for he seeth that his day is coming.**

    13. The Imagination, the Infinite Intelligence, the Lord, will laugh at those thoughts: for the Lord can see when the day of the demise of the evil thoughts are to come.

¹⁴ **The wicked have drawn out the sword, and have bent their bow, to cast down the poor and needy, and to slay such as be of upright conversation.**

    14. The wicked thoughts have drawn out the sword, and have bent their bow in retaliation of the just, to cast down those that lack and suffer from wisdom, and to slay such thoughts that have conversation of justice.

¹⁵ **Their sword shall enter into their own heart, and their bows shall be broken.**

    15. The sword of the evil thoughts, the evil doers, will enter into their own heart, and their bows shall be broken.

¹⁶ **A little that a righteous man hath is better than the riches of many wicked.**

> 16. A man that has few righteous thoughts, is better off than the man with an abundance of wicked thoughts.

¹⁷ **For the arms of the wicked shall be broken: but the LORD upholdeth the righteous.**

> 17. For the strength upon the mind exerted by the wicked thoughts shall be broken: but the Lord, the Universal Mind shall uphold righteousness.

¹⁸ **The LORD knoweth the days of the upright: and their inheritance shall be for ever.**

> 18. The Imagination knows the days of the righteous: and knows that their inheritance shall last forever.

¹⁹ **They shall not be ashamed in the evil time: and in the days of famine they shall be satisfied.**

> 19. The righteous thoughts will not be ashamed in the congregation of the evil thoughts: and in the days of famine, the righteous thoughts will be fed.

²⁰ **But the wicked shall perish, and the enemies of the LORD shall be as the fat of lambs: they shall consume; into smoke shall they consume away.**

> 20. But the wicked thoughts shall perish, and the enemies of the Imagination, God's temple, will be forced to feed upon themselves: they will consume; into smoke will they eat themselves away.

²¹ **The wicked borroweth, and payeth not again: but the righteous sheweth mercy, and giveth.**

> 21. The wicked thought only exist on borrowed time, and cannot give reward: the righteous shows mercy and reward is given.

²² **For such as be blessed of him shall inherit the earth; and they that be cursed of him shall be cut off.**

22. For the man that is rewarded shall inherit the earth; and those negative thoughts that once cursed will be cut off.

²³ The steps of a good man are ordered by the LORD: and he delighteth in his way.

23. The steps of a good man are planned by the Imagination: and the Lord is delighted in his way.

²⁴ Though he fall, he shall not be utterly cast down: for the LORD upholdeth him with his hand.

24. Though the man stumble with negative faults, he shall not be cast down: for the Imagination upholds such a man with the hand of the Lord.

²⁵ I have been young, and now am old; yet have I not seen the righteous forsaken, nor his seed begging bread.

25. As a thought, I have been young, and now I have manifested; yet I haven't seen the righteous of thought turned away, or any of the offspring of the righteous thoughts face famine.

²⁶ He is ever merciful, and lendeth; and his seed is blessed.

26. Universal Intelligence is ever merciful, and lends a hand to the righteous; and offspring of the righteous is also rewarded.

²⁷ Depart from evil, and do good; and dwell for evermore.

27. Leave the evil thoughts alone and perform good; and dwell in righteousness of the Lord forever.

²⁸ For the LORD loveth judgment, and forsaketh not his saints; they are preserved for ever: but the seed of the wicked shall be cut off.

28. For the Imagination, Universal Mind loves judgment, and does not turn away those that are for him; but he preserves them forever; the seed of the wicked thoughts will be cut off forever.

²⁹ The righteous shall inherit the land, and dwell therein for ever.

29. The righteous will inherit the land, heaven, and dwell in their Imagination forever.

30 **The mouth of the righteous speaketh wisdom, and his tongue talketh of judgment.**

30. The mouth of those that practice righteousness speak wisdom, and he shall make judgment of negative thoughts.

31 **The law of his God is in his heart; none of his steps shall slide.**

31. The law of the righteous thought rests in the heart, the Imagination; thus never shall he miss a step in his path of righteousness.

32 **The wicked watcheth the righteous, and seeketh to slay him.**

32. The wicked always watch the righteous, and looks to slay him.

33 **The LORD will not leave him in his hand, nor condemn him when he is judged.**

33. The Imagination, the Lord, will not abandon the righteous, nor condemn him when such thoughts surrounding him are judged.

34 **Wait on the LORD, and keep his way, and he shall exalt thee to inherit the land: when the wicked are cut off, thou shalt see it.**

34. Wait on the Lord, and keep his way, and he will raise you to inherit the land: when the wicked thoughts are cut off, you will see it.

35 **I have seen the wicked in great power, and spreading himself like a green bay tree.**

35. I have seen the wicked in great dominance, and spread itself like a bay tree, where fresh leaves release bitter substances.

36 **Yet he passed away, and, lo, he was not: yea, I sought him, but he could not be found.**

36. Yet the thought passed away, and no longer: yes, I search for the negative thought, but it could not be found.

37 **Mark the perfect man, and behold the upright: for the end of that man is peace.**

37. Mark the righteous manifestation, and hold on to the affirmed positive thought: for the end of that manifestation is peace.

[38] But the transgressors shall be destroyed together: the end of the wicked shall be cut off.

38. But the evil plotters will be destroyed together: the end of the wicked thoughts will be cut off.

[39] But the salvation of the righteous is of the LORD: he is their strength in the time of trouble.

39. But the salvation of the righteous is the Imagination: he is the strength of the righteous in times of trouble.

[40] And the LORD shall help them, and deliver them: he shall deliver them from the wicked, and save them, because they trust in him.

40. And the Imagination, Infinite Intelligence will help the positive thoughts, and deliver them: he will deliver them from the wicked, and save them, because they trust in him.

ANALYSIS OF THE SCRIPTURE

Don't fear your evil thoughts, neither be envious against the workers of wickedness. For they will soon be cut down like the grass, and wither away as the truth is seen in the green of a plant. Trust in the Imagination and do good. You must dwell in the land of the mind, and verily you will be fed.

Give praise for the workings of the mind, God in action, and he shall give you all the desires of your heart. Make a commitment unto your Imagination; trust, and the Lord will bring your desires to pass.

And all things, whatsoever ye shall ask in prayer, believing, ye shall receive.
Matthew 21:22

The Lord will bring forth the righteousness you seek in your witness of the truth, and your judgment will be seen clearly. Rest in the

Imagination and wait patiently for the Lord. Don't worry yourself regarding those who choose not to prosper in the way of the Lord. The subconscious mind will bring forth their unwanted manifestations of wickedness.

Stop your anger and turn away from the wrath of wicked thoughts. Don't worry yourself, for they choose to do evil. Those thoughts that do evil, will be cut off: but those that wait upon the Lord, shall inherit the earth.

Blessed are the meek: for they shall inherit the earth.

Matthew 5:5

Wait a little while, and in the time of God, the time of harvest, the wicked thoughts shall be no longer. Yes, you must diligently recognize their place in your mind, but in time, they shall no longer be.

But with patience and without resentment, the righteous thoughts will inherit the earth; and shall delight themselves in the abundance of peace. The wicked thoughts certainly plot against the righteous thoughts, and grind upon the mind with their teeth.

The Imagination, the Infinite Intelligence, the Lord, will laugh at those thoughts: for the Lord can see when the day of the demise of the evil thoughts are to come. The wicked thoughts have drawn out their swords, bending their bow in retaliation of the just. They seek to cast down those that lack and suffer from wisdom; only to slay such thoughts that have conversation of justice.

The sword of the evil thoughts, the evil doers, will enter their own heart, and their bows shall be broken.

In that day I will also make a covenant for them With the beasts of the field, The birds of the sky And the creeping things of the ground And I will abolish the bow, the sword and war from the land, And will make them lie down in safety.

Hosea 2:18

A man that has few righteous thoughts, is better off than the man with an abundance of wicked thoughts. For the strength upon the mind exerted by the wicked thoughts shall be broken, but the Lord, the Universal Mind, shall uphold righteousness.

The Imagination knows the days of the righteous and know that their inheritance shall last forever. The righteous thoughts will not be ashamed in the congregation of the evil thoughts, and in the days of famine, the righteous thoughts will be fed. But the wicked thoughts shall perish, and the enemies of the Imagination, God's temple, will be forced to feed upon themselves. They will consume the air and turn into smoke; eating themselves away.

The wicked thoughts only exist on borrowed time and cannot give reward. The Lord shows righteous mercy, and reward is given. For the man that is rewarded, shall inherit the earth; and those negative thoughts that once cursed him will be cut off. The steps of a good man are planned by the Imagination, and the Lord is delighted in his way.

Though a man stumble with negative faults, he shall not be cast down; for the Imagination upholds such a man with the hand of the Lord. As a thought, I have been young, and now I have manifested; yet I haven't seen the righteous of thought turned away, or any of the offspring of the righteous thoughts face famine.

Universal Intelligence is ever merciful and lends a hand to the righteous; and offspring of the righteous is also rewarded. Leave the evil thoughts alone and perform good; and dwell in righteousness of the Lord forever.

For the Imagination, Universal Mind loves judgment, and does not turn away those that are for him. He preserves them forever; the seed of the wicked thoughts will be cut off forever. The righteous will inherit the land, heaven, and dwell in their Imagination forever.

The mouth of those that practice righteousness speak wisdom, and the Lord shall make judgment of negative thoughts. The law of the righteous thought rests in the heart, the Imagination; thus, never shall you miss a step in your path of righteousness. The wicked always watch the righteous and looks to slay him.

The Imagination, the Lord, will neither abandon the righteous, nor condemn him when such thoughts surrounding him are judged. Wait on the Lord, and keep his way, and he will raise you to inherit the land: when the wicked thoughts are cut off, you will see it.

I have seen the wicked in great dominance, and spread itself like a bay tree, where fresh leaves release bitter substances. Yet the thought passed away and was no longer. Yes, you can search for the negative thought, but it will not be found.

Mark the righteous manifestation and hold on to the affirmed positive thought: for the end of that manifestation is peace. But the evil plotters will be destroyed together. The end of the wicked thoughts will be cut off.

But the salvation of the righteous is the Imagination: he is the strength of the righteous in times of trouble. And the Imagination, Infinite Intelligence will help the positive thoughts, and deliver them. He will deliver them from the wicked, and save them, because they trust in him.

CHAPTER THIRTY-EIGHT

PSALM 38

ORIGINAL TEXT

38 O Lord, rebuke me not in thy wrath: neither chasten me in thy hot displeasure.

² For thine arrows stick fast in me, and thy hand presseth me sore.

³ There is no soundness in my flesh because of thine anger; neither is there any rest in my bones because of my sin.

⁴ For mine iniquities are gone over mine head: as an heavy burden they are too heavy for me.

⁵ My wounds stink and are corrupt because of my foolishness.

⁶ I am troubled; I am bowed down greatly; I go mourning all the day long.

⁷ For my loins are filled with a loathsome disease: and there is no soundness in my flesh.

⁸ I am feeble and sore broken: I have roared by reason of the disquietness of my heart.

⁹ Lord, all my desire is before thee; and my groaning is not hid from thee.

¹⁰ My heart panteth, my strength faileth me: as for the light of mine eyes, it also is gone from me.

¹¹ My lovers and my friends stand aloof from my sore; and my kinsmen stand afar off.

¹² They also that seek after my life lay snares for me: and they that seek my hurt speak mischievous things, and imagine deceits all the day long.

¹³ But I, as a deaf man, heard not; and I was as a dumb man that openeth not his mouth.

¹⁴ Thus I was as a man that heareth not, and in whose mouth are no reproofs.

¹⁵ For in thee, O Lord, do I hope: thou wilt hear, O Lord my God.

¹⁶ For I said, Hear me, lest otherwise they should rejoice over me: when my foot slippeth, they magnify themselves against me.

¹⁷ For I am ready to halt, and my sorrow is continually before me.

¹⁸ For I will declare mine iniquity; I will be sorry for my sin.

¹⁹ But mine enemies are lively, and they are strong: and they that hate me wrongfully are multiplied.

²⁰ They also that render evil for good are mine adversaries; because I follow the thing that good is.

²¹ Forsake me not, O Lord: O my God, be not far from me.

²² Make haste to help me, O Lord my salvation.

THEME

Troubled Heart – Troubled Mind

POWER OF PSALM

Attack from Evil; Unfortunate Circumstance or Situation; Unwanted Company of Others; Confusion, Concern

THOUGHT FOR THE PSALM

Use your creative powers and change the way you think. No longer disapprove of yourself, a situation or circumstance. Ask the Lord within you to provide you the answers and remain in the faith that your troubled mind is resolved.

> *Examine yourselves, to see whether you are in the faith. Test yourselves. Or do you not realize this about yourselves, that Jesus Christ is in you?—unless indeed you fail to meet the test!*
>
> 2 Corinthians 13:5

INTERPRETATION OF EACH VERSE

38 O Lord, rebuke me not in thy wrath: neither chasten me in thy hot displeasure.

1. Infinite Intelligence, don't let me disapprove of myself in anger, nor let me suffer in displeasure.

² For thine arrows stick fast in me, and thy hand presseth me sore.

2. For the arrows of the wicked thoughts continue to wound me, and I ache in trying to defend.

³ There is no soundness in my flesh because of thine anger; neither is there any rest in my bones because of my sin.

3. There is nothing left of me to defend the arrows of negative thoughts that pierce me; neither can I sleep because I miss the mark.

⁴ For mine iniquities are gone over mine head: as an heavy burden they are too heavy for me.

4. For my wicked thoughts continue to circle in my mind: for not only are they a heavy burden, they are a burden too heavy for me.

⁵ My wounds stink and are corrupt because of my foolishness.

5. My wounds reek from sin, and I am faced with corrupted thoughts because of my foolishness.

⁶ I am troubled; I am bowed down greatly; I go mourning all the day long.

6. I am troubled; I am brought to a low point; I am disappointed all day long.

⁷ For my loins are filled with a loathsome disease: and there is no soundness in my flesh.

7. For the path I choose to walk, I am not able because I am diseased with corrupted thoughts: and there is nothing left of my flesh to defend.

⁸ I am feeble and sore broken: I have roared by reason of the disquietness of my heart.

8. I am feeble and sore broken: I have shouted because of the troubles of the mind.

⁹ Lord, all my desire is before thee; and my groaning is not hid from thee.

9. Imagination, all of my desires have been placed before you

¹⁰ My heart panteth, my strength faileth me: as for the light of mine eyes, it also is gone from me.

10. My mind races, my strength to withstand such thoughts have failed: as for me, I can no longer see my way.

¹¹ My lovers and my friends stand aloof from my sore; and my kinsmen stand afar off.

11. Those thoughts that love and admire me stand distant from wounds; and those thoughts that are related to circumstances also stand at a distance.

¹² They also that seek after my life lay snares for me: and they that seek my hurt speak mischievous things, and imagine deceits all the day long.

12. The wicked thoughts seek after my life and set traps for me to fall into: and those thoughts that wish me harm speak mischievous things about me, and lies to tell me all day long.

¹³ But I, as a deaf man, heard not; and I was as a dumb man that openeth not his mouth.

13. But I, a man in charge of my own hearing, did not hear the call of the wicked thoughts; and I was the quiet man that chose not to speak to them.

¹⁴ Thus I was as a man that heareth not, and in whose mouth are no reproofs.

14. I was the man that does not hear the cry of such negative thoughts, for their mouths have nothing to offer me for righteousness.

¹⁵ For in thee, O LORD, do I hope: thou wilt hear, O Lord my God.

15. For in you, hear me Lord, for I hope: that you will hear my cry.

¹⁶ For I said, Hear me, lest otherwise they should rejoice over me: when my foot slippeth, they magnify themselves against me.

16. For I said, Hear me, otherwise those negative thoughts will rejoice in their way over me: when my foot slips into their snare, they will congregate upon me in high numbers.

¹⁷ For I am ready to halt, and my sorrow is continually before me.

17. For I am ready to stop, and my sorrow continues to be with me.

¹⁸ For I will declare mine iniquity; I will be sorry for my sin.

18. For I will declare my wicked thoughts; I will be sorry for missing the mark.

¹⁹ But mine enemies are lively, and they are strong: and they that hate me wrongfully are multiplied.

19. But my enemies are still alive and with me, and they are strong: and they hate me, wrongfully multiplying against me.

²⁰ They also that render evil for good are mine adversaries; because I follow the thing that good is.

> 20. Such negative thoughts that declare their evil for good are my adversaries; because I follow what can be declared righteous.

²¹ Forsake me not, O LORD: O my God, be not far from me.

> 21. Don't turn away from me Infinite Intelligence: hear me God, and don't be distant from me.

²² Make haste to help me, O Lord my salvation.

> 22. With swiftness, help me, Imagination hear me, for you are my salvation.

ANALYSIS OF THE SCRIPTURE

Troubled Heart – Troubled Mind

Ask of Infinite Intelligence, not to let you disapprove of yourself in anger, nor let you suffer in displeasure. For the arrows of your wicked thoughts continue to wound you, and you ache in trying to defend against them.

You may have the feeling that there is nothing left of you to defend the arrows of negative thoughts that pierce your flesh. It is hard for you to sleep because you miss the mark. For your wicked thoughts continue to circle in your mind. They are not only a heavy burden, but they are a burden too heavy for you.

Your wounds reek from sin, and you are faced with corrupted thoughts because of your foolishness. You are troubled and have been brought to a low point. You are disappointed all day long.

> "The Lord your God is with you, the Mighty Warrior who saves. He will take great delight in you; in his love he will no longer rebuke you, but will rejoice over you with singing."
>
> Zephaniah 3:17

For the path you choose to walk, you are not able because you are diseased with corrupted thoughts. You believe that there is nothing left of your flesh to defend. You feel feeble and broken down. You have shouted because of the troubles of your mind.

Declare to your Imagination that all your desires have been placed before him. For your mind races, and your strength to withstand such thoughts have failed. At this time, you can no longer see your way.

Those thoughts that love and admire you seem distant because of your wounds from negative thoughts. It may seem all your desires that are related to your current circumstances also stand at a distance. The wicked thoughts seek after your life and set traps for you to fall into. Those punishing thoughts that wish you harm, speak mischievous things about you. They speak lies to you all day long.

You are to be a man in charge of your own hearing. You are to declare to Infinite Intelligence that you no longer respond to the call of the wicked thoughts. You are to be the quiet man that chooses not to speak to them. You are to be the man that does not hear the cry of such negative thoughts, for their mouths have nothing to offer you in righteousness.

For in God, ask for the Lord to hear you. It is your hope that Infinite Intelligence will hear your cry. For you are to declare for the Lord to hear you, because those negative thoughts will rejoice in their way over you. When your foot slips into their snare, they will congregate upon you in high numbers.

For you are ready to stop, and your sorrow continues to be with you. For you are to declare your wicked thoughts before the Lord, your Imagination. You are to declare that you are sorry for missing the mark. You know that your enemies are still alive and with you; and you know they are strong. You know they hate you, and that they wrongfully multiply against you.

Such negative thoughts that declare their evil for good are your adversaries; because you follow what you can now declare as righteous. Ask the Universal Creator not to turn away from you, but to hear you; for you never want the Creator to be distant from you. You are to declare with swiftness, help. You are to ask your Imagination to hear you, for your Imagination is your salvation.

CHAPTER THIRTY-NINE

PSALM 39

39 I said, I will take heed to my ways, that I sin not with my tongue: I will keep my mouth with a bridle, while the wicked is before me.

² I was dumb with silence, I held my peace, even from good; and my sorrow was stirred.

³ My heart was hot within me, while I was musing the fire burned: then spake I with my tongue,

⁴ LORD, make me to know mine end, and the measure of my days, what it is: that I may know how frail I am.

⁵ Behold, thou hast made my days as an handbreadth; and mine age is as nothing before thee: verily every man at his best state is altogether vanity. Selah.

⁶ Surely every man walketh in a vain shew: surely they are disquieted in vain: he heapeth up riches, and knoweth not who shall gather them.

⁷ And now, Lord, what wait I for? my hope is in thee.

⁸ Deliver me from all my transgressions: make me not the reproach of the foolish.

⁹ I was dumb, I opened not my mouth; because thou didst it.

¹⁰ Remove thy stroke away from me: I am consumed by the blow of thine hand.

¹¹ When thou with rebukes dost correct man for iniquity, thou makest his beauty to consume away like a moth: surely every man is vanity. Selah.

¹² Hear my prayer, O LORD, and give ear unto my cry; hold not thy peace at my tears: for I am a stranger with thee, and a sojourner, as all my fathers were.

¹³ O spare me, that I may recover strength, before I go hence, and be no more.

THEME

FEELING OF SUFFERING

POWER OF PSALM

Suffering; Need the Right Thing to Say; Need to Strengthen Personal Values;

THOUGHT FOR THE PSALM

Observe the words that are spoken from your mouth, for no words are excluded from manifestation.

INTERPRETATION OF EACH VERSE

39 **I said, I will take heed to my ways, that I sin not with my tongue: I will keep my mouth with a bridle, while the wicked is before me.**

1. I said, I will pay attention to my ways, that I will not miss the mark with my tongue. I will keep my mouth with a bit which will silence me while the wicked thought is before me.

² I was dumb with silence, I held my peace, even from good; and my sorrow was stirred.

2. I lacked words with my silence, I held my peace, even from good; and my sorrow was stirred.

³ **My heart was hot within me, while I was musing the fire burned: then spake I with my tongue,**

3. My mental thoughts are sparked within me, while I was meditating, the thoughts came into existence; then with the right thoughts, I spoke with my tongue.

⁴ **LORD, make me to know mine end, and the measure of my days, what it is: that I may know how frail I am.**

4. Imagination, allow me to know when the persecution of my thoughts are going to end, and the length of my days remaining: that I may know how much longer I must suffer this persecution.

⁵ **Behold, thou hast made my days as an handbreadth; and mine age is as nothing before thee: verily every man at his best state is altogether vanity. Selah.**

5. Behold, I make my days for you simple; the time in not your concern: truthfully, every man should, at any time, consider and continue his own business.

⁶ **Surely every man walketh in a vain shew: surely they are disquieted in vain: he heapeth up riches, and knoweth not who shall gather them.**

6. Certainly, every man walks with their own expectation of pride: surely, they are not comfortable with their own thoughts about themselves: he piles up his own wealth of negative thoughts and shall not need to know how to gather them all.

⁷ **And now, Lord, what wait I for? my hope is in thee.**

7. And now, Lord, what do I need to wait for? My hope is in your deliverance.

⁸ **Deliver me from all my transgressions: make me not the reproach of the foolish.**

8. Deliver me from all my sins: don't let me be mocked by my foolish thoughts.

⁹ **I was dumb, I opened not my mouth; because thou didst it.**

9. I was quiet, for I did not open my mouth; because you delivered me.

¹⁰ **Remove thy stroke away from me: I am consumed by the blow of thine hand.**

10. Remove my attention of your swift blow of destruction to my negative thoughts away from me: I am in awe by the blow of your hand.

¹¹ **When thou with rebukes dost correct man for iniquity, thou makest his beauty to consume away like a moth: surely every man is vanity. Selah.**

11. When you judge to rebuke, you correct man's mind of wicked thoughts, and they all wither away as you bring forth the true beauty of every man.

¹² **Hear my prayer, O LORD, and give ear unto my cry; hold not thy peace at my tears: for I am a stranger with thee, and a sojourner, as all my fathers were.**

12. Hear my desire, Imagination, and listen to my cry; I will not stop meditating with my feelings: for I am a stranger with you, and a visitor to your ways, as all my previous thoughts I believed ruled me.

¹³ **O spare me, that I may recover strength, before I go hence, and be no more.**

13. Spare me, so that I may recover strength, before I go from this place on earth, and be no more here.

ANALYSIS OF THE SCRIPTURE

FEELING OF SUFFERING

Pay attention to your ways. Declare that you will not miss the mark with your tongue. Declare that you will keep your lips sealed in silence, while the wicked thoughts act before you. Keep your thoughts righteous, meaning keep rightful thinking.

You may lack words with your silence, but you are to hold your peace, even in what the negative thoughts have you picture what appears to be good. Any sorrow of within your current thoughts will be recognized.

> *Not only so, but we also glory in our sufferings, because we know that suffering produces perseverance; perseverance, character; and character, hope.*
>
> *Romans 5:3-4*

Your mental thoughts will be sparked within you even while you meditate. During meditation, new thoughts will come into existence. They will be the right thoughts, and you will speak such thoughts with your tongue.

You may want to ask of your Imagination, by creating the objective you desire, when the persecution of your negative thoughts will end? You may want to know the day and time remaining that the suffering is to take place? Though scripture tells you, behold, the Lord, Infinite Intelligence makes the days for you simple. The time in not your concern: truthfully, every man should, at any time, consider and continue his own business. Selah

Certainly, every man walks with their own expectation of pride: surely, they are not comfortable with their own thoughts about themselves. Man piles up his own wealth of negative thoughts and will not need to know how to gather them all.

You may want to ask the Lord, what do you need to wait for? For your hope is in your deliverance. You may even ask to be delivered from all your sins; for you no longer want to be mocked by your foolish thoughts, and that is not necessary.

Just know that you remained quiet, and that you didn't open your mouth in front of foolish thoughts; for you are to know that the Lord has delivered you. Remove your attention of the swift blow of destruction that will reign upon your negative thoughts that stand distant. When the time comes, you will be in awe by the swift blow of the hand of God.

When you judge to rebuke, you correct your own mind of wicked thoughts, and they all wither away as you bring forth the true beauty and truth of yourself; thus, this goes for every man. Selah.

Look to the Imagination to capture your desire. The Imagination will hear your cry and will listen to your cry. You are to continue to meditate with your feelings. You are a stranger to yourself but known by the Lord. You are a visitor in the eyes of all your previous negative thoughts you believed to rule your life; but knowing the Lord, that is short-lived. Though you may feel weak, ask the Higher Self to spare you, so that you can recover strength and righteously manifest throughout the remaining days you have on earth.

CHAPTER FORTY

PSALM 40

40 I waited patiently for the LORD; and he inclined unto me, and heard my cry.

² He brought me up also out of an horrible pit, out of the miry clay, and set my feet upon a rock, and established my goings.

³ And he hath put a new song in my mouth, even praise unto our God: many shall see it, and fear, and shall trust in the LORD.

⁴ Blessed is that man that maketh the LORD his trust, and respecteth not the proud, nor such as turn aside to lies.

⁵ Many, O LORD my God, are thy wonderful works which thou hast done, and thy thoughts which are to us-ward: they cannot be reckoned up in order unto thee: if I would declare and speak of them, they are more than can be numbered.

⁶ Sacrifice and offering thou didst not desire; mine ears hast thou opened: burnt offering and sin offering hast thou not required.

⁷ Then said I, Lo, I come: in the volume of the book it is written of me,

⁸ I delight to do thy will, O my God: yea, thy law is within my heart.

⁹ I have preached righteousness in the great congregation: lo, I have not refrained my lips, O LORD, thou knowest.

¹⁰ I have not hid thy righteousness within my heart; I have declared thy faithfulness and thy salvation: I have not concealed thy lovingkindness and thy truth from the great congregation.

¹¹ Withhold not thou thy tender mercies from me, O LORD: let thy lovingkindness and thy truth continually preserve me.

¹² For innumerable evils have compassed me about: mine iniquities have taken hold upon me, so that I am not able to look up; they are more than the hairs of mine head: therefore my heart faileth me.

¹³ Be pleased, O LORD, to deliver me: O LORD, make haste to help me.

¹⁴ Let them be ashamed and confounded together that seek after my soul to destroy it; let them be driven backward and put to shame that wish me evil.

¹⁵ Let them be desolate for a reward of their shame that say unto me, Aha, aha.

¹⁶ Let all those that seek thee rejoice and be glad in thee: let such as love thy salvation say continually, The LORD be magnified.

¹⁷ But I am poor and needy; yet the Lord thinketh upon me: thou art my help and my deliverer; make no tarrying, O my God.

THEME

THE LORD HEARS YOUR CRY

POWER OF PSALM

Patience; Darkness; Despair; Depression; Lack of Knowledge or Wisdom; Anxiety

THOUGHT FOR THE PSALM

The suffering of wicked thoughts will end; in a time only determined by God.

> *"For My thoughts* are *not your thoughts, Nor* are *your ways My ways," says the* LORD. *"For* as *the heavens are higher than the earth, So are My ways higher than your ways, And My thoughts than your thoughts.*
>
> *Isaiah 55:8-9*

INTERPRETATION OF EACH VERSE

40 I waited patiently for the LORD; and he inclined unto me, and heard my cry.

1. I waited patiently for the Law to be cast upon my thoughts, and he delivered unto me, as he heard my cry.

² He brought me up also out of an horrible pit, out of the miry clay, and set my feet upon a rock, and established my goings.

2. He brought me up out of the horrible pit of negative and deceitful thoughts, out of the marsh of nothingness, and set my feet upon a foundation, and established my directions.

³ **And he hath put a new song in my mouth, even praise unto our God: many shall see it, and fear, and shall trust in the Lord.**

3. And he hath put a new song in my mouth, even praise unto our Imagination: many will see it, and fear, and will trust in their Imagination.

⁴ **Blessed is that man that maketh the Lord his trust, and respecteth not the proud, nor such as turn aside to lies.**

4. Rewarded is that man that trusts his own Imagination, and doesn't respect the boastful thoughts, nor such thoughts that turn away from the Lord and tell lies.

⁵ **Many, O Lord my God, are thy wonderful works which thou hast done, and thy thoughts which are to us-ward: they cannot be reckoned up in order unto thee: if I would declare and speak of them, they are more than can be numbered.**

5. Many, in the Imagination, my God, are my own wonderful works which you have done, and your thoughts which are to be guarded: such works cannot accounted for that were given by your hand: if I would declare and speak of such works, they are more than can be numbered.

⁶ **Sacrifice and offering thou didst not desire; mine ears hast thou opened: burnt offering and sin offering hast thou not required.**

6. Sacrifice and offering you didn't desire; my ears have opened: and you don't require of me a burnt offering or me missing the mark.

⁷ **Then said I, Lo, I come: in the volume of the book it is written of me,**

7. Upon the offering, then I said, look, for now I come: in the volume of the book, the book of the Law, it is written of me,

⁸ **I delight to do thy will, O my God: yea, thy law is within my heart.**

8. I delight to do the will of God: yes, it is your Law that is within my mind.

⁹ **I have preached righteousness in the great congregation: lo, I have not refrained my lips, O LORD, thou knowest.**

> 9. I have preached righteousness in the great congregation of negative and deceitful thoughts: look, I have said nothing but the good, and you the Lord, the Imagination know this.

¹⁰ **I have not hid thy righteousness within my heart; I have declared thy faithfulness and thy salvation: I have not concealed thy lovingkindness and thy truth from the great congregation.**

> 10. I have not hidden your righteousness within my mind; I have openly declared my faithfulness and my salvation: I have not hidden your loving kindness and your truth from the great congregation of wicked thoughts.

¹¹ **Withhold not thou thy tender mercies from me, O LORD: let thy lovingkindness and thy truth continually preserve me.**

> 11. Don't hold back your mercy from me, my own human Imagination: let your loving kindness and your truth continually preserve me.

¹² **For innumerable evils have compassed me about: mine iniquities have taken hold upon me, so that I am not able to look up; they are more than the hairs of mine head: therefore my heart faileth me.**

> 12. For so many evils have occupied my mind: my wicked thoughts have taken hold upon me, so that I am not able to look up; there are more evil thoughts in my mind than there are hairs on my own head: therefore my mind fails me.

¹³ **Be pleased, O LORD, to deliver me: O LORD, make haste to help me.**

> 13. Be pleased dear God, my own Imagination, to deliver me: Lord, with your swiftness, help me.

¹⁴ **Let them be ashamed and confounded together that seek after my soul to destroy it; let them be driven backward and put to shame that wish me evil.**

14. Let those ugly thoughts be ashamed and confused in their congregation together that seek after my mind to destroy it; let those negative thoughts be driven backward and put to shame that wish me evil.

¹⁵ Let them be desolate for a reward of their shame that say unto me, Aha, aha.

15. Let those ungodly thoughts be deserted for a reward of their shame that say unto me, Aha, aha.

¹⁶ Let all those that seek thee rejoice and be glad in thee: let such as love thy salvation say continually, The LORD be magnified.

16. Let all those ungodly thoughts seek you and rejoice and be glad in you: let such as love of your salvation continually say, The Imagination, Infinite Intelligence be larger than them.

¹⁷ But I am poor and needy; yet the Lord thinketh upon me: thou art my help and my deliverer; make no tarrying, O my God.

17. But I lack knowledge and wisdom; yet the Lord uses my Imagination to thinketh upon me: you are my help and my deliverer; you make me no longer linger dear God.

ANALYSIS OF THE SCRIPTURE

You have waited patiently for the Law of God to be cast upon your thoughts, and he delivered unto you, as he heard your cry.

He brought you up out of the horrible pit of negative and deceitful thoughts. Out of the marsh of nothingness, he set your feet upon a foundation, and established your direction. He has put a new song in your mouth. Give praise unto your Imagination, for many negative thoughts will see your praise. Those thoughts will fear the Lord and you are to continue to trust in your Imagination.

Rewarded is that man that trusts his own Imagination, and doesn't respect the boastful thoughts, nor such thoughts that turn away from the Lord and tell lies. Many thoughts, in the Imagination, your God, are your own wonderful works which you have done, and your thoughts of goodness are to be guarded. Such works cannot be accounted for that were given by the hand of God in you. When you declare and speak of such works, you will find that there are more than can be numbered.

> *"And if we know that he hears us—whatever we ask—we know that we have what we asked of him."*
>
> John 5:15

Sacrifice and offering at one time, you didn't desire. Now, your ears have opened. You are not required to supply a burnt offering or need to miss the mark. You just need to believe in the Imagination.

Upon an offering, you will declare to come forth before the Lord. For in the volume of the book of the gospel, the book of the Law, it is written of you and your ways. It is for you to delight in the will of God. Yes, it is the Law that should occupy your mind.

You may have at one time preached righteousness in the great congregation of negative and deceitful thoughts. You will try to convince yourself that you have said nothing but good, and you the Lord, the Imagination know this. Thus, you do not need to preach to negative thoughts; for they know the truth.

Be sure not to keep the righteousness within your mind hidden. Openly declare your faithfulness and your Imagination as your salvation. Neither keep hidden the loving kindness of the Lord, nor your truth from the great congregation of wicked thoughts.

Don't hold back on your Imagination, for that is where your mercy is given. Let your loving kindness, the truth of the Lord, continually preserve you.

You know that so many evils have occupied your mind. Your wicked thoughts have even taken a hold upon you, and thus you are not even able to move forward. There are more evil thoughts in your mind than there are hairs on your own head, making it hard to defend.

Ask of your own Imagination, to deliver you. The Imagination is Lord, and he will respond to your negative thoughts with a swiftness. Let those ugly thoughts be ashamed and confused in their congregation.

Remember, they seek after your mind, only to destroy it. Let those negative thoughts be driven backward and put to shame that wish you evil.

Let those ungodly thoughts be deserted for a reward of their shame that say unto you, Aha, aha. Let all those ungodly thoughts seek you and rejoice in you. Because in the end, in your salvation, you will declare: Imagination, Infinite Intelligence, is larger than them.

Knowing you lack knowledge and wisdom, just know that the Lord uses your Imagination to think upon you. He is your helper and your deliverer. Trust in him, and you will no longer linger in your life.

CHAPTER FORTY-ONE

PSALM 41

41 Blessed is he that considereth the poor: the LORD will deliver him in time of trouble.

² The LORD will preserve him, and keep him alive; and he shall be blessed upon the earth: and thou wilt not deliver him unto the will of his enemies.

³ The LORD will strengthen him upon the bed of languishing: thou wilt make all his bed in his sickness.

⁴ I said, LORD, be merciful unto me: heal my soul; for I have sinned against thee.

⁵ Mine enemies speak evil of me, When shall he die, and his name perish?

⁶ And if he come to see me, he speaketh vanity: his heart gathereth iniquity to itself; when he goeth abroad, he telleth it.

⁷ All that hate me whisper together against me: against me do they devise my hurt.

⁸ An evil disease, say they, cleaveth fast unto him: and now that he lieth he shall rise up no more.

⁹ Yea, mine own familiar friend, in whom I trusted, which did eat of my bread, hath lifted up his heel against me.

¹⁰ But thou, O LORD, be merciful unto me, and raise me up, that I may requite them.

¹¹ By this I know that thou favourest me, because mine enemy doth not triumph over me.

¹² And as for me, thou upholdest me in mine integrity, and settest me before thy face for ever.

¹³ Blessed be the LORD God of Israel from everlasting, and to everlasting. Amen, and Amen.

THEME

THE STRENGTH OF YOUR FAITH

POWER OF PSALM

Perseverance; Strength; Improvement; Reverie

THOUGHT FOR THE PSALM

Be strong and courageous. Do not be afraid or terrified because of them, for the LORD your God goes with you; he will never leave you nor forsake you."

Deuteronomy 31:6

INTERPRETATION OF EACH VERSE

41 **Blessed is he that considereth the poor: the LORD will deliver him in time of trouble.**

1. Rewarded is he that considers those thoughts that are lacking: Imagination, Universal Mind will deliver him in time of trouble.

²The LORD will preserve him, and keep him alive; and he shall be blessed upon the earth: and thou wilt not deliver him unto the will of his enemies.

    2. The Imagination will preserve him and keep him alive; and he will be rewarded upon the earth: and the Lord will not deliver him unto the will of his enemies; his enemy thoughts.

³The LORD will strengthen him upon the bed of languishing: thou wilt make all his bed in his sickness.

    3. The Imagination will strengthen him in his bed of weakness: God will make his bed in his sickness.

⁴I said, LORD, be merciful unto me: heal my soul; for I have sinned against thee.

    4. I said, Universal Mind, be merciful unto me: heal my mind; for I have missed the mark regarding the Lord.

⁵Mine enemies speak evil of me, When shall he die, and his name perish?

    5. My negative thoughts speak evil of me, When will they die, and in the name of the Lord, the Imagination will they perish.

⁶And if he come to see me, he speaketh vanity: his heart gathereth iniquity to itself; when he goeth abroad, he telleth it.

    6. And if he come to see me, my enemy, he boast an ungodly pride: his heart attracts other wicked thoughts to itself; when he leaves the Lord and tells his story.

⁷All that hate me whisper together against me: against me do they devise my hurt.

    7. All those thoughts that hate me whisper together against me: against me do they devise my hurt.

⁸An evil disease, say they, cleaveth fast unto him: and now that he lieth he shall rise up no more.

8. An evil disease, say those negative thoughts, attaching fast unto that one wicked thought and now that the single thought has chosen to lie, he shall no longer rise in the Kingdom.

⁹ Yea, mine own familiar friend, in whom I trusted, which did eat of my bread, hath lifted up his heel against me.

9. Yes, my own familiar friend, my created thought in whom I trusted, which did eat of my bread, has turned his direction against me.

¹⁰ But thou, O LORD, be merciful unto me, and raise me up, that I may requite them.

10. But as for me, hear me Imagination, hear me Lord, be merciful unto me, and raise me up, that I may retaliate against them.

¹¹ By this I know that thou favourest me, because mine enemy doth not triumph over me.

11. By having faith in the Lord, the Imagaination, I know that you favor me, because my enemy thought doesn't triumph over me.

¹² And as for me, thou upholdest me in mine integrity, and settest me before thy face for ever.

12. And as for me, you Infinite Intelligence, uphold me for my honesty, and set me before your face forever.

¹³ Blessed be the LORD God of Israel from everlasting, and to everlasting. Amen, and Amen.

13. Rewarded is the Imagination of the enlightened forever and forever. Amen, and Amen. (To all manifestations, and to all manifestations).

ANALYSIS OF THE SCRIPTURE

Rewarded is he that considers those negative thoughts that are lacking. The Imagination, Universal Mind will deliver you in time of trouble. The Imagination will preserve you and keep your wonderful thoughts alive. The Lord in you, the God that you are, will be rewarded upon the earth. The Lord will not deliver you unto the will of your enemies.

The Imagination will strengthen you in your bed of weakness. God will make your bed in your sickness. Ask of Universal Mind, to be merciful unto you. Ask Higher Intelligence to heal your mind; for you have missed the mark regarding the Lord.

Trust in the LORD with all your heart, and do not lean on your own understanding. In all your ways acknowledge him, and he will make straight your paths.

Proverbs 3:5-6

Your negative thoughts speak evil of you. You will question as to when they will die? Imagine new thoughts, loving thoughts, and declare in the name of the Lord, that the negative thoughts will perish.

And if negative thoughts, your enemy, come to cloud your vision, he will boast an ungodly pride. Careful, for his heart attracts other wicked thoughts to itself as he leaves the Lord and tells his story.

All those thoughts that hate you will certainly whisper together against you. Those thoughts that desire to do so, devise your hurt. Like an evil disease, negative thoughts attach fast unto other wicked thoughts, and coerce lies from other thoughts. That thought too will no longer be welcomed in the Kingdom of heaven. Yes, your own familiar friend, your created thought in whom you trusted, was the same thought that ate of your bread. Once a friend, now turned his direction against you.

But as for you, ask to be heard by your own Imagination. Declare: Hear me Lord, be merciful unto you, and raise you up, that you may retaliate against such wicked thoughts. By having faith in the Lord, the

Imagination, you will know that you are favored. Because your enemy thought shall not triumph over you.

And as for you, request Infinite Intelligence, uphold you for your honesty, and set you before the face of God forever. Rewarded is the Imagination of the enlightened forever and forever. Amen, and Amen. (Amen means: To all manifestations).

CHAPTER FORTY-TWO

PSALM 42

42 As the hart panteth after the water brooks, so panteth my soul after thee, O God.

² My soul thirsteth for God, for the living God: when shall I come and appear before God?

³ My tears have been my meat day and night, while they continually say unto me, Where is thy God?

⁴ When I remember these things, I pour out my soul in me: for I had gone with the multitude, I went with them to the house of God, with the voice of joy and praise, with a multitude that kept holyday.

⁵ Why art thou cast down, O my soul? and why art thou disquieted in me? hope thou in God: for I shall yet praise him for the help of his countenance.

⁶ O my God, my soul is cast down within me: therefore will I remember thee from the land of Jordan, and of the Hermonites, from the hill Mizar.

⁷ Deep calleth unto deep at the noise of thy waterspouts: all thy waves and thy billows are gone over me.

⁸ Yet the LORD will command his lovingkindness in the day time, and in the night his song shall be with me, and my prayer unto the God of my life.

⁹ I will say unto God my rock, Why hast thou forgotten me? why go I mourning because of the oppression of the enemy?

¹⁰ As with a sword in my bones, mine enemies reproach me; while they say daily unto me, Where is thy God?

¹¹ Why art thou cast down, O my soul? and why art thou disquieted within me? hope thou in God: for I shall yet praise him, who is the health of my countenance, and my God.

THEME

TRUST NOT WHAT YOU SEE BEFORE YOU

POWER OF PSALM

Insomnia; Feeling Hopeless; Need of Inspiration; Trust

THOUGHT FOR THE PSALM

Whatever you desire, with faith, so shall it be.

INTERPRETATION OF EACH VERSE

42 As the hart panteth after the water brooks, so panteth my soul after thee, O God.

1. As a deer breathes heavy, the deer thirsts after water in brooks. So do you, when you exhale your breath hurriedly in seeking after the truth of the gospel.

² **My soul thirsteth for God, for the living God: when shall I come and appear before God?**

2. My mind longs for the use of Imagination, for the living God: when shall I come and use it?

³ **My tears have been my meat day and night, while they continually say unto me, Where is thy God?**

3. My negative thoughts have been my substance day and night, apparent good times and bad, while they continually say unto me, Where is your God?

⁴ **When I remember these things, I pour out my soul in me: for I had gone with the multitude, I went with them to the house of God, with the voice of joy and praise, with a multitude that kept holyday.**

4. When I remember these things, I empty my mind: for I had at one time gone with the multitude of negative and doubtful thoughts, I went with them to the house of God, with the voice of joy and praise, with the good thoughts that kept the faith in the Imagination; faith in God.

⁵ **Why art thou cast down, O my soul? and why art thou disquieted in me? hope thou in God: for I shall yet praise him for the help of his countenance.**

5. Why aren't my negative thoughts cast down, out of my mind? And why are they not silenced within me? Hope is in God, Imagination: for I will also praise him for the help of his expression upon my thoughts.

⁶ **O my God, my soul is cast down within me: therefore will I remember thee from the land of Jordan, and of the Hermonites, from the hill Mizar.**

6. My God, my Imagination is buried inside of me: therefore I will remember you from the holy streams of truth or higher consciousness, and of the Hermonites from the hill Mizar.

⁷ **Deep calleth unto deep at the noise of thy waterspouts: all thy waves and thy billows are gone over me.**

7. Negative thoughts in the pit of darkness call upon their own in the deep at the expression of their extensions: all my emotions are swayed back and forth all throughout the calls unto their own.

⁸ Yet the LORD will command his lovingkindness in the day time, and in the night his song shall be with me, and my prayer unto the God of my life.

8. Yet the Imagination will command his loving kindness in the good times, and in the times of trouble his song will be with me, and my desire unto the Imagination of my life.

⁹ I will say unto God my rock, Why hast thou forgotten me? why go I mourning because of the oppression of the enemy?

9. I will imagine within my own mind, my foundation, Why have you forgotten me? Why do I continue to grieve due to the oppression of my negative thoughts?

¹⁰ As with a sword in my bones, mine enemies reproach me; while they say daily unto me, Where is thy God?

10. Like a dagger in my flesh, my negative thoughts continue to approach me; while they continue to taunt me, Where is thy God?

¹¹ Why art thou cast down, O my soul? and why art thou disquieted within me? hope thou in God: for I shall yet praise him, who is the health of my countenance, and my God.

11. Why aren't my negative thoughts cast down, out of my mind? And why are they not silenced within me? Hope is in God, Imagination: for I will also praise him for the help of his expression upon my thoughts of my Imagination and my God.

ANALYSIS OF THE SCRIPTURE

As a deer breathes heavy, the deer thirsts after water in brooks. So do you, when you exhale your breath hurriedly in seeking after the truth of the gospel. Your mind longs for the use of Imagination, for the living God. The question is, when shall you decide to use it?

Your negative thoughts have been your substance day and night; apparent in good times and bad, while they continually say unto you, where is your God?

While we look not at the things which are seen, but at the things which are not seen; for the things which are seen are temporal, but the things which are not seen are eternal.

2 Corinthians 4:18

When you remember these things, you are to empty your mind. For you had at one time gone with the multitude of negative and doubtful thoughts. Now you are to embrace good with righteous thoughts in the house of God. Do this with a voice of joy and praise. For it were those good thoughts that kept the faith in the Imagination; faith in God.

Why aren't your negative thoughts cast down, out of your mind you may ask? And why are they not silenced within you? Hope must be in God, your own Imagination. For you are to also praise the Lord for the help of his expression upon your thoughts.

"I am a stranger and a sojourner among you; give me a burial site among you that I may bury my dead out of my sight."

Genesis 23:4

Your God, your Imagination is buried inside of you. Therefore, you are to remember him from the holy streams of truth or higher consciousness, and of the Hermonites from the hill Mizar.

Negative thoughts in the pit of darkness call upon their own in the deep. They do so at the expression of their extensions; their evil branches. All your emotions sway back and forth all throughout the calls of negative thoughts unto their own.

Yet the Imagination will command his loving kindness in the good times, and in times of trouble. The song of the Lord will be with you, and your desire unto the Imagination of your life.

You are to imagine within your own mind, your own foundation. You will question, why has the Lord forgotten you? Why do you continue to grieve due to the oppression of your negative thoughts? Like a dagger in your flesh, your negative thoughts continue to approach you; while they continue to taunt you. They continue to question and ask: where is your God?

CHAPTER FORTY-THREE

PSALM 43

43 Judge me, O God, and plead my cause against an ungodly nation: O deliver me from the deceitful and unjust man.

² For thou art the God of my strength: why dost thou cast me off? why go I mourning because of the oppression of the enemy?

³ O send out thy light and thy truth: let them lead me; let them bring me unto thy holy hill, and to thy tabernacles.

⁴ Then will I go unto the altar of God, unto God my exceeding joy: yea, upon the harp will I praise thee, O God my God.

⁵ Why art thou cast down, O my soul? and why art thou disquieted within me? hope in God: for I shall yet praise him, who is the health of my countenance, and my God.

THEME

SEARCHING

POWER OF PSALM

Avoidance; Strength; Searching for Answers; Improve Health

THOUGHT FOR THE PSALM

The only nation spoken of in scripture, is the nation within your mind. The people of that nation are your thoughts.

INTERPRETATION OF EACH VERSE

43 Judge me, O God, and plead my cause against an ungodly nation: O deliver me from the deceitful and unjust man.

1. Imagination, place before me what I have been thinking. Hear me, and plead my cause against the nation of negative thoughts: and deliver me from the deceitful and unjust manifestation.

² For thou art the God of my strength: why dost thou cast me off? why go I mourning because of the oppression of the enemy?

2. For you are the God of my strength: why don't you just cast me off? Why do I continue to grieve because of the oppression of negative thoughts?

³ O send out thy light and thy truth: let them lead me; let them bring me unto thy holy hill, and to thy tabernacles.

3. Hear me and send out your light and your truth: let them be my guidance; let them bring me unto my own Imagination and the tabernacle of the Holy Spirit.

⁴ **Then will I go unto the altar of God, unto God my exceeding joy: yea, upon the harp will I praise thee, O God my God.**

4. Then I will go unto the altar of God, unto the Imagination my exceeding joy: yes, upon the sounds will I praise you, hear me Imagination, my God.

⁵ **Why art thou cast down, O my soul? and why art thou disquieted within me? hope in God: for I shall yet praise him, who is the health of my countenance, and my God.**

5. Why are you cast down, O my mind? And why are you disturbed within me? Hope in God: for I will soon praise him, who is the health of my savior, and my Imagination.

ANALYSIS OF THE SCRIPTURE

It is for you to declare: Imagination, place before me what I have been thinking. Ask that Infinite Intelligence hear you and handle trouble caused by your nation of negative thoughts. Ask, not beg. Ask to be delivered from the deceitful and unjust manifestations.

For you are to declare that God is your strength. You may be the one that questions: why don't you just cast me off? You may question: why do you continue to grieve because of the oppression of negative thoughts? Ask to be heard and request that the Lord, your Higher Mind, send out his light and his truth. Ask the Father to let them be your guidance. Ask for him to let them both bring you unto your own Imagination and the tabernacle of the Holy Spirit.

It is for you to go unto the altar of God, unto the Imagination which is your exceeding joy. Yes, upon the music of his voice, you are to praise him. Ask for your Imagination to hear your call.

The question you may raise is: Why are you cast down, O my mind? You may ask: And why are you disturbed within me? For you are to have hope in God. You are to praise him now, for he is your health, your savior, and your Imagination.

CHAPTER FORTY-FOUR

PSALM 44

44 We have heard with our ears, O God, our fathers have told us, what work thou didst in their days, in the times of old.

² How thou didst drive out the heathen with thy hand, and plantedst them; how thou didst afflict the people, and cast them out.

³ For they got not the land in possession by their own sword, neither did their own arm save them: but thy right hand, and thine arm, and the light of thy countenance, because thou hadst a favour unto them.

⁴ Thou art my King, O God: command deliverances for Jacob.

⁵ Through thee will we push down our enemies: through thy name will we tread them under that rise up against us.

⁶ For I will not trust in my bow, neither shall my sword save me.

⁷ But thou hast saved us from our enemies, and hast put them to shame that hated us.

⁸ In God we boast all the day long, and praise thy name for ever. Selah.

⁹ But thou hast cast off, and put us to shame; and goest not forth with our armies.

¹⁰ Thou makest us to turn back from the enemy: and they which hate us spoil for themselves.

¹¹ Thou hast given us like sheep appointed for meat; and hast scattered us among the heathen.

¹² Thou sellest thy people for nought, and dost not increase thy wealth by their price.

¹³ Thou makest us a reproach to our neighbours, a scorn and a derision to them that are round about us.

¹⁴ Thou makest us a byword among the heathen, a shaking of the head among the people.

¹⁵ My confusion is continually before me, and the shame of my face hath covered me,

¹⁶ For the voice of him that reproacheth and blasphemeth; by reason of the enemy and avenger.

¹⁷ All this is come upon us; yet have we not forgotten thee, neither have we dealt falsely in thy covenant.

¹⁸ Our heart is not turned back, neither have our steps declined from thy way;

¹⁹ Though thou hast sore broken us in the place of dragons, and covered us with the shadow of death.

²⁰ If we have forgotten the name of our God, or stretched out our hands to a strange god;

²¹ Shall not God search this out? for he knoweth the secrets of the heart.

²² Yea, for thy sake are we killed all the day long; we are counted as sheep for the slaughter.

²³ Awake, why sleepest thou, O Lord? arise, cast us not off for ever.

²⁴ Wherefore hidest thou thy face, and forgettest our affliction and our oppression?

²⁵ For our soul is bowed down to the dust: our belly cleaveth unto the earth.

²⁶ Arise for our help, and redeem us for thy mercies' sake.

THEME

Understanding the Commands of Scripture

POWER OF PSALM

Possession; Hearing; Receiving the Right Hand of God; Positive Mindset; Deter your Enemies

THOUGHT FOR THE PSALM

All commands of scripture are addressed to and fulfilled by Universal Mind, Supreme Intelligence, who is all Imagination. It is your own Imagination who is called upon to "Awake" or "Rouse thyself!."

INTERPRETATION OF EACH VERSE

44 We have heard with our ears, O God, our fathers have told us, what work thou didst in their days, in the times of old.

> 1. We have heard with our ears, hear me Imagination, our fathers have told us, what work you had done in their days, in the times of the past.

² How thou didst drive out the heathen with thy hand, and plantedst them; how thou didst afflict the people, and cast them out.

> 2. You have driven out the all those thoughts that didn't acknowledge God with your hand, and stopped them in their tracks; you've afflicted the thoughts, and cast them out.

³ For they got not the land in possession by their own sword, neither did their own arm save them: but thy right hand, and thine arm, and the light of thy countenance, because thou hadst a favour unto them.

> 3. Those thoughts did not obtain the possession of my mind by their own sword, neither did their own strength save them: but the hand of truth and righteousness, and arm of strength, and

the light of your expression, because I imagined them and because you had placed favor unto them that manifest.

⁴ Thou art my King, O God: command deliverances for Jacob.

4. You are my King, hear me Imagination, Infinite Intelligence: command deliverances for higher consciousness.

⁵ Through thee will we push down our enemies: through thy name will we tread them under that rise up against us.

5. Through you, we will push down our negative thoughts: through your name will we tread those thoughts under that rise up against us.

⁶ For I will not trust in my bow, neither shall my sword save me.

6. For I will not trust in my bow, my ego, neither shall my sword save me.

⁷ But thou hast saved us from our enemies, and hast put them to shame that hated us.

7. But you have saved us from our negative thoughts, and have placed such thoughts to shame that hated us.

⁸ In God we boast all the day long, and praise thy name for ever. Selah.

8. In God we declare our pride all day long, and praise your name forever. Selah

⁹ But thou hast cast off, and put us to shame; and goest not forth with our armies.

9. But you have cast off, and put the negative thoughts to shame; and does not move forward with our negative collective thoughts.

¹⁰ Thou makest us to turn back from the enemy: and they which hate us spoil for themselves.

10. You make us turn back from negative thoughts: and they which hate us bask in their own glory of themselves; until ruin.

¹¹ **Thou hast given us like sheep appointed for meat; and hast scattered us among the heathen.**

> 11. Negative mind of myself has given power unto my negative thoughts for me to be devoured; and has scattered us among those other thoughts that do not acknowledge my Imagination, my God.

¹² **Thou sellest thy people for nought, and dost not increase thy wealth by their price.**

> 12. Negative thoughts do not sell anything of value, and they don't increase their own power by their belief or conviction of their own evil.

¹³ **Thou makest us a reproach to our neighbours, a scorn and a derision to them that are round about us.**

> 13. You create us to disapprove our sinful thoughts that are near in mind, a hateful and showing of contempt to those thoughts that surround us.

¹⁴ **Thou makest us a byword among the heathen, a shaking of the head among the people.**

> 14. You create us notorious among the sinful, a shaking of the head among the negative thoughts.

¹⁵ **My confusion is continually before me, and the shame of my face hath covered me,**

> 15. My confusion is continually before me, and the shame of my negative manifestations show their reflection of me,

¹⁶ **For the voice of him that reproacheth and blasphemeth; by reason of the enemy and avenger.**

> 16. For the voice of that thought which disapproves and shows lack of reverence for God; by reason of the negative thought and avenger.

¹⁷ All this is come upon us; yet have we not forgotten thee, neither have we dealt falsely in thy covenant.

> 17. All this negativity has come upon us; yet, we have not forgotten our Imagination, Infinite Intelligence, Lord, neither have we imagined the ungodly in our Imagination.

¹⁸ Our heart is not turned back, neither have our steps declined from thy way;

> 18. Our mind is not negative, neither have our steps turned away from the righteous path.

¹⁹ Though thou hast sore broken us in the place of dragons, and covered us with the shadow of death.

> 19. Though you have shown us the defeat of our negative thoughts in the place of wisdom, and shielded us from those thoughts with the shadow of death.

²⁰ If we have forgotten the name of our God, or stretched out our hands to a strange god;

> 20. If we have forgotten the name of our Imagination, our God, or stretched out our hands to a false god, a god believed to be something outside of ourselves;

²¹ Shall not God search this out? for he knoweth the secrets of the heart.

> 21. Will God find this out? For he knows the secrets of the mind.

²² Yea, for thy sake are we killed all the day long; we are counted as sheep for the slaughter.

> 22. Yes, for our sake, are negative thoughts killed all day long; we are counted negative thoughts for the slaughter.

²³ Awake, why sleepest thou, O Lord? arise, cast us not off for ever.

> 23. Awake, why do you remain still, O Imagination? Arise, don't cast us from positive manifestation forever.

²⁴ Wherefore hidest thou thy face, and forgettest our affliction and our oppression?

    24. Where do you hide your face dear Lord, Universal Mind, and not address our affliction and our oppression?

²⁵ For our soul is bowed down to the dust: our belly cleaveth unto the earth.

    25. For our mind is guarded from top to bottom: our belly is full manifestations upon the earth.

²⁶ Arise for our help, and redeem us for thy mercies' sake.

    26. Arise for our help, and redeem us for the sake of compassion.

ANALYSIS OF THE SCRIPTURE

You have heard with your own ears, through your own Imagination, what your prior creations and prior thoughts have taught you. You have learned from what you imagined in the past; the days of old.

You have driven out all those thoughts that didn't acknowledge God with your hand, and you have stopped them in their tracks. Through Infinite Intelligence, Imagination, the Lord, you have afflicted the negative thoughts that came upon you, and casted them out.

> *"When the unclean spirit has gone out of a person, it passes through waterless places seeking rest, but finds none. Then it says, 'I will return to my house from which I came.' And when it comes, it finds the house empty, swept, and put in order. Then it goes and brings with it seven other spirits more evil than itself, and they enter and dwell there, and the last state of that person is worse than the first. So also will it be with this evil generation."*
>
> Matthew 12:43-45

Those negative thoughts did not obtain the possession of your mind by their own sword, neither did their own strength save them. It is because of the hand of truth and righteousness, the arm of strength, and the light of the expression of the subconscious mind that they have not been able to obtain possession. It is only because when you imagined such negative thoughts and because you had placed favor unto them, that they manifested at any time.

Claim that your own wonderful human Imagination is God. Ask of God, Universal Mind, to hear you and deliver wisdom to you from Higher Consciousness. Through you, through your Imagination, God will push down your negative thoughts. Through the Law, the Law of God, you will tread upon those negative thoughts under you that try to rise up against you.

For you are not to trust in your bow, your ego. Using your sword of ego will not save you from such negative thoughts. Acknowledge that your own Imagination, the God within you, the God Mind, always saved you from your negative thoughts before, and will do so now. For the Lord can place such thoughts to shame.

In God within you, you are to declare your pride of love all day long and praise his name forever. (Selah)

Knowing that the Lord has cast off negative thoughts, and put the negative thoughts to shame, you are to know that no longer will negative thoughts move forward with other negative collective thoughts within you.

It is the Lord that makes you turn back from negative thoughts. All those negative thoughts which hate you will bask in their own glory of themselves; until their ruin.

The negative mind of yourself has given power unto your negative thoughts for the destruction of your own self. By the Lord, such thoughts have scattered among your other thoughts. Those negative thoughts are the thoughts that do not acknowledge your Imagination, your God.

Negative thoughts do not sell anything of value, and they don't increase their own power by their belief or conviction of their own evil. God has created man (manifestation) to disapprove of his sinful thoughts that are near in mind. He will show a disapproval and contempt to those thoughts that surround him.

God creates man to be notorious among the sinful; a shaking of the head among the negative thoughts. Your confusion is continually before you, and the shame of your negative manifestations show their reflection of yourself. For the voice of that thought which disapproves and shows lack of reverence for God, is due to the reason of the ego; regarding the negative thought and being the avenger.

Negativity has come upon you; yet, you are not to forget your Imagination, Infinite Intelligence, or Lord. At no time are you to imagine the ungodly in your Imagination. Declare that neither your mind is negative, nor have your steps turned away from the righteous path.

Your Imagination has shown the defeat of your negative thoughts. In their place, he inserted wisdom, and shielded you from those thoughts with the shadow of death among those thoughts.

If you have forgotten the name of your Imagination, your God, or stretched out your hands to a false god, a god believed to be something outside of yourself, you have the wrong god. Will God find this out? For he knows the secrets of the mind.

Yes, for your sake, are negative thoughts killed all day long. Negative thoughts may be countless, but all are ready for slaughter.

Your declaration within yourself:

Awake, why do you remain still, O Imagination? Arise, don't cast us from positive manifestation forever. Where do you hide your face dear Lord, Universal Mind, and not address my affliction and my oppression? For my mind is guarded from top to bottom. My belly is full of manifestations upon the earth. Arise for help of self and receive redemption of yourself for the sake of compassion.

CHAPTER FORTY-FIVE

PSALM 45

45 My heart is inditing a good matter: I speak of the things which I have made touching the king: my tongue is the pen of a ready writer.

² Thou art fairer than the children of men: grace is poured into thy lips: therefore God hath blessed thee for ever.

³ Gird thy sword upon thy thigh, O most mighty, with thy glory and thy majesty.

⁴ And in thy majesty ride prosperously because of truth and meekness and righteousness; and thy right hand shall teach thee terrible things.

⁵ Thine arrows are sharp in the heart of the king's enemies; whereby the people fall under thee.

⁶ Thy throne, O God, is for ever and ever: the sceptre of thy kingdom is a right sceptre.

⁷ Thou lovest righteousness, and hatest wickedness: therefore God, thy God, hath anointed thee with the oil of gladness above thy fellows.

⁸ All thy garments smell of myrrh, and aloes, and cassia, out of the ivory palaces, whereby they have made thee glad.

⁹ Kings' daughters were among thy honourable women: upon thy right hand did stand the queen in gold of Ophir.

¹⁰ Hearken, O daughter, and consider, and incline thine ear; forget also thine own people, and thy father's house;
¹¹ So shall the king greatly desire thy beauty: for he is thy Lord; and worship thou him.

¹² And the daughter of Tyre shall be there with a gift; even the rich among the people shall intreat thy favour.

¹³ The king's daughter is all glorious within: her clothing is of wrought gold.

¹⁴ She shall be brought unto the king in raiment of needlework: the virgins her companions that follow her shall be brought unto thee.

¹⁵ With gladness and rejoicing shall they be brought: they shall enter into the king's palace.

¹⁶ Instead of thy fathers shall be thy children, whom thou mayest make princes in all the earth.

¹⁷ I will make thy name to be remembered in all generations: therefore shall the people praise thee for ever and ever.

THEME

READY TO MAKE A CHANGE

POWER OF PSALM

Attitude Change; Affirmation for Good Things; Prosperity

THOUGHT FOR THE PSALM

You are the author of your thoughts. You are the operant power to create your own mental novel; your mental bestseller.

INTERPRETATION OF EACH VERSE

45 My heart is inditing a good matter: I speak of the things which I have made touching the king: my tongue is the pen of a ready writer.

1. My mind brings forth the conviction of good things: I speak of things which I have made that represent the Lord's delight: my tongue is the pen of an author ready to write.

² Thou art fairer than the children of men: grace is poured into thy lips: therefore God hath blessed thee for ever.

2. You are merciful as opposed to the negative thoughts of the many manifestations I created: grace is poured into my lips: therefore I know God, Universal Mind has blessed me forever.

³ Gird thy sword upon thy thigh, O most mighty, with thy glory and thy majesty.

3. Keep your sword of justice close at hand, the sword of the Most High, where you will find his glory and his power.

⁴ And in thy majesty ride prosperously because of truth and meekness and righteousness; and thy right hand shall teach thee terrible things.

4. And I will ride in the way of prosperity because of truth and patience without resentment and righteousness; and your hand of truth will teach those negative thoughts terrible things.

⁵ Thine arrows are sharp in the heart of the king's enemies; whereby the people fall under thee.

5. Your arrows are sharp in the heart of the Imagination's enemies; whereby the deceitful thoughts fall under you.

⁶ Thy throne, O God, is for ever and ever: the sceptre of thy kingdom is a right sceptre.

6. Your throne, hear me Father, is forever in my mind: the staff of authority of your tabernacle is the staff of truth.

⁷ Thou lovest righteousness, and hatest wickedness: therefore God, thy God, hath anointed thee with the oil of gladness above thy fellows.

7. The Imagination where God dwells in you, loves righteousness, and hates wicked thoughts. Therefore, in your Mind, God has anointed you with the substance of gladness above your negative thoughts.

⁸**All thy garments smell of myrrh, and aloes, and cassia, out of the ivory palaces, whereby they have made thee glad.**

> 8. All my garments smell of myrrh, and aloes, and cassia, out of the pure palaces of mind, whereby they have made the Imagination joyous.

⁹**Kings' daughters were among thy honourable women: upon thy right hand did stand the queen in gold of Ophir.**

> 9. Of the ruler, his manifestations gave birth to noble thoughts: upon the truth did stand the subconscious mind, brilliant in the truth of Ophir.

¹⁰**Hearken, O daughter, and consider, and incline thine ear; forget also thine own people, and thy father's house;**

> 10. Listen, noble branch of manifestation, and consider, and give your ear; forget those negative thoughts that call upon you and your father's house;

¹¹**So shall the king greatly desire thy beauty: for he is thy Lord; and worship thou him.**

> 11. The ruler that manifested such negative thoughts will desire their beauty; for he is their maker, and they worship him.

¹²**And the daughter of Tyre shall be there with a gift; even the rich among the people shall intreat thy favour.**

> 12. And the manifestation of a ruler will be present to give a gift; and the greatest of the wicked thoughts will rejoice in the favor of the ruler.

¹³**The king's daughter is all glorious within: her clothing is of wrought gold.**

> 13. The subconscious mind is glorious unto herself: her manifestations are delivered in a covering of perfection.

¹⁴**She shall be brought unto the king in raiment of needlework: the virgins her companions that follow her shall be brought unto thee.**

14. She will have her robe of will be brought before her ruler or creator of thoughts, with the finest of stitching: for she is filled with uninfluenced companions that follow her, and will be brought unto the ruler.

¹⁵ With gladness and rejoicing shall they be brought: they shall enter into the king's palace.

15. With gladness and rejoicing will the new thoughts be brought: they will enter into the king's palace.

¹⁶ Instead of thy fathers shall be thy children, whom thou mayest make princes in all the earth.

16. Instead of the thoughts of maturity, new thoughts or offspring of the thoughts of maturity, whom may make princes in all the earth.

¹⁷ I will make thy name to be remembered in all generations: therefore shall the people praise thee for ever and ever.

17. I will make your name to be remembered in all generations: therefore, will the thoughts of mind praise God forever and forever.

ANALYSIS OF THE SCRIPTURE

Your mind is to bring forth the conviction of good things. Speak of things which you have made that represent the Lord's delight. Your tongue is to represent the pen of an author ready to write.

Acknowledge that the God within you, is merciful as opposed to the words of negative thoughts of the many manifestations you created may have told you. Know that grace is poured into your lips, and that you know God, Spirit, Universal Mind has blessed you forever.

> *Therefore no one will be declared righteous in God's sight by the works of the law; rather, through the law we become conscious of our sin. But now apart from the law the righteousness of God has been made known, to which the Law and the Prophets testify. This righteousness is given through faith in Jesus Christ to all who believe. There is no difference between Jew and Gentile, for all have sinned and fall short of the glory of God, and all are justified freely by his grace through the redemption that came by Christ Jesus.*

Romans 3:20-24

Keep your sword of justice, your righteous thoughts, close at hand; for it is the sword of the Most High. There, you will find his glory and his power. You will ride in the way of prosperity, because truth, patience without resentment and righteousness are what you are to desire. From the hand of truth will God teach those negative thoughts terrible things.

His arrows are sharp in the heart of the Imagination's enemies; whereby the deceitful thoughts fall under you. His throne, where he hears from, is forever in your mind. The staff of authority of your tabernacle is the staff of truth; the palace where the Lord resides.

The Imagination where God dwells in you, loves righteousness, and hates wicked thoughts. Therefore, in your Mind, God has anointed you with the substance of gladness above your negative thoughts.

In your Imagination, all your garments are to smell of myrrh, and aloes, and cassia. These are wonderful scents (thoughts) that are to be visualized in the pure palaces of mind. Such thoughts make the Imagination joyous.

You are the ruler, and your manifestations have given birth to noble thoughts. Upon this truth stands the subconscious mind; brilliant in the truth of Ophir. Listen to your noble thoughts and have them consider hearing you. Forget those negative thoughts that call upon you and your father's house;

The ruler that manifests negative thoughts will desire their beauty; for he is their maker, and they worship him. And the manifestation of a ruler will be present to give a gift to him, and the greatest of the wicked thoughts will rejoice in the favor of the ruler.

The subconscious mind is glorious unto herself: her manifestations are delivered in a covering of perfection. She will have her robe of manifestation brought before her ruler or creator of thoughts, with the finest of stitching. She, the subconscious, is filled with uninfluenced companions that follow her, and will be brought unto the ruler.

With gladness and rejoicing will the new thoughts of wickedness be brought forward. They will enter the king's palace. Instead of the thoughts of maturity, new thoughts or offspring of the thoughts of maturity are whom the rulers shall make princes of all the earth. It is for you to make your name to be remembered in all generations. Therefore, must the thoughts of your mind praise God forever and forever.

CHAPTER FORTY-SIX

PSALM 46

46 God is our refuge and strength, a very present help in trouble.

²Therefore will not we fear, though the earth be removed, and though the mountains be carried into the midst of the sea;

³Though the waters thereof roar and be troubled, though the mountains shake with the swelling thereof. Selah.

⁴There is a river, the streams whereof shall make glad the city of God, the holy place of the tabernacles of the most High.

⁵God is in the midst of her; she shall not be moved: God shall help her, and that right early.

⁶The heathen raged, the kingdoms were moved: he uttered his voice, the earth melted.

⁷The LORD of hosts is with us; the God of Jacob is our refuge. Selah.

⁸Come, behold the works of the LORD, what desolations he hath made in the earth.
⁹He maketh wars to cease unto the end of the earth; he breaketh the bow, and cutteth the spear in sunder; he burneth the chariot in the fire.

¹⁰Be still, and know that I am God: I will be exalted among the heathen, I will be exalted in the earth.

¹¹The LORD of hosts is with us; the God of Jacob is our refuge. Selah.

THEME

In Need of Refuge

POWER OF PSALM

Faith in a New Venture; Overcoming Obstacles; Need of Hearing Truth

THOUGHT FOR THE PSALM

There is no obstacle too great for you, as long as you know where and how to use the Kingdom within you.

INTERPRETATION OF EACH VERSE

46 **God is our refuge and strength, a very present help in trouble.**

1. Imagination is our refuge and strength, a very present help in trouble.

² Therefore will not we fear, though the earth be removed, and though the mountains be carried into the midst of the sea;

2. Therefore we have no fear, because the negative thoughts upon the earth shall be removed;

³ Though the waters thereof roar and be troubled, though the mountains shake with the swelling thereof. Selah.

3. The truth speaks loudly, and the negative thoughts are to be troubled, though the obstacles tremble on unsolid ground. Selah.

⁴ There is a river, the streams whereof shall make glad the city of God, the holy place of the tabernacles of the Most High.

4. There is a righteous understanding that flows forth, and where the truth will appear and create glory in the City of God, the holy place of the Imagination, the tabernacles of the Most High.

⁵ **God is in the midst of her; she shall not be moved: God shall help her, and that right early.**

    5. God is in the midst of the subconscious mind, the Imagination; the subconscious (mind) shall not be deterred: God shall play a role, and that is the initial role of righteousness.

⁶ **The heathen raged, the kingdoms were moved: he uttered his voice, the earth melted.**

    6. Those that fail to acknowledge God raged with anger, the kingdoms were once replaced by negative thoughts: he uttered his voice, the voice of God, and the past thoughts melted.

⁷ **The LORD of hosts is with us; the God of Jacob is our refuge. Selah.**

    7. The Lord is Mind and the ruler of Mind; the God of the Higher Mind is our heaven. Selah.

⁸ **Come, behold the works of the LORD, what desolations he hath made in the earth.**

    8. Come and witness the works of the Lord, what ruin he has made upon the earth.

⁹ **He maketh wars to cease unto the end of the earth; he breaketh the bow, and cutteth the spear in sunder; he burneth the chariot in the fire.**

    9. He makes wars upon the negative thoughts that follow man to the ends of the earth; he stops the weapons and arrows that afflict; he burns the vehicle that allows such thoughts to travel.

¹⁰ **Be still, and know that I am God: I will be exalted among the heathen, I will be exalted in the earth.**

    10. Be still, meditate and know that I am God: I will reign supreme among the negative thoughts that fail to acknowledge me, I will reign supreme of the earth.

¹¹ The LORD of hosts is with us; the God of Jacob is our refuge. Selah.
> 11. The Lord is Mind and the ruler of Mind; the God of the Higher Mind is our heaven. Selah.

ANALYSIS OF THE SCRIPTURE

Imagination is our refuge and strength, the immediate present help when in trouble. Therefore, we are to have no fear, because all the negative thoughts upon the earth created by your own manifestations shall be removed.

According to your faith be it unto you.

Matthew 9:29

The truth speaks loudly, and the negative thoughts will be troubled. Obstacles, negative thinking, will tremble on unsolid ground. Selah. There is a righteous understanding that flows forth, and one will find the truth appearing with glory in the City of God. The holy place is the Imagination, the tabernacles of the Most High.

God works in the midst of the subconscious mind, the Imagination; and the subconscious (mind) shall not be deterred. God shall play a role, and that is the initial role of righteousness. Those thoughts that fail to acknowledge God shall rage with anger. All the kingdoms created by man will be replaced. When God speaks with his voice, the negative thoughts within those kingdoms will melt away.

The Lord is Mind and the ruler of Mind; the God of the Higher Mind is our heaven. Selah. Come and witness the works of the Lord, see what ruin man has made upon the earth. God makes wars upon the negative thoughts that follow man to the ends of the earth. He stops the weapons and arrows that afflict. He burns the vehicle that allows such thoughts to travel.

Scripture tells us: "Be still, meditate and know that I am God." Know that you are God. Know that you will reign supreme among the negative thoughts that fail to acknowledge you, and you reign supreme of the earth. The Lord is Mind and the ruler of Mind; the God of the Higher Mind is our heaven. Selah.

CHAPTER FORTY-SEVEN

PSALM 47

47 O clap your hands, all ye people; shout unto God with the voice of triumph.

² For the LORD most high is terrible; he is a great King over all the earth.

³ He shall subdue the people under us, and the nations under our feet.

⁴ He shall choose our inheritance for us, the excellency of Jacob whom he loved. Selah.

⁵ God is gone up with a shout, the LORD with the sound of a trumpet.

⁶ Sing praises to God, sing praises: sing praises unto our King, sing praises.

⁷ For God is the King of all the earth: sing ye praises with understanding.

⁸ God reigneth over the heathen: God sitteth upon the throne of his holiness.

⁹ The princes of the people are gathered together, even the people of the God of Abraham: for the shields of the earth belong unto God: he is greatly exalted.

THEME

SUBDUE NEGATIVE THINKING

POWER OF PSALM

Gaining Control; Learning to Let Go; Focus

THOUGHT FOR THE PSALM

Take control of your thought, take control of your life.

INTERPRETATION OF EACH VERSE

47 O clap your hands, all ye people; shout unto God with the voice of triumph.

1. Doubtful, deceitful, negative thoughts, clap your hands; shout unto the Imagination, God, with the voice of victory.

² For the LORD most high is terrible; he is a great King over all the earth.

2. For the Imagination, the Law of the Lord is ruthless; he is a great King over all the manifestations on earth.

³ He shall subdue the people under us, and the nations under our feet.

3. He will subdue such thoughts that come to mind, and the congregation of thoughts that already lay before you.

⁴ He shall choose our inheritance for us, the excellency of Jacob whom he loved. Selah.

4. From righteous thoughts, he will choose our inheritance for us, the perfection of the Higher Mind whom he loved; meaning himself. Selah.

⁵ **God is gone up with a shout, the LORD with the sound of a trumpet.**

    5.   God loudly vibrates in the mind of man, in the Imagination, with the sound of his declaration.

⁶ **Sing praises to God, sing praises: sing praises unto our King, sing praises.**

    6.   Sing praises to the Higher Mind, sing praises: sing praises unto our King, sing praises.

⁷ **For God is the King of all the earth: sing ye praises with understanding.**

    7.   For the Imagination is the King of all the earth: sing ye praises with understanding.

⁸ **God reigneth over the heathen: God sitteth upon the throne of his holiness.**

    8.   Goodness reigns over those thoughts that fail to acknowledge God: God sits upon the throne in the Imagination, the abode of his holiness.

⁹ **The princes of the people are gathered together, even the people of the God of Abraham: for the shields of the earth belong unto God: he is greatly exalted.**

    9.   The chief persuader of all the negative and doubtful thoughts gathers like thoughts to him, even the thoughts of the God of Abraham: for the shields of the earth belong unto Imagination: he is greatly held to the Most High.

ANALYSIS OF THE SCRIPTURE

Declare unto doubtful, deceitful, and negative thoughts to clap their hands for mercy. Have them shout unto the Imagination, God, with the voice of victory if they please. For they know, the Imagination, the Law of the Lord is ruthless. Remind them that God is a great King over all the manifestations on earth.

He will subdue negative thinking, and the congregation of negative thoughts that already lay before you. From righteous thoughts, he will choose our inheritance for us. This is done through the perfection of the Higher Mind whom he favors. Selah.

God loudly vibrates in the mind of man, in the Imagination, with the sound of his declaration. Sing praises to the Higher Mind! Sing praises! Sing praises unto our King! Sing praises! For the Imagination is the King of all the earth. Sing all your praises with understanding that God is King.

> *So the people shouted when the priests blew with the trumpets: and it came to pass, when the people heard the sound of the trumpet, and the people shouted with a great shout, that the wall fell down flat, so that the people went up into the city, every man straight before him, and they took the city.*
>
> *Joshua 6:20*

Goodness reigns over those thoughts that fail to acknowledge God. God sits upon the throne in the Imagination, the abode of his holiness. The chief persuader of all the negative and doubtful thoughts collectively gathers like thoughts to him; even the thoughts of the God of Abraham. For the shields of the earth belong unto the Imagination. We are to know that all things happen through the Most High.

CHAPTER FORTY-EIGHT

PSALM 48

48 Great is the LORD, and greatly to be praised in the city of our God, in the mountain of his holiness.

² Beautiful for situation, the joy of the whole earth, is mount Zion, on the sides of the north, the city of the great King.

³ God is known in her palaces for a refuge.

⁴ For, lo, the kings were assembled, they passed by together.

⁵ They saw it, and so they marvelled; they were troubled, and hasted away.

⁶ Fear took hold upon them there, and pain, as of a woman in travail.

⁷ Thou breakest the ships of Tarshish with an east wind.

⁸ As we have heard, so have we seen in the city of the LORD of hosts, in the city of our God: God will establish it for ever. Selah.

⁹ We have thought of thy lovingkindness, O God, in the midst of thy temple.

¹⁰ According to thy name, O God, so is thy praise unto the ends of the earth: thy right hand is full of righteousness.

¹¹ Let mount Zion rejoice, let the daughters of Judah be glad, because of thy judgments.

¹² Walk about Zion, and go round about her: tell the towers thereof.
¹³ Mark ye well her bulwarks, consider her palaces; that ye may tell it to the generation following.

¹⁴ For this God is our God for ever and ever: he will be our guide even unto death.

THEME

SHELTER FROM DISTRESS

POWER OF PSALM

Mental Health; Impatience; Clear Vision; Compassion

THOUGHT FOR THE PSALM

Begin with a simple thought in mind and build upon your own mountain.

INTERPRETATION OF EACH VERSE

48 Great is the LORD, and greatly to be praised in the city of our God, in the mountain of his holiness.

1. Imagination, Infinite Intelligence is great, and greatly to be praised in the temple of our mind, in the foundation of his holiness.

² Beautiful for situation, the joy of the whole earth, is mount Zion, on the sides of the north, the city of the great King.

2. Such perfection, the joy of the whole earth, is the pinnacle. Between the ears rests the mind. In the mind is the great King.

³ God is known in her palaces for a refuge.

3. Subconscious Mind, Universal Mind, knows that the Mind is the shelter for distress.

⁴ For, lo, the kings were assembled, they passed by together.

4. The princes of negative thoughts were gathered together, and they exchanged wickedness between themselves.

⁵ They saw it, and so they marvelled; they were troubled, and hasted away.

5. They saw the tabernacle, and they were in awe; they were troubled, and moved with great swiftness.

⁶ Fear took hold upon them there, and pain, as of a woman in travail.

6. A strong unpleasant emotion took hold upon the negative thoughts, including pain, where the subconscious mind exerts new righteous thoughts upon them.

⁷ Thou breakest the ships of Tarshish with an east wind.

7. The force of the Lord breaks all vessels of negative thinking with a strong affirmation.

⁸ As we have heard, so have we seen in the city of the LORD of hosts, in the city of our God: God will establish it for ever. Selah.

8. As we have heard, so have we seen in the abode of the Lord of hosts, Lord of all thoughts,

⁹ We have thought of thy lovingkindness, O God, in the midst of thy temple.

9. We have thought of your loving kindness, hear me God, in the midst of my Imagination.

¹⁰ According to thy name, O God, so is thy praise unto the ends of the earth: thy right hand is full of righteousness.

10. According to your name, hear me God, so is my praise unto the ends of the earth: the truth is full of righteousness.

¹¹ Let mount Zion rejoice, let the daughters of Judah be glad, because of thy judgments.

11. Let the pinnacle of mind rejoice, let the creators of the choice of God be glad, because of my judgments.

¹² Walk about Zion, and go round about her: tell the towers thereof.

> 12. Walk about in the Imagination, and seek to tell all thoughts within the subconscious mind about your ascent to the top

¹³ Mark ye well her bulwarks, consider her palaces; that ye may tell it to the generation following.

> 13. Know that your mind is a solid structure, consider the subconscious mind the supreme palace in which to tell the next generation of thoughts to follow.

¹⁴ For this God is our God for ever and ever: he will be our guide even unto death.

> 14. For this God Power, is our Imagination forever and forever. He will be our guide until the day we die.

ANALYSIS OF THE SCRIPTURE

Imagination, Infinite Intelligence is great, and greatly to be praised in the temple of our mind; in the foundation of his holiness. Such perfection, the joy of the whole earth, is the pinnacle. Between the ears rests the mind. In the mind is the great King; the King meaning God.

Subconscious Mind, Universal Mind, knows that the Mind is the shelter for distress. The princes of negative thoughts were gathered, and they exchanged wickedness between themselves. However, when they saw the tabernacle, they were in awe. So much in awe, they were troubled, and moved with great swiftness.

> *And they said one to another, We [are] verily guilty concerning our brother, in that we saw the anguish of his soul, when he besought us, and we would not hear; therefore is this distress come upon us.*
>
> *Genesis 42:21*

A strong unpleasant emotion took hold upon the negative thoughts, including pain, where the subconscious mind exerts new righteous thoughts upon them. The force of the Lord breaks all vessels of negative thinking with a strong affirmation. You must be strong in your affirmation; for your thoughts will always look to rise up against you.

We have seen in the abode, the Lord of hosts, Lord of all thoughts. Thus, we are to adore the thought of loving kindness and know that God will hear you. God is to be your praise unto the ends of the earth: his truth is full of righteousness.

> *And thou shalt eat the fruit of thine own body, the flesh of thy sons and of thy daughters, which the LORD thy God hath given thee, in the siege, and in the straitness, wherewith thine enemies shall distress thee:*
>
> *Deuteronomy 28:53*

Let the pinnacle of mind rejoice. Let the creators of the choice of God be glad because of my righteous judgments. Walk about in the Imagination and seek to tell all thoughts within the subconscious mind about your ascent to the top. Know that your mind is a solid structure. Consider the subconscious mind the supreme palace in which to tell the next generation of thoughts to follow. For this God Power, is our Imagination forever and forever. He will be our guide until the day we die.

> *The eternal God is thy refuge, and underneath are the everlasting arms: and he shall thrust out the enemy from before thee; and shall say, Destroy them.*
>
> *Deuteronomy 33:27*

CHAPTER FORTY-NINE

PSALM 49

49 Hear this, all ye people; give ear, all ye inhabitants of the world:

² Both low and high, rich and poor, together.

³ My mouth shall speak of wisdom; and the meditation of my heart shall be of understanding.

⁴ I will incline mine ear to a parable: I will open my dark saying upon the harp.

⁵ Wherefore should I fear in the days of evil, when the iniquity of my heels shall compass me about?

⁶ They that trust in their wealth, and boast themselves in the multitude of their riches;

⁷ None of them can by any means redeem his brother, nor give to God a ransom for him:

⁸ (For the redemption of their soul is precious, and it ceaseth for ever:)

⁹ That he should still live for ever, and not see corruption.

¹⁰ For he seeth that wise men die, likewise the fool and the brutish person perish, and leave their wealth to others.

¹¹ Their inward thought is, that their houses shall continue for ever, and their dwelling places to all generations; they call their lands after their own names.

¹² Nevertheless man being in honour abideth not: he is like the beasts that perish.

¹³ This their way is their folly: yet their posterity approve their sayings. Selah.

¹⁴ Like sheep they are laid in the grave; death shall feed on them; and the upright shall have dominion over them in the morning; and their beauty shall consume in the grave from their dwelling.

¹⁵ But God will redeem my soul from the power of the grave: for he shall receive me. Selah.

¹⁶ Be not thou afraid when one is made rich, when the glory of his house is increased;

¹⁷ For when he dieth he shall carry nothing away: his glory shall not descend after him.

¹⁸ Though while he lived he blessed his soul: and men will praise thee, when thou doest well to thyself.

¹⁹ He shall go to the generation of his fathers; they shall never see light.

²⁰ Man that is in honour, and understandeth not, is like the beasts that perish.

THEME

Honor and Understand the Law of God

POWER OF PSALM

Distinguishing Good and Bad Thoughts; Redemption; Relief from Folly

THOUGHT FOR THE PSALM

Honor and understanding are within all men. Take time to stop and meditate on all matters; both night and day.

INTERPRETATION OF EACH VERSE

49 **Hear this, all ye people; give ear, all ye inhabitants of the world:**

1. Hear this, all thoughts; listen, all of the manifestations of the world.

² Both low and high, rich and poor, together.

2. Both those thoughts manifested, and those that have not manifested from heaven. Both thoughts that are abundant in likeness, and those that are lacking.

³ My mouth shall speak of wisdom; and the meditation of my heart shall be of understanding.

3. My mouth will speak of wisdom; and the meditation of my mind will give understanding.

⁴ I will incline mine ear to a parable: I will open my dark saying upon the harp.

4. I will raise my ear to a story within a story, intended to teach a truth: I will open my hidden words upon the sweet sound of my voice.

⁵ Wherefore should I fear in the days of evil, when the iniquity of my heels shall compass me about?

5. For this reason, should I be in fear of evil moments, when the wickedness of my burdens directs me about?

⁶ They that trust in their wealth, and boast themselves in the multitude of their riches;

6. Those thoughts that trust in their own satisfaction, and boast of themselves among the many thoughts that are already in abundance;

⁷ **None of them can by any means redeem his brother, nor give to God a ransom for him:**

7. None of them can by any means win back the attention of their fellow thoughts that have converted to the righteous path, nor give to God a ransom to have such negative thought back:

⁸ **(For the redemption of their soul is precious, and it ceaseth for ever:)**

8. (For the returning of consciousness of mind is precious, and the troubled mind will stop forever:)

⁹ **That he should still live for ever, and not see corruption.**

9. Consciousness in man should still live forever, and not see corruption.

¹⁰ **For he seeth that wise men die, likewise the fool and the brutish person perish, and leave their wealth to others.**

10. For he sees men of judgment die, likewise the fool and the brutish die, and leave their negative energy to other wicked manifestations.

¹¹ **Their inward thought is, that their houses shall continue for ever, and their dwelling places to all generations; they call their lands after their own names.**

11. The thoughts of the wicked are, that their houses that carry burden will continue forever, and so shall it be for all the manifestations made in their likeness; they call their estate after their own names.

¹² **Nevertheless man being in honour abideth not: he is like the beasts that perish.**

12. Nevertheless, for the man that fails to adhere to the Law of God, the Law of Imagination: he is like the beasts that die.

¹³ **This their way is their folly: yet their posterity approve their sayings. Selah.**

13. The way of the wicked, wicked thoughts, results in folly: yet the descendants of the wicked will approve their declarations as if it were truth. Selah

¹⁴ Like sheep they are laid in the grave; death shall feed on them; and the upright shall have dominion over them in the morning; and their beauty shall consume in the grave from their dwelling.

14. Like negative thoughts are placed in the grave; death will feed on them; and the righteous thoughts will have dominion over them from the start; and their beauty will consume in the grave from where they reside.

¹⁵ But God will redeem my soul from the power of the grave: for he shall receive me. Selah.

15. But the Imagination, Infinite Intelligence will redeem my mind from the power of the grave: for Infinite Intelligence shall receive me.

¹⁶ Be not thou afraid when one is made rich, when the glory of his house is increased;

16. Don't be afraid when you create an abundance of righteous thoughts, when the glory of the Imagination is increased;

¹⁷ For when he dieth he shall carry nothing away: his glory shall not descend after him.

17. For when negative thoughts die, there will be nothing left of them to attach to the abundance: the glory of God will not come down to save them.

¹⁸ Though while he lived he blessed his soul: and men will praise thee, when thou doest well to thyself.

18. Though while the thought existed, he rewarded the mind: and men will praise you, when I do well to think for myself.

¹⁹ He shall go to the generation of his fathers; they shall never see light.

19. A negative thought will go to the creation of negative thoughts that follow him in darkness, their creators of darkness, and they shall never see light.

²⁰ Man that is in honour, and understandeth not, is like the beasts that perish.

> 20. The man that fails to honor and understand the Law of God, is like the beasts that die.

ANALYSIS OF THE SCRIPTURE

A call is being made upon all your thoughts in mind and in manifestation to hear the Word of God. This pertains to those thoughts that have manifested, and those that have yet to mature in heaven. The call is upon both thoughts that are abundant in likeness, and those that are lacking.

The mouth will speak wisdom, and the meditation of your mind will give understanding. Infinite Intelligence will raise your ear to a story within a story; intended to teach a truth or principle. God will reveal his hidden words upon the sweet sound of his voice. For this reason, should you be in fear of evil moments, when the wickedness of your burdens directs you about?

> *Now to the King eternal, immortal, invisible, the only God, be honor and glory for ever and ever. Amen.*
>
> 1 Timothy 1:17

Those thoughts that trust in their own satisfaction and boast of themselves among the many thoughts that are already in abundance, cannot redeem any other thoughts. Whether it is a good thought or not, God will not be held hostage or bribed for the collection of additional wicked thoughts to be among you.

In other words, none of those negative thoughts can win back the attention of their fellow thoughts by any means; particularly thoughts that have converted to the righteous path. Wicked thoughts cannot offer God a ransom to win a negative thought back to the legion of wicked thoughts.

(For the returning of consciousness of mind is precious, and the troubled mind will stop forever.) Consciousness in man should still live forever, and not see corruption. For he sees men of judgment die. Likewise, the fool and the brutish die and leave their negative energy to other wicked manifestations.

The thoughts of the wicked from their houses, carry a burden that will endure forever. So, shall it be for all the manifestations made in their likeness. Wicked thoughts will call their estate after their own names.

> *He received honor and glory from God the Father when the voice came to him from the Majestic Glory, saying, "This is my Son, whom I love; with him I am well pleased."*
>
> *2 Peter 1:17*

Nevertheless, for the man that fails to adhere to the Law of God, the Law of Imagination, he is like the negative thoughts that will eventually die. The way of the wicked, wicked thoughts, results in folly. Yet, the descendants of the wicked will approve their declarations as if it were truth. Selah.

Similar negative thoughts are placed in a grave. Death will feed upon them, and the righteous thoughts will have dominion over them from the start. Negative thoughts may turn to righteous thoughts. The beauty of positive thoughts among the wicked, will consume in the grave from where they reside.

But the Imagination, Infinite Intelligence will redeem your mind from the power of the grave. Infinite Intelligence will receive you. Don't be afraid when you create an abundance of righteous thoughts. Only glory comes out of the Imagination when the amount of righteous thoughts is increased. For when negative thoughts die, there will be nothing left of them to attach to the abundance of the righteous thoughts. The glory of God will not come down to save them.

Men will praise you when they see you do well to think righteousness for yourself. A negative thought on the other hand, will go to the creation of like thoughts that follow him in darkness, and they will praise you only for their deeds of influence. They are creators of darkness, and they shall never see light. The man that fails to honor and understand the Law of God, is like the negative thoughts that die.

CHAPTER FIFTY

PSALM 50

50 The mighty God, even the Lord, hath spoken, and called the earth from the rising of the sun unto the going down thereof.

² Out of Zion, the perfection of beauty, God hath shined.

³ Our God shall come, and shall not keep silence: a fire shall devour before him, and it shall be very tempestuous round about him.

⁴ He shall call to the heavens from above, and to the earth, that he may judge his people.

⁵ Gather my saints together unto me; those that have made a covenant with me by sacrifice.

⁶ And the heavens shall declare his righteousness: for God is judge himself. Selah.

⁷ Hear, O my people, and I will speak; O Israel, and I will testify against thee: I am God, even thy God.

⁸ I will not reprove thee for thy sacrifices or thy burnt offerings, to have been continually before me.

⁹ I will take no bullock out of thy house, nor he goats out of thy folds.

¹⁰ For every beast of the forest is mine, and the cattle upon a thousand hills.

¹¹ I know all the fowls of the mountains: and the wild beasts of the field are mine.

¹² If I were hungry, I would not tell thee: for the world is mine, and the fulness thereof.

¹³ Will I eat the flesh of bulls, or drink the blood of goats?

¹⁴ Offer unto God thanksgiving; and pay thy vows unto the most High:

¹⁵ And call upon me in the day of trouble: I will deliver thee, and thou shalt glorify me.

¹⁶ But unto the wicked God saith, What hast thou to do to declare my statutes, or that thou shouldest take my covenant in thy mouth?

¹⁷ Seeing thou hatest instruction, and casteth my words behind thee.

¹⁸ When thou sawest a thief, then thou consentedst with him, and hast been partaker with adulterers.

¹⁹ Thou givest thy mouth to evil, and thy tongue frameth deceit.

²⁰ Thou sittest and speakest against thy brother; thou slanderest thine own mother's son.

²¹ These things hast thou done, and I kept silence; thou thoughtest that I was altogether such an one as thyself: but I will reprove thee, and set them in order before thine eyes.

²² Now consider this, ye that forget God, lest I tear you in pieces, and there be none to deliver.

²³ Whoso offereth praise glorifieth me: and to him that ordereth his conversation aright will I shew the salvation of God.

THEME

KNOW GOD IS THE ULTIMATE THOUGHT - CREATOR

POWER OF PSALM

Faulty Direction; Judgment; Agreements;

THOUGHT FOR THE PSALM

Seeking earnest instruction from God, provides freedom.

INTERPRETATION OF EACH VERSE

50 The mighty God, even the LORD, hath spoken, and called the earth from the rising of the sun unto the going down thereof.

1. The mighty Universal Mind, the Imagination has spoken, and calls all manifestations from beginning to what appears to be the end.

² Out of Zion, the perfection of beauty, God hath shined.

2. Out of the Imagination, the perfection of beauty, thoughts have shined.

³ Our God shall come, and shall not keep silence: a fire shall devour before him, and it shall be very tempestuous round about him.

3. Our Imagination will come, and will not keep quiet: a fire for all negative thoughts will destroy them directly before God, the Universal Mind, and will be very tumultuous around him.

⁴ He shall call to the heavens from above, and to the earth, that he may judge his people.

4. God will make his voice heard in the Imagination above, and to the earth, that he may judge negative and doubtful thoughts.

⁵ **Gather my saints together unto me; those that have made a covenant with me by sacrifice.**

5. Gather my wonderful thoughts together unto me; those that have made an agreement with me by sacrifice, meaning faith.

⁶ **And the heavens shall declare his righteousness: for God is judge himself. Selah.**

6. And the heavens will declare his righteousness: for the Imagination, Infinite Intelligence is judge himself. Selah.

⁷ **Hear, O my people, and I will speak; O Israel, and I will testify against thee: I am God, even thy God.**

7. Hear, listen all thoughts, and I will speak; recognize God, and I will testify against those negative thoughts: I am God, even your God.

⁸ **I will not reprove thee for thy sacrifices or thy burnt offerings, to have been continually before me.**

8. I will not scold you for your sacrifices or your tribulations from a world like fire, or your remnants of the fire, to have been continually before me.

⁹ **I will take no bullock out of thy house, nor he goats out of thy folds.**

9. I will take no breath from the Imagination, nor interrupt the flow of good thoughts already created.

¹⁰ **For every beast of the forest is mine, and the cattle upon a thousand hills.**

10. For every beast of the forest is of my creation, and the herd of thoughts that come from the heavens.

¹¹ **I know all the fowls of the mountains: and the wild beasts of the field are mine.**

11. I know all the thoughts in flight in the heavens: and the unruly thoughts of the field are mine.

¹² **If I were hungry, I would not tell thee: for the world is mine, and the fulness thereof.**

> 12. If I were hungry, I would not tell you: for the world is mine, and the world is full of all me.

¹³ **Will I eat the flesh of bulls, or drink the blood of goats?**

> 13. Will I eat the flesh of the manifestation of breath, or drink the blood of something unruly that appears outside of myself?

¹⁴ **Offer unto God thanksgiving; and pay thy vows unto the most High:**

> 14. Offer unto the Imagination thanksgiving; and pay your respect unto the Universal Mind:

¹⁵ **And call upon me in the day of trouble: I will deliver thee, and thou shalt glorify me.**

> 15. And call upon me, the Universal Mind in the day of trouble: I will deliver you, and you must glorify me.

¹⁶ **But unto the wicked God saith, What hast thou to do to declare my statutes, or that thou shouldest take my covenant in thy mouth?**

> 16. But unto the wicked God said, What do you have to do to declare my laws, or for you to speak of agreement with me from your mouth?

¹⁷ **Seeing thou hatest instruction, and casteth my words behind thee.**

> 17. Seeing you ignore my instructions, and you cast them behind you without acknowledgement.

¹⁸ **When thou sawest a thief, then thou consentedst with him, and hast been partaker with adulterers.**

> 18. When you witnessed stealing, you agreed with the actions of the thief, and he has taken part in irreverence and adulterating my name and existence.

¹⁹ **Thou givest thy mouth to evil, and thy tongue frameth deceit.**

19. You give your mouth to speaking evil, and your tongue is filled with deceit.

²⁰ **Thou sittest and speakest against thy brother; thou slanderest thine own mother's son.**

20. You sit and speak against your brother god; you slander your own manifestation.

²¹ **These things hast thou done, and I kept silence; thou thoughtest that I was altogether such an one as thyself: but I will reprove thee, and set them in order before thine eyes.**

21. These things you have done, and I kept silent; you thought that all circumstances and situations are a product of chance: but I will correct you, and set those thoughts in order right before your eyes.

²² **Now consider this, ye that forget God, lest I tear you in pieces, and there be none to deliver.**

22. Now consider this, you that forget God, those negative thoughts, I shall tear you into pieces and there will nothing left for wickedness to offer.

²³ **Whoso offereth praise glorifieth me: and to him that ordereth his conversation aright will I shew the salvation of God.**

23. For those who offer praise and glorify me: and to him that ask me to speak with him will be set aright and I will show him the salvation of God.

ANALYSIS OF THE SCRIPTURE

The mighty Universal Mind, the Imagination has spoken, and calls all manifestations from beginning to end. Out of your Imagination, the perfection of beauty, thoughts shine.

God will work in your Imagination and will not keep quiet. God shall place a wrath upon all negative thoughts, that will destroy them. The wrath of God, Universal Mind, will be very tumultuous around you.

God will make his voice heard in the Imagination above and upon the earth. Infinite Intelligence will also be the judge of both negative and doubtful thoughts. Gather your wonderful thoughts together unto yourself. It is you that must make an agreement with God, of sacrifice; meaning faith in the All that Is.

> *"I will be a father to him and he will be a son to Me; when he commits iniquity, I will correct him with the rod of men and the strokes of the sons of men,"*
>
> *2 Samuel 7:14*

And the heavens will declare his righteousness. The Imagination, Infinite Intelligence, is the judge of himself. Selah. Hear, listen all thoughts, and I will speak. Recognize God, and I will testify against those negative thoughts: I am God, meaning your God.

The Father will not scold you for your sacrifices or your tribulations from a world subjected to fire. All that may be left of you are remnants of the fire, but Father will still be there for you.

Infinite Intelligence will take no breath from the Imagination, nor interrupt the flow of good thoughts that you already created. For every beast of the forest, meaning your ungodly thoughts in mind, are of your creation. And if not careful, all the future thoughts that come from your mind can be like thoughts.

You know that all the thoughts in flight comes from the mind; and are unruly thoughts from the field of your mind. If you were hungry, you would not tell the Father of your hunger. For the world is yours, and the world is full of all the thoughts necessary to satisfy your hunger.

Will you eat the flesh of the manifestation by your breath, or drink the blood of something unruly that appears outside of yourself? Offer unto the Imagination thanksgiving and pay your respect unto the Universal Mind.

Call upon God, the Imagination in the time of trouble. God will deliver you, and you must glorify him. God asks a simple question. What do you have to do to declare my laws, or for you to speak of agreement with me from your mouth? He can see when you ignore his instructions, and those instructions of thought are cast behind you.

There came a time when you witnessed stealing of your wonderful thoughts. You agreed with the actions of the thief, and you have taken part in the irreverence and adulterating of God's name and existence. When that happens, you give your mouth to speaking evil, and your tongue is filled with deceit.

You sit and speak against your brother god, meaning your brother thought. When you do so, you slander your own manifestation. These things you have done, and the God within kept silent. You convinced yourself that all circumstances and situations are a product of chance. However, Infinite Intelligence will correct you, and set those thoughts in order right before your eyes.

Now consider this, you that forget God, those negative thoughts, God shall tear those thoughts into pieces and there will be nothing left for wickedness within you to offer. For those who offer praise and glorify Universal Mind, the Lord, and the man that asks for the counsel of God, will be set aright; for God will show you salvation.

END OF VOLUME 1

ABOUT THE AUTHOR

DAVID E. SMITH JR.

Author and publisher of numerous books, plays and screenplays. David continues to break new ground in the area of publishing; especially in the field of Mind Science. More volumes are soon to be released as of the printing of this edition.

David has created a full learning series that encompasses learning for adults and children in the areas of Vedic Mathematics, Esoteric Sciences, Consciousness, Inspirational Lectures, Cybersecurity Technology, Law, Coaching and Mentoring. Many of his achievements can be found throughout his podcasts, Youtube Channel, blog, and website at Aspoonful.com.

Volume II & III of Mind Science coming soon!

Other acclaimed books by

David E. Smith Jr.

Looking to start a new romance or keep your current soulmate, but don't know how to go about it? Perhaps you would like to know what a relationship has in store for you before you sign that contract or hold hands with that potential love one? Then this book is for you. If you are looking for that soulmate secret that will make you happy for the rest of your life, look no further.

Here is a dating book for women and men that will help you narrow down finding that perfect someone that you may have been searching for in earnest in other relationship books. Finding Your Perfect Soulmate or Business Partner will help you make more sense of the dating scene and help you find the love and respect for your values that you have been searching for.

Whether you are interested in business partnering or looking to know what kind of love relationship you are about to get into before you commit, then this book is for you. It is time to have your questions about partnerships and soulmates answered once and for all!

When it comes to mindfulness, do you really understand the term and what it means to you and your relationships? Are you looking to once and for all master your relationships you encounter each and every day? Are you ready to be true to what you see in the mirror each day? This book, love inspired, is about you.

This book provides the self-help as to what you need to understand, and how you can develop your powers to return to the Knowing being you truly are. Yes, a Universal Knowing; a knowing apart from false teachings in text books, declared religious dogma or treatises disseminated by scientist about your existence on this planet.

Now comes a book that challenges your spirituality; reminding you, who you truly are. Whether you subscribe to a religion or not, this book will help you identify the truth in the interpretations of religious books; helping you change your life forever.

Web & Social Media

Website: Aspoonful.com
Podcast: Aspoonful of Knowledge
Youtube Channel: Aspoonful of Knowledge
Instagram: Aspoonful_love
Facebook: /David.e.smith.391

www.ingramcontent.com/pod-product-compliance
Lightning Source LLC
Chambersburg PA
CBHW032032150426
43194CB00006B/250